# RAND McNALLY

# The 2014 Easy to Read Road Atlas

## Contents

Photo credits: p.2 ©Rand McNally, ©John Wright / Murray Ledger & Times, Murray, KY; p.3 ©Rand McNally, town Courtesy Bardstown CVB, all others Courtesy Delray Beach Marketing Cooperative; p.4 class Courtesy Santa Fe School of Cooking, art gallery ©Luc Novovitch/Alamy, all others ©Rand McNally; p. 6-7 in chronological order: ©Rand McNally, ©istockphoto, Courtesy Library of Congress, ©FPG/Hulton Archive/Getty Images, ©Rand McNally, ©Rand McNally, ©istockphoto, ©Car Culture Collection/Getty Images, ©Philipus/Alamy, ©istockphoto, ©Rand McNally, ©RV/MH Hall of Fame in Elkhart, Indiana, Courtesy NASA, ©istockphoto, ©Culture-images GmbH/Alamy, ©Rand McNally, ©imagebroker/Alamy, last 4 photos ©Rand McNally; back cover ©Tetra Images/Corbis.

Published in U.S.A.
Printed in U.S.A.

For licensing information and copyright permissions, contact us at
permissions@randmcnally.com

If you have a question or even a compliment, please visit us at randmcnally.com/contact or e-mail us at consumeraffairs@randmcnally.com

or write to
Rand McNally Consumer Affairs
P.O. Box 7600
Chicago, Illinois 60680-9915

1 2 3 TN 14 13

## TRAVEL INFORMATION

### Best of the Road® 2-4
Meet the winning towns from our Best of the Road® search, celebrating the Best Small Towns in America.

### Mileage Chart 5
Driving distances between 77 North American cities.

### Road Travel Over the Last 90 Years 6-7
A timeline that looks back at how Rand McNally's history is entwined with that of American road travel.

### Mileage and Driving Times Map inside back cover
Distances and driving times between hundreds of North American cities and national parks.

## MAPS

**Map legend** inside front cover
**United States overview map** 8-9
**U.S. states** 10-109
**Canada overview map** 110-111
**Canadian provinces** 112-127
**Mexico overview map and**
**Puerto Rico** 160
**U.S. and Canadian cities** 128-159

SUSTAINABLE FORESTRY INITIATIVE
**Certified Chain of Custody**
Promoting Sustainable Forestry
www.sfiprogram.org
SFI-00993

## TELL RAND!
For over 155 years, Rand McNally has been collecting road travel information and publishing industry-leading maps and atlases. Each year our geographic information systems (GIS) specialists research road conditions and construction projects to update our atlas. Of course, conditions change quickly and new construction projects begin frequently.

If you see something that we haven't captured in our atlas let us know at **randmcnally.com/tellrand**. If we can verify the accuracy of your tip and use it in our next edition, you may be eligible for a discount to our online store.

# 2012 Best Small Towns in America

The 2012 Best Small Towns were chosen from more than 650 communities voted for by our readers—many of them proud residents of their nominees. Five teams of two people each explored six of 30 finalist towns. They drove from Washington, DC, to Seattle, WA, in four weeks—taking America along for the ride through stories, photos, and videos. When the teams arrived in Seattle, five towns were crowned **Most Beautiful, Most Patriotic, Friendliest, Most Fun,** and **Best for Food** in America!

Choosing the winners wasn't easy. Each community showed off the best of its down-home experiences, sights, and spirit. Teams were often welcomed with ceremonies or parades and always welcomed with hospitality and town pride. The rally was made even more exciting thanks to Travel Channel crews who filmed three teams and 15 finalist towns for a heartwarming *Best of the Road*® program. You can still see rally highlights on both TravelChannel.com and **bestoftheroad.com.**

And the excitement continues: Download the Rand McNally Road Atlas and Trip Planner App for your tablet! Create your own road trip to America's small towns and beyond, follow one of ours, or do a bit of both. The app includes all of the Rand McNally Road Atlas maps for offline use. Enjoy America!

Scan this TAG for more of the Best Small Towns in America, with reviews and photos from Best of the Road® users.

## ★Winner★

## Friendliest: Murray, KY

Murray State athletes

The Friendliest Small Town title only adds to Murray's accolades as one of the 100 Best Communities for Young People and a Playful City USA recipient. Not only is this a prime location for young people as the home of Murray State University, but it's also certified as a retirement community, and, with such friendly residents, it's an ideal location for people all ages. The Murray State campus hosts athletic and other events and has such arts and cultural institutions as the Clara M. Eagle Gallery and the Wrather West Kentucky Museum. Must-see local landmarks include Murray Court Square; Central Park; and the Kentucky and Barkley lakes, which are connected by a canal. There's plenty of scenic beauty, not to mention outdoor activities: from go-kart and water-park attractions to camping, fishing, and hunting. Murray hosts several seasonal festivals each year, but it's best known for its Freedom Fest, with street fairs, cookouts, concerts, a parade, a 5K run, and a fireworks finale.

Central Park spraypark

## Things to do in Murray:
### Mary's Kitchen
Come for breakfast at this local staple where the Breakfast Club meets each Sunday.
**1205 Stadium View Dr., Murray, KY 42071, 270-759-2036**

### Central Park
Enjoy the outdoors, disc golf, soccer, swimming, and Playhouse in the Park at Murray's biggest green space.
**Arcadia Circle, Murray, KY 42071, www.murrayparks.org**

### Murray State
Tour the grounds or attend athletics or arts events at the local university of about 9,000 students.
**102 Curris Center, Murray, KY 42071, 800-272-4678**
**www.murraystate.edu**

# ★Winner★

## Most Beautiful: Bardstown, KY

Heaven Hill Distillery

The Bourbon Capital of the World, Bardstown is a Kentucky landmark and quintessentially hospitable. Kick off your visit in downtown's Courthouse Square where distinct small town storefronts lead to the picturesque, distinguished courthouse. From here a walking tour, carriage ride, or trolley trip will transport you through history and traditions. The first stop on Kentucky's Bourbon Trail, this town's tastings are most visitor's first stop upon arrival. From small, family-owned distilleries to world-famous Jim Beam and Maker's Mark, bourbon is an art form here and a part of Bardstown's identity. My Old Kentucky Home is another must-stop, the state park where Stephen Foster wrote the song locals still hold dear. For a feel of that time ride the My Old Kentucky Dinner Train, which offers a first-class meal through beautiful Bluegrass Country. The town's history is further commemorated at the Civil War Museum and Kentucky Railway Museum, where visitors can ride a locomotive and view model trains and artifacts. With 30 annual events, there's always something happening here, with food, music, history and spirits bringing the community together.

### Things to do in Bardstown:

### Heaven Hill Distillery
Discover the heritage and history behind Kentucky's most popular spirit with a tour and tasting.
**Bourbon Heritage Center, 1311 Gilkey Run Rd., Bardstown, KY 40004, 502-337-1000, www.heavenhill.com**

### My Old Kentucky Dinner Train
Step back in time with an elegant dinner along Kentucky's countryside reminiscent of 19th-century rail travel.
**602 N. 3rd St., Bardstown, KY 40004, 866-801-3463 www.kydinnertrain.com**

### Beautiful Dreamer B&B
Stay in charming and relaxing accommodations across from the famed My Old Kentucky Home within walking distance of Historic Bardstown.
**440 E. Stephen Foster Ave., Bardstown, KY 40004, 502-348-4004, www.bdreamerbb.com**

Downtown Bardstown

# ★Winner★

## Most Fun: Delray Beach, FL

Lifeguards at Delray Beach

Delray Beach uniquely ties beach days and downtown nights together for an experience that offers everything. The small town is as known for its art and nightlife as it is for beautiful beaches and water sports. Start the day combing the shore for sea turtles then snorkeling, and end it at a trendy restaurant and funky bar. Delray offers over a hundred restaurants, distinctly original boutique shops, local art galleries and spas downtown with surfing, snorkeling, kayaking and sailing on the water. Visit a local gallery by day and likely meet the artist, then try antiques shopping, a show or performance, or a museum. From the Cornell Museum of Art and American Culture to the Morikami Museum and Japenese Gardens, history and culture abound here. Community events range from craft shows or concerts to Civil War re-enactments or farmers markets. Each year Delray hosts a Seafood & Wine Festival in November, a summer music festival in July, several family nights throughout the year, and events for nearly every holiday.

Arts Garage

### Things to do in Delray Beach:

### Kevros Art Bar
Discover Delray's unique bar, gallery, and studio all in one for a creative, one-of-a-kind experience.
**166 S.E. 2nd Ave., Delray Beach, FL 33444, 561-278-9675 www.kevroart.com**

### Kismet Recycled Vintage & Designer Clothing
Shop a local boutique with designer and vintage clothing in Pineapple Grove.
**157 N.E. 2nd Ave., Delray Beach, FL 33444, 561-865-7895 kismetvintage.com**

### William DeBilzan's Gallery
View this local fine artist's paintings right in the town where he's inspired.
**38 E. Atlantic Ave., Delray Beach, FL 33444, 561-274-8532**

## ★Winner★

## Most Patriotic: Gainesville, TX

Patriotic home in Gainesville

Named after Edmund Pendleton Gaines, Gainesville is a town deeply rooted in its past with historic homes, traditional events and long standing educational institutions. The town is home to North Central Texas College and North Texas Medical Center and has the largest school system in its county. It most notably plays host to the Medal of Honor program, welcoming every recipient in the nation. The local train station was used by the Amtrak *Lone Star*, which stopped operating in 1979. The station's reopening in 1999 brought a renewed prosperity to the town. One of Gainesville's noteworthy events is the annual Depot Day. Every October the town celebrates railroad history with a car show, an art show, and other entertainment. Visit the Morton Museum to get a glimpse into the town's history, and take a tour of the historic downtown and sites in the area including two theaters and a performing arts center. Families will particularly enjoy Frank Buck Zoo in Leonard Park.

Frank Buck Zoo

### Things to do in Gainesville:

### Frank Buck Zoo

See a wide variety of animals within Gainesville's largest park, where you can feed giraffes or ride a train.

**1000 W. California St., Gainesville, TX 76240, 940-668-4539**
**www.frankbuckzoo.com**

### Morton Museum

The building that once served as the city hall, fire station, *and* jail now houses the local history museum.

**210 S. Dixon St., Gainesville, TX 76240, 940-668-8900**
**www.mortonmuseum.org**

### Sarah's on the Square

Enjoy lunch at a local staple in the heart of downtown, serving American fare.

**115 W. California St., Gainesville, TX 76240, 940-612-4782**

## ★Winner★

## Best for Food: Santa Fe, NM

Santa Fe cuisine

Claiming to be the most exotic city in North America, Santa Fe is cultured and diverse. Spanish and Native American influences make for fascinating food, art and entertainment with a rich heritage evident all over town. While the food stands out, Santa Fe has so much more in store. Santa Fe's food focuses on the local staple—chile—and visitors should prepare to answer red or green? You can't miss the New Mexican, Southwestern offerings, but the town has every other cuisine imaginable. With the third largest art market in the U.S., Santa Fe boasts hundreds of art galleries, a variety of museums, opera and trademark architecture. Outdoor recreation is also a must in a destination that promises 300 sunny days each year. Hike, bike or swim in the summer and ski or ice skate in the

A class at Santa Fe School of Cooking

winter. Families can choose between horseback riding, rafting, fishing or even riding a hot air balloon over the beautiful view in the valley below the Rocky Mountains.

### Things to do in Santa Fe:

### The Pantry Restaurant

Don't miss this family-owned local favorite, especially for breakfast, but there will be a line!

**1820 Cerrillos Rd., Santa Fe, NM 87505, 505-986-0022**
**www.pantrysantafe.com**

### Santa Fe School of Cooking

Take advantage of a southwest cooking class where the area's best chefs instruct.

**125 N. Guadalupe St., Santa Fe, NM 87501, 505-983-4511**
**santafeschoolofcooking.com**

### La Posada de Santa Fe

For the full experience in Santa Fe, indulge in a favorite resort, spa and restaurant in one.

**330 E. Palace Ave., Santa Fe, NM 87501, 855-278-5276**
**www.laposadadesantafe.com**

Art gallery in Santa Fe

# Mile Markers | Mileage Chart

This handy chart offers more than 2,400 mileages covering 77 North American cities. Want more mileages? Visit **randmcnally.com/MC** and type in any two cities or addresses.

| | Albuquerque, NM | Atlanta, GA | Billings, MT | Boston, MA | Charlotte, NC | Chicago, IL | Cincinnati, OH | Dallas, TX | Denver, CO | Detroit, MI | Houston, TX | Indianapolis, IN | Kansas City, MO | Los Angeles, CA | Memphis, TN | Miami, FL | Milwaukee, WI | Minneapolis, MN | New Orleans, LA | New York, NY | Omaha, NE | Orlando, FL | Philadelphia, PA | Phoenix, AZ | Pittsburgh, PA | Portland, OR | Saint Louis, MO | Salt Lake City, UT | San Francisco, CA | Seattle, WA | Washington, DC | Wichita, KS |
|---|---|---|---|---|---|---|---|---|---|---|---|---|---|---|---|---|---|---|---|---|---|---|---|---|---|---|---|---|---|---|---|---|
| Albuquerque, NM | | 1386 | 998 | 2219 | 1626 | 1333 | 1387 | 647 | 446 | 1570 | 884 | 1279 | 784 | 786 | 1008 | 1952 | 1354 | 1225 | 1165 | 2001 | 863 | 1730 | 1924 | 462 | 1641 | 1363 | 1037 | 599 | 1086 | 1438 | 1885 | 591 |
| Amarillo, TX | 284 | 1102 | 965 | 1935 | 1342 | 1049 | 1103 | 363 | 424 | 1286 | 589 | 995 | 570 | 1072 | 720 | 1668 | 1132 | 1009 | 881 | 1716 | 647 | 1446 | 1640 | 746 | 1357 | 1669 | 752 | 883 | 1370 | 1743 | 1600 | 382 |
| Atlanta, GA | 1386 | | 1831 | 1095 | 244 | 715 | 461 | 780 | 1404 | 722 | 794 | 533 | 800 | 2174 | 379 | 661 | 809 | 1127 | 468 | 882 | 992 | 440 | 780 | 1844 | 684 | 2603 | 555 | 1878 | 2472 | 2649 | 637 | 955 |
| Atlantic City, NJ | 1985 | 831 | 2072 | 338 | 590 | 818 | 632 | 1518 | 1792 | 644 | 1598 | 703 | 1187 | 2774 | 1063 | 1248 | 910 | 1232 | 1273 | 126 | 1272 | 1038 | 60 | 2447 | 365 | 2922 | 948 | 2201 | 2934 | 2889 | 188 | 1379 |
| Austin, TX | 705 | 920 | 1495 | 1959 | 1164 | 1121 | 1128 | 193 | 950 | 1358 | 157 | 1067 | 702 | 1381 | 643 | 1341 | 1204 | 1136 | 503 | 1737 | 839 | 1124 | 1658 | 1010 | 1411 | 2068 | 825 | 1304 | 1760 | 2143 | 1524 | 542 |
| Baltimore, MD | 1887 | 683 | 1953 | 400 | 442 | 699 | 513 | 1368 | 1673 | 524 | 1448 | 584 | 1068 | 2670 | 914 | 1082 | 792 | 1112 | 1124 | 192 | 1153 | 889 | 98 | 2349 | 246 | 2804 | 829 | 2081 | 2816 | 2771 | 39 | 1260 |
| Billings, MT | 998 | 1831 | | 2236 | 1990 | 1246 | 1546 | 1425 | 551 | 1535 | 1652 | 1435 | 1026 | 1240 | 1477 | 2497 | 1173 | 838 | 1868 | 2041 | 845 | 2275 | 2011 | 1210 | 1713 | 891 | 1278 | 552 | 1173 | 818 | 1951 | 1064 |
| Birmingham, AL | 1241 | 146 | 1780 | 1177 | 390 | 660 | 466 | 636 | 1329 | 724 | 668 | 478 | 749 | 2030 | 235 | 746 | 754 | 1072 | 343 | 960 | 939 | 534 | 880 | 1700 | 748 | 2551 | 502 | 1826 | 2327 | 2598 | 745 | 810 |
| Boise, ID | 938 | 2177 | 621 | 2660 | 2336 | 1693 | 1943 | 1702 | 830 | 1960 | 1930 | 1835 | 1372 | 842 | 1825 | 2844 | 1732 | 1461 | 2216 | 2465 | 1225 | 2622 | 2435 | 914 | 2137 | 428 | 1622 | 339 | 639 | 503 | 2375 | 1338 |
| Boston, MA | 2219 | 1095 | 2236 | | 841 | 983 | 870 | 1764 | 1970 | 724 | 1844 | 937 | 1421 | 2983 | 1312 | 1482 | 1074 | 1396 | 1520 | 207 | 1436 | 1288 | 306 | 2681 | 570 | 3086 | 1182 | 2365 | 3098 | 3054 | 439 | 1613 |
| Branson, MO | 864 | 652 | 1241 | 1433 | 868 | 545 | 601 | 435 | 806 | 784 | 602 | 493 | 209 | 1651 | 274 | 1284 | 630 | 643 | 597 | 1201 | 402 | 1062 | 1138 | 1326 | 851 | 2013 | 249 | 1288 | 1950 | 2060 | 1081 | 292 |
| Calgary, AB | 1542 | 2357 | 541 | 2615 | 2400 | 1627 | 1925 | 1967 | 1096 | 1916 | 2209 | 1814 | 1567 | 1557 | 2028 | 3018 | 1555 | 1221 | 2419 | 2439 | 1387 | 2797 | 2391 | 1524 | 2093 | 787 | 1820 | 869 | 1500 | 678 | 2334 | 1606 |
| Charleston, SC | 1703 | 317 | 2133 | 970 | 207 | 908 | 620 | 1099 | 1706 | 826 | 1105 | 726 | 1103 | 2491 | 696 | 583 | 1002 | 1324 | 742 | 768 | 1294 | 380 | 668 | 2165 | 654 | 2904 | 857 | 2180 | 2789 | 2951 | 532 | 1272 |
| Charlotte, NC | 1626 | 244 | 1990 | 841 | | 769 | 477 | 1023 | 1566 | 616 | 1038 | 583 | 961 | 2414 | 619 | 728 | 867 | 1180 | 712 | 641 | 1151 | 526 | 539 | 2088 | 446 | 2761 | 714 | 2037 | 2712 | 2808 | 398 | 1092 |
| Chicago, IL | 1333 | 715 | 1246 | 983 | 769 | | 289 | 926 | 1002 | 280 | 1085 | 181 | 526 | 2015 | 531 | 1381 | 90 | 408 | 923 | 787 | 470 | 1153 | 757 | 1795 | 459 | 2118 | 296 | 1398 | 2130 | 2063 | 697 | 724 |
| Cincinnati, OH | 1387 | 461 | 1546 | 870 | 477 | 289 | | 934 | 1187 | 259 | 1055 | 108 | 584 | 2172 | 482 | 1127 | 381 | 703 | 804 | 637 | 722 | 905 | 571 | 1849 | 288 | 2369 | 348 | 1647 | 2380 | 2363 | 512 | 779 |
| Cleveland, OH | 1598 | 714 | 1597 | 638 | 514 | 342 | 248 | 1194 | 1330 | 168 | 1315 | 315 | 799 | 2342 | 729 | 1240 | 434 | 756 | 1057 | 460 | 797 | 1043 | 428 | 2060 | 131 | 2446 | 560 | 1725 | 2458 | 2414 | 370 | 992 |
| Columbus, OH | 1457 | 567 | 1606 | 763 | 426 | 354 | 106 | 1039 | 1261 | 191 | 1174 | 176 | 657 | 2244 | 587 | 1164 | 445 | 766 | 910 | 533 | 792 | 954 | 468 | 1920 | 184 | 2439 | 421 | 1718 | 2451 | 2425 | 411 | 851 |
| Corpus Christi, TX | 855 | 1001 | 1622 | 2051 | 1244 | 1338 | 1262 | 410 | 1077 | 1542 | 207 | 1228 | 919 | 1494 | 782 | 1394 | 1421 | 1353 | 554 | 1844 | 1056 | 1172 | 1754 | 1122 | 1561 | 2218 | 1042 | 1454 | 1873 | 2292 | 1619 | 758 |
| Dallas, TX | 647 | 780 | 1425 | 1764 | 1023 | 926 | 934 | | 880 | 1163 | 228 | 873 | 489 | 1437 | 453 | 1307 | 1010 | 928 | 519 | 1548 | 656 | 1086 | 1467 | 1066 | 1221 | 2128 | 630 | 1403 | 1734 | 2193 | 1332 | 361 |
| Denver, CO | 446 | 1404 | 551 | 1970 | 1566 | 1002 | 1187 | 880 | | 1270 | 1035 | 1083 | 603 | 1015 | 1097 | 2069 | 1042 | 913 | 1398 | 1775 | 534 | 1851 | 1732 | 908 | 1447 | 1256 | 854 | 533 | 1268 | 1320 | 1671 | 519 |
| Des Moines, IA | 983 | 902 | 946 | 1299 | 1057 | 332 | 580 | 683 | 670 | 599 | 938 | 474 | 193 | 1682 | 617 | 1567 | 371 | 242 | 1008 | 1105 | 137 | 1339 | 1074 | 1445 | 777 | 1786 | 354 | 1065 | 1798 | 1764 | 1015 | 391 |
| Detroit, MI | 1570 | 722 | 1535 | 724 | 616 | 280 | 259 | 1163 | 1270 | | 1319 | 288 | 764 | 2281 | 742 | 1354 | 374 | 696 | 1066 | 613 | 736 | 1144 | 583 | 2032 | 285 | 2385 | 533 | 1664 | 2397 | 2353 | 522 | 964 |
| Duluth, MN | 1375 | 1187 | 860 | 1370 | 1239 | 466 | 760 | 1092 | 1063 | 754 | 1331 | 651 | 586 | 2076 | 963 | 1852 | 394 | 152 | 1354 | 1264 | 530 | 1632 | 1230 | 1838 | 932 | 1749 | 679 | 1458 | 2033 | 1677 | 1171 | 785 |
| Edmonton, AB | 1724 | 2391 | 722 | 2549 | 2443 | 1670 | 1968 | 2149 | 1278 | 1958 | 2391 | 1857 | 1626 | 1755 | 2147 | 3058 | 1598 | 1264 | 2538 | 2482 | 1445 | 2836 | 2434 | 1721 | 2136 | 966 | 1878 | 1069 | 1695 | 793 | 2377 | 1787 |
| El Paso, TX | 260 | 1418 | 1257 | 2373 | 1662 | 1455 | 1569 | 635 | 707 | 1702 | 744 | 1398 | 929 | 796 | 1089 | 1934 | 1497 | 1377 | 1095 | 2202 | 1004 | 1712 | 2102 | 424 | 1774 | 1630 | 1157 | 866 | 1175 | 1705 | 1967 | 730 |
| Fargo, ND | 1318 | 1361 | 607 | 1629 | 1414 | 641 | 937 | 1079 | 873 | 930 | 1321 | 825 | 600 | 1848 | 1054 | 2025 | 569 | 235 | 1445 | 1438 | 420 | 1807 | 1405 | 1780 | 1107 | 1497 | 841 | 1160 | 1781 | 1424 | 1348 | 685 |
| Gatlinburg, TN | 1439 | 196 | 1803 | 922 | 202 | 578 | 290 | 884 | 1376 | 552 | 964 | 396 | 773 | 2226 | 431 | 865 | 672 | 994 | 640 | 707 | 964 | 640 | 625 | 1901 | 493 | 2574 | 527 | 1850 | 2525 | 2621 | 490 | 905 |
| Guadalajara, JA | 1194 | 1739 | 2194 | 2789 | 1982 | 1954 | 1962 | 1028 | 1639 | 2191 | 948 | 1901 | 1535 | 1501 | 1482 | 2131 | 2037 | 1969 | 1292 | 2592 | 1672 | 1910 | 2492 | 1212 | 2261 | 2545 | 1658 | 1792 | 1963 | 2631 | 2356 | 1377 |
| Gulfport, MS | 1221 | 399 | 1912 | 1482 | 643 | 896 | 767 | 562 | 1386 | 1025 | 403 | 780 | 883 | 1949 | 365 | 792 | 988 | 1196 | 78 | 1266 | 1073 | 572 | 1180 | 1577 | 1052 | 2633 | 647 | 1909 | 2307 | 2730 | 1036 | 867 |
| Houston, TX | 884 | 794 | 1652 | 1844 | 1038 | 1085 | 1055 | 228 | 1035 | 1319 | | 1021 | 732 | 1550 | 575 | 1186 | 1163 | 1171 | 347 | 1632 | 898 | 965 | 1547 | 1178 | 1354 | 2356 | 784 | 1634 | 1929 | 2431 | 1411 | 595 |
| Indianapolis, IN | 1279 | 533 | 1435 | 937 | 583 | 181 | 108 | 873 | 1083 | 288 | 1021 | | 482 | 2068 | 464 | 1198 | 272 | 591 | 818 | 707 | 613 | 968 | 643 | 1742 | 359 | 2260 | 243 | 1541 | 2273 | 2253 | 582 | 674 |
| Jacksonville, FL | 1636 | 346 | 2183 | 1146 | 379 | 1068 | 796 | 992 | 1756 | 1002 | 871 | 874 | 1152 | 2421 | 677 | 349 | 1163 | 1474 | 547 | 939 | 1344 | 141 | 844 | 2050 | 825 | 2954 | 907 | 2230 | 2723 | 3001 | 706 | 1272 |
| Kansas City, MO | 784 | 800 | 1026 | 1421 | 961 | 526 | 584 | 489 | 603 | 764 | 732 | 482 | | 1616 | 451 | 1466 | 565 | 436 | 844 | 1196 | 187 | 1246 | 1127 | 1246 | 840 | 1797 | 250 | 1073 | 1808 | 1844 | 1066 | 193 |
| Key West, FL | 2099 | 809 | 2646 | 1659 | 886 | 1534 | 1275 | 1455 | 2222 | 1515 | 1334 | 1348 | 1617 | 2884 | 1159 | 162 | 1632 | 1944 | 1010 | 1446 | 1807 | 387 | 1357 | 2514 | 1332 | 3417 | 1370 | 2693 | 3186 | 3464 | 1213 | 1735 |
| Las Vegas, NV | 572 | 1959 | 973 | 2714 | 2199 | 1746 | 1932 | 1220 | 747 | 2013 | 1457 | 1828 | 1349 | 270 | 1581 | 2525 | 1786 | 1656 | 1739 | 2518 | 1278 | 2303 | 2480 | 286 | 2190 | 1023 | 1600 | 419 | 569 | 1128 | 2428 | 1164 |
| Lexington, KY | 1371 | 369 | 1610 | 917 | 400 | 370 | 83 | 876 | 1186 | 344 | 996 | 184 | 581 | 2158 | 423 | 1030 | 464 | 782 | 745 | 701 | 771 | 817 | 638 | 1833 | 370 | 2381 | 334 | 1657 | 2392 | 2428 | 533 | 773 |
| Little Rock, AR | 877 | 515 | 1407 | 1447 | 754 | 650 | 617 | 319 | 965 | 885 | 439 | 583 | 381 | 1666 | 137 | 1147 | 724 | 815 | 425 | 1230 | 574 | 925 | 1150 | 1340 | 905 | 2211 | 345 | 1488 | 1963 | 2275 | 1015 | 446 |
| Los Angeles, CA | 786 | 2174 | 1240 | 2983 | 2414 | 2015 | 2172 | 1437 | 1015 | 2281 | 1550 | 2068 | 1616 | | 1794 | 2735 | 2055 | 1925 | 1894 | 2787 | 1546 | 2515 | 2713 | 370 | 2428 | 963 | 1821 | 688 | 380 | 1134 | 2670 | 1377 |
| Memphis, TN | 1008 | 379 | 1477 | 1312 | 619 | 531 | 482 | 453 | 1097 | 742 | 575 | 464 | 451 | 1794 | | 1012 | 622 | 831 | 394 | 1094 | 641 | 778 | 1014 | 1471 | 768 | 2245 | 283 | 1524 | 2095 | 2299 | 879 | 577 |
| Mexico City, DF | 1404 | 1718 | 2301 | 2768 | 1962 | 2017 | 1979 | 1090 | 1756 | 2254 | 924 | 1963 | 1598 | 1839 | 1500 | 2111 | 2100 | 2032 | 1272 | 2571 | 1735 | 1889 | 2471 | 1469 | 2279 | 2768 | 1721 | 2003 | 2218 | 2842 | 2336 | 1440 |
| Miami, FL | 1952 | 661 | 2497 | 1482 | 728 | 1381 | 1127 | 1307 | 2069 | 1354 | 1186 | 1198 | 1466 | 2735 | 1012 | | 1475 | 1791 | 861 | 1288 | 1658 | 229 | 1180 | 2362 | 1173 | 3260 | 1221 | 2544 | 3038 | 3315 | 1044 | 1587 |
| Milwaukee, WI | 1354 | 809 | 1173 | 1074 | 867 | 90 | 381 | 1010 | 1042 | 374 | 1163 | 272 | 565 | 2055 | 622 | 1475 | | 336 | 1015 | 879 | 509 | 1258 | 849 | 1817 | 551 | 2062 | 379 | 1437 | 2170 | 1990 | 788 | 763 |
| Minneapolis, MN | 1225 | 1127 | 838 | 1396 | 1180 | 408 | 703 | 928 | 913 | 696 | 1171 | 591 | 436 | 1925 | 831 | 1791 | 336 | | 1223 | 1204 | 372 | 1573 | 1171 | 1687 | 874 | 1727 | 563 | 1308 | 2040 | 1655 | 1110 | 634 |
| Mobile, AL | 1234 | 328 | 1874 | 1427 | 571 | 917 | 721 | 589 | 1414 | 978 | 468 | 733 | 850 | 2014 | 382 | 719 | 1011 | 1224 | 144 | 1202 | 1038 | 497 | 1101 | 1643 | 1000 | 2661 | 645 | 1936 | 2320 | 2727 | 965 | 894 |
| Montréal, QC | 2129 | 1218 | 2099 | 310 | 980 | 847 | 824 | 1722 | 1832 | 560 | 1884 | 847 | 1330 | 2845 | 1314 | 1647 | 938 | 1262 | 1640 | 382 | 1302 | 1437 | 454 | 2591 | 603 | 2948 | 1092 | 2228 | 2960 | 2916 | 587 | 1529 |
| Nashville, TN | 1219 | 248 | 1586 | 1099 | 407 | 469 | 273 | 664 | 1158 | 534 | 786 | 287 | 555 | 2006 | 212 | 913 | 564 | 881 | 532 | 884 | 747 | 692 | 802 | 1682 | 560 | 2357 | 310 | 1633 | 2306 | 2404 | 667 | 688 |
| New Orleans, LA | 1165 | 468 | 1868 | 1520 | 712 | 923 | 804 | 519 | 1398 | 1066 | 347 | 818 | 844 | 1894 | 394 | 861 | 1015 | 1223 | | 1304 | 1032 | 641 | 1222 | 1523 | 1090 | 2642 | 675 | 1920 | 2252 | 2716 | 1087 | 880 |
| New York, NY | 2001 | 882 | 2041 | 207 | 641 | 787 | 637 | 1548 | 1775 | 613 | 1632 | 707 | 1196 | 2787 | 1094 | 1288 | 879 | 1204 | 1304 | | 1245 | 1089 | 97 | 2463 | 369 | 2891 | 954 | 2170 | 2902 | 2858 | 228 | 1391 |
| Norfolk, VA | 1910 | 558 | 2132 | 569 | 328 | 878 | 605 | 1350 | 1758 | 704 | 1362 | 720 | 1155 | 2707 | 898 | 950 | 969 | 1295 | 1026 | 370 | 1335 | 755 | 271 | 2373 | 425 | 2962 | 911 | 2238 | 2973 | 2949 | 189 | 1349 |
| Oklahoma City, OK | 542 | 844 | 1203 | 1678 | 1084 | 792 | 846 | 204 | 631 | 1029 | 437 | 739 | 348 | 1326 | 466 | 1476 | 876 | 788 | 722 | 1460 | 452 | 1254 | 1384 | 1005 | 1101 | 1922 | 496 | 1200 | 1627 | 1948 | 1344 | 158 |
| Omaha, NE | 863 | 992 | 845 | 1436 | 1151 | 470 | 722 | 656 | 534 | 736 | 898 | 613 | 187 | 1546 | 641 | 1658 | 509 | 372 | 1032 | 1245 | | 1436 | 1212 | 1325 | 914 | 1650 | 439 | 930 | 1662 | 1663 | 1151 | 298 |
| Orlando, FL | 1730 | 440 | 2275 | 1288 | 526 | 1153 | 905 | 1086 | 1851 | 1144 | 965 | 968 | 1246 | 2515 | 778 | 229 | 1258 | 1573 | 641 | 1089 | 1436 | | 986 | 2145 | 975 | 3048 | 999 | 2323 | 2816 | 3093 | 849 | 1365 |
| Ottawa, ON | 2039 | 1158 | 1768 | 428 | 920 | 760 | 732 | 1632 | 1748 | 471 | 1804 | 757 | 1240 | 2763 | 1230 | 1618 | 859 | 1032 | 1582 | 440 | 1213 | 1408 | 447 | 2501 | 546 | 2660 | 1002 | 2142 | 2877 | 2586 | 366 | 1439 |
| Philadelphia, PA | 1924 | 780 | 2011 | 306 | 539 | 757 | 571 | 1467 | 1732 | 583 | 1547 | 643 | 1127 | 2713 | 1014 | 1180 | 849 | 1171 | 1222 | 97 | 1212 | 986 | | 2387 | 304 | 2861 | 888 | 2140 | 2873 | 2828 | 137 | 1319 |
| Phoenix, AZ | 462 | 1844 | 1210 | 2681 | 2088 | 1795 | 1849 | 1066 | 908 | 2032 | 1178 | 1742 | 1246 | 370 | 1471 | 2362 | 1817 | 1687 | 1523 | 2463 | 1325 | 2145 | 2387 | | 2104 | 1332 | 1499 | 653 | 749 | 1414 | 2348 | 1053 |
| Pittsburgh, PA | 1641 | 684 | 1713 | 570 | 446 | 459 | 288 | 1221 | 1447 | 285 | 1354 | 359 | 840 | 2428 | 768 | 1173 | 551 | 874 | 1090 | 369 | 914 | 975 | 304 | 2104 | | 2563 | 604 | 1842 | 2574 | 2530 | 244 | 1035 |
| Portland, ME | 2315 | 1192 | 2333 | 110 | 938 | 1079 | 967 | 1861 | 2067 | 825 | 1940 | 1034 | 1518 | 3082 | 1408 | 1585 | 1176 | 1492 | 1616 | 304 | 1533 | 1385 | 402 | 2778 | 666 | 3186 | 1279 | 2461 | 3196 | 3151 | 535 | 1710 |
| Portland, OR | 1363 | 2603 | 891 | 3086 | 2761 | 2118 | 2369 | 2128 | 1256 | 2385 | 2356 | 2260 | 1797 | 963 | 2245 | 3260 | 2062 | 1727 | 2642 | 2891 | 1650 | 3048 | 2861 | 1332 | 2563 | | 2050 | 765 | 635 | 172 | 2800 | 1764 |
| Rapid City, SD | 843 | 1508 | 323 | 1900 | 1670 | 912 | 1208 | 1061 | 397 | 1200 | 1291 | 1100 | 704 | 1312 | 1160 | 2173 | 840 | 575 | 1551 | 1708 | 525 | 1956 | 1675 | 1305 | 1378 | 1215 | 959 | 649 | 1384 | 1142 | 1618 | 699 |
| Reno, NV | 1019 | 2396 | 958 | 2881 | 2555 | 1913 | 2163 | 1668 | 1051 | 2180 | 1904 | 2056 | 1591 | 470 | 2029 | 3063 | 1953 | 1818 | 2186 | 2685 | 1445 | 2841 | 2656 | 733 | 2357 | 578 | 1844 | 518 | 217 | 720 | 2595 | 1558 |
| Richmond, VA | 1832 | 532 | 2051 | 547 | 293 | 797 | 512 | 1278 | 1671 | 622 | 1329 | 627 | 1069 | 2620 | 824 | 944 | 888 | 1210 | 1002 | 334 | 1259 | 742 | 245 | 2294 | 344 | 2869 | 822 | 2145 | 2880 | 2868 | 108 | 1261 |
| Saint Louis, MO | 1037 | 555 | 1278 | 1182 | 714 | 296 | 348 | 630 | 854 | 533 | 784 | 243 | 250 | 1821 | 283 | 1221 | 379 | 563 | 675 | 954 | 439 | 999 | 888 | 1499 | 604 | 2050 | | 1326 | 2061 | 2096 | 827 | 442 |
| Salt Lake City, UT | 599 | 1878 | 552 | 2365 | 2037 | 1398 | 1647 | 1403 | 533 | 1664 | 1634 | 1541 | 1073 | 688 | 1524 | 2544 | 1437 | 1308 | 1920 | 2170 | 930 | 2323 | 2140 | 653 | 1842 | 765 | 1326 | | 735 | 839 | 2079 | 1042 |
| San Antonio, TX | 712 | 986 | 1480 | 2039 | 1230 | 1202 | 1210 | 276 | 935 | 1439 | 197 | 1149 | 766 | 1357 | 727 | 1379 | 1285 | 1205 | 541 | 1822 | 920 | 1160 | 1742 | 985 | 1495 | 2076 | 906 | 1311 | 1736 | 2150 | 1607 | 625 |
| San Diego, CA | 810 | 2138 | 1302 | 3046 | 2381 | 2080 | 2196 | 1359 | 1077 | 2346 | 1472 | 2089 | 1597 | 120 | 1819 | 2656 | 2118 | 1986 | 1816 | 2809 | 1613 | 2430 | 2738 | 352 | 2452 | 1083 | 1845 | 750 | 501 | 1256 | 2693 | 1401 |
| San Francisco, CA | 1086 | 2472 | 1173 | 3098 | 2712 | 2130 | 2380 | 1734 | 1268 | 2397 | 1929 | 2273 | 1808 | 380 | 2095 | 3038 | 2170 | 2040 | 2252 | 2902 | 1662 | 2816 | 2873 | 749 | 2574 | 635 | 2061 | 735 | | 807 | 2812 | 1775 |
| Santa Fe, NM | 58 | 1379 | 943 | 2212 | 1618 | 1313 | 1379 | 640 | 391 | 1562 | 877 | 1272 | 766 | 846 | 998 | 1944 | 1336 | 1207 | 1158 | 1994 | 891 | 1723 | 1917 | 520 | 1634 | 1388 | 1029 | 625 | 1144 | 1463 | 1879 | 572 |
| Sault Ste. Marie, ON | 1777 | 1040 | 1273 | 923 | 947 | 471 | 577 | 1370 | 1428 | 347 | 1527 | 540 | 951 | 2465 | 972 | 1685 | 398 | 538 | 1355 | 921 | 850 | 1475 | 911 | 2240 | 614 | 2166 | 740 | 1848 | 2581 | 2090 | 854 | 1150 |
| Seattle, WA | 1438 | 2649 | 818 | 3054 | 2808 | 2063 | 2363 | 2193 | 1320 | 2353 | 2431 | 2253 | 1844 | 1134 | 2299 | 3315 | 1990 | 1655 | 2716 | 2858 | 1663 | 3093 | 2828 | 1414 | 2530 | 172 | 2096 | 839 | 807 | | 2768 | 1828 |
| Spokane, WA | 1320 | 2369 | 541 | 2774 | 2528 | 1785 | 2084 | 1964 | 1091 | 2075 | 2192 | 1973 | 1564 | 1216 | 2018 | 3035 | 1712 | 1377 | 2409 | 2580 | 1383 | 2814 | 2550 | 1381 | 2252 | 351 | 1817 | 720 | 874 | 278 | 2490 | 1600 |
| Tampa, FL | 1746 | 451 | 2293 | 1342 | 578 | 1166 | 916 | 1102 | 1860 | 1178 | 980 | 984 | 1252 | 2525 | 779 | 255 | 1260 | 1578 | 651 | 1138 | 1445 | 84 | 1040 | 2153 | 1023 | 3064 | 1008 | 2340 | 2832 | 3111 | 904 | 1381 |
| Toronto, ON | 1800 | 963 | 1771 | 548 | 756 | 519 | 493 | 1393 | 1504 | 232 | 1551 | 518 | 1001 | 2517 | 983 | 1483 | 609 | 933 | 1306 | 489 | 974 | 1284 | 497 | 2262 | 316 | 2620 | 763 | 1899 | 2632 | 2588 | 486 | 1188 |
| Tulsa, OK | 645 | 782 | 1234 | 1576 | 1022 | 687 | 738 | 258 | 692 | 927 | 487 | 635 | 243 | 1433 | 402 | 1414 | 773 | 704 | 671 | 1350 | 380 | 1192 | 1282 | 1107 | 994 | 1938 | 392 | 1215 | 1731 | 2012 | 1234 | 173 |
| Vancouver, BC | 1575 | 2785 | 953 | 3188 | 2944 | 2198 | 2499 | 2338 | 1465 | 2487 | 2565 | 2389 | 1980 | 1275 | 2437 | 3451 | 2125 | 1790 | 2851 | 2993 | 1799 | 3229 | 2963 | 1550 | 2665 | 313 | 2232 | 973 | 947 | 141 | 2903 | 1973 |
| Washington, DC | 1885 | 637 | 1951 | 439 | 398 | 697 | 512 | 1332 | 1671 | 522 | 1411 | 582 | 1066 | 2670 | 879 | 1044 | 788 | 1110 | 1087 | 228 | 1151 | 849 | 137 | 2348 | 244 | 2800 | 827 | 2079 | 2812 | 2768 | | 1258 |
| Wichita, KS | 591 | 955 | 1064 | 1613 | 1092 | 724 | 779 | 361 | 519 | 964 | 595 | 674 | 193 | 1377 | 577 | 1587 | 763 | 634 | 880 | 1391 | 298 | 1365 | 1319 | 1053 | 1035 | 1764 | 442 | 1042 | 1775 | 1828 | 1258 | |

Mileages in this chart are based upon the routes usually followed by motorists. Highway systems include interstate, U.S., and state highways.

# ROAD TRAVEL: THE LAST 90 YEARS

It all began in 1868, when William Rand and Andrew McNally first published railroad tickets and timetables. By 1880, their company offered a whole line of maps, geography textbooks, and globes. The innovations continued. In 1907, Rand McNally published its *Photo Auto Guide* with route maps and photos of actual road segments and intersections (some taken by Andrew McNally's grandson while on his honeymoon). In 1917, the company released a map that debuted a highway numbering system on which today's system is based. And, in 1924, Rand McNally published its first road atlas. **In this, the 90th edition, we look back to see how the company's history is entwined with that of American road travel.**

**1947**
First self-service gas station opens in Los Angeles.

**1963**
Family Motor Coach Association (FMCA) forms.

**1924**
Rand McNally releases its first road atlas.

First Chrysler car debuts.

American Motorcycle Association is formed.

**1932**
The pricey Stout Scarab minivan is released; fewer than a dozen were ever made, all of them hand-built.

**1936**
Rand McNally publishes *The Official Transportation Mileage Guide*.

**1951**
Chrysler releases the Imperial, the first vehicle with power steering.

**1967**
Winnebago releases five mass-produced models from 16 to 27 feet long. They were among the first RVs to be priced accessibly, starting at $5,000.

**1940**
Packard introduces the first factory-installed automobile A/C.

**1956**
Construction begins on the Interstate Highway System, a project championed by Eisenhower.

**1920** — **1930** — **1940** — **1950** — **1960**

**1927**
Noted aviator Charles Lindbergh uses Rand McNally railroad maps for navigation over land during his historic flight across the Atlantic Ocean.

**1939**
Within 24 hours of Germany's invasion of Poland in 1939, stores across the United States sell out of Rand McNally's map of Europe.

**1950**
The first mass-produced minivan debuts: the Volkswagen Type 2 (a.k.a. "the minibus").

**1969**
Rand McNally publishes the first edition of *The New International Atlas*. The result: American cartographic standards triumph over the traditional dominance of European publishers.

**1926**
Route 66 is commissioned.

**1932**
Ford revolutionizes the auto industry by mass producing the V8 engine, leaving the competition in its dust.

**1948**
The Tucker Sedan (a.k.a., the Car of Tomorrow) incorporates safety and other innovations that later become standard in the auto industry.

**1960**
Rand McNally publishes the first full-color edition of *The Road Atlas*.

**1980**
Motor Carrier Act deregulates the trucking industry.

Rand McNally acquires a small company called Transportation Data Management (TDM). TDM marries Rand McNally's enormous maps database to an electronic system for delivery of routing and mileage information to the trucking industries.

**1974**
Cadillac, Buick, and Oldsmobile are the first cars with airbags.

**1985**
Becker introduces factory-installed dashboard CD players.

**1994**
Rand McNally introduces its first consumer software product, TripMaker®, for planning trips on personal computers.

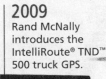

**2004**
Toyota Prius is the first car with self-parking.

**2009**
Rand McNally introduces the IntelliRoute® TND™ 500 truck GPS.

**BEST OF THE ROAD**

**2011**
Rand McNally and USA TODAY launch the inaugural Best of the Road® Rally

**2013**
The 90th edition of the *Rand McNally Road Atlas* is released.

---

**1970** **1980** **1990** **2000** **2010**

---

**1973**
Advent of the GPS project for the Department of Defense; it's fully operational in 1994 and available to civilians in 2007.

**1986**
The futuristic DeLorean DMC-12 is made famous with its role as a time machine in the film phenomenon, *Back to the Future*.

**1981**
The U.S. limits the number of imported Japanese cars; the Japanese then begin building auto-manufacturing plants in America.

**1997**
Toyota introduces the first mass-produced hybrid car, the Prius, in Japan. It's made available in the U.S. in 2000.

**1990**
The RV power slide-out is invented.

**2006**
Honda releases the first production motorcycle airbag system.

**2013**
Rand McNally releases it's first digital road atlas.

**2010**
Rand McNally releases the first GPS device designed for RVers, the RVND™ 5510.

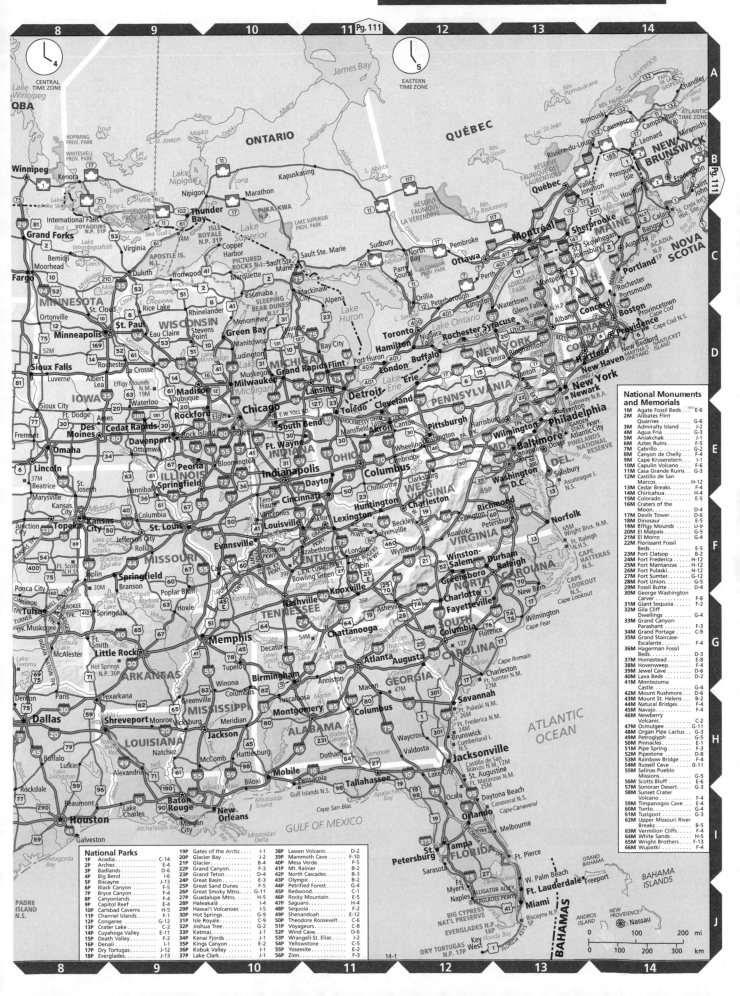

**National Parks**

| | | |
|---|---|---|
| 1P Acadia | C-14 |
| 2P Arches | E-4 |
| 3P Badlands | D-5 |
| 4P Big Bend | I-6 |
| 5P Biscayne | J-13 |
| 6P Black Canyon | F-5 |
| 7P Bryce Canyon | F-4 |
| 8P Canyonlands | F-4 |
| 9P Capitol Reef | E-4 |
| 10P Carlsbad Caverns | H-5 |
| 11P Channel Islands | F-1 |
| 12P Congaree | G-12 |
| 13P Crater Lake | C-2 |
| 14P Cuyahoga Valley | E-11 |
| 15P Death Valley | F-2 |
| 16P Denali | I-1 |
| 17P Dry Tortugas | J-12 |
| 18P Everglades | J-13 |
| 19P Gates of the Arctic | I-1 |
| 20P Glacier Bay | J-2 |
| 21P Glacier | B-4 |
| 22P Grand Canyon | F-3 |
| 23P Grand Teton | D-4 |
| 24P Great Basin | E-3 |
| 25P Great Sand Dunes | F-5 |
| 26P Great Smoky Mtns. | G-11 |
| 27P Guadalupe Mtns. | H-5 |
| 28P Haleakalā | I-4 |
| 29P Hawai'i Volcanoes | I-5 |
| 30P Hot Springs | G-9 |
| 31P Isle Royale | C-9 |
| 32P Joshua Tree | G-2 |
| 33P Katmai | J-1 |
| 34P Kenai Fjords | J-1 |
| 35P Kings Canyon | E-2 |
| 36P Kobuk Valley | I-1 |
| 37P Lake Clark | J-1 |
| 38P Lassen Volcanic | D-2 |
| 39P Mammoth Cave | F-10 |
| 40P Mesa Verde | F-5 |
| 41P Mt. Rainier | B-2 |
| 42P North Cascades | B-3 |
| 43P Olympic | B-2 |
| 44P Petrified Forest | G-4 |
| 45P Redwood | C-1 |
| 46P Rocky Mountain | E-5 |
| 47P Saguaro | H-4 |
| 48P Sequoia | F-2 |
| 49P Shenandoah | E-12 |
| 50P Theodore Roosevelt | C-6 |
| 51P Voyageurs | C-8 |
| 52P Wind Cave | D-6 |
| 53P Wrangell-St. Elias | J-2 |
| 54P Yellowstone | C-5 |
| 55P Yosemite | E-2 |
| 56P Zion | F-3 |

**National Monuments and Memorials**

| | | |
|---|---|---|
| 1M Agate Fossil Beds | E-6 |
| 2M Alibates Flint Quarries | G-6 |
| 3M Admiralty Island | J-2 |
| 4M Agua Fria | G-3 |
| 5M Aniakchak | J-1 |
| 6M Aztec Ruins | F-5 |
| 7M Cabrillo | G-2 |
| 8M Canyon de Chelly | F-4 |
| 9M Cape Krusenstern | I-1 |
| 10M Capulin Volcano | F-6 |
| 11M Casa Grande Ruins | G-3 |
| 12M Castillo de San Marcos | H-12 |
| 13M Cedar Breaks | F-4 |
| 14M Chiricahua | H-4 |
| 15M Colorado | E-5 |
| 16M Craters of the Moon | D-4 |
| 17M Devils Tower | D-6 |
| 18M Dinosaur | E-5 |
| 19M Effigy Mounds | D-9 |
| 20M El Malpais | G-4 |
| 21M El Morro | G-4 |
| 22M Florissant Fossil Beds | E-5 |
| 23M Fort Clatsop | B-2 |
| 24M Fort Frederica | H-12 |
| 25M Fort Mantanzas | H-12 |
| 26M Fort Pulaski | G-12 |
| 27M Fort Sumter | G-12 |
| 28M Fort Union | G-5 |
| 29M Fossil Butte | D-4 |
| 30M George Washington Carver | F-8 |
| 31M Giant Sequoia | F-2 |
| 32M Gila Cliff Dwellings | G-4 |
| 33M Grand Canyon-Parashant | F-3 |
| 34M Grand Portage | C-9 |
| 35M Grand Staircase-Escalante | F-4 |
| 36M Hagerman Fossil Beds | D-3 |
| 37M Homestead | E-8 |
| 38M Hovenweep | F-4 |
| 39M Jewel Cave | D-6 |
| 40M Lava Beds | D-2 |
| 41M Montezuma Castle | G-4 |
| 42M Mount Rushmore | D-6 |
| 43M Mount St. Helens | B-2 |
| 44M Natural Bridges | F-4 |
| 45M Navajo | F-4 |
| 46M Newberry Volcanic | C-2 |
| 47M Ocmulgee | G-11 |
| 48M Organ Pipe Cactus | G-3 |
| 49M Petroglyph | G-5 |
| 50M Pinnacles | E-1 |
| 51M Pipe Spring | F-3 |
| 52M Pipestone | D-8 |
| 53M Rainbow Bridge | F-4 |
| 54M Russell Cave | G-10 |
| 55M Salinas Pueblo Missions | G-5 |
| 56M Scotts Bluff | E-6 |
| 57M Sonoran Desert | G-3 |
| 58M Sunset Crater Volcano | F-4 |
| 59M Timpanogos Cave | E-4 |
| 60M Tonto | G-3 |
| 61M Tuzigoot | G-3 |
| 62M Upper Missouri River Breaks | B-5 |
| 63M Vermilion Cliffs | F-4 |
| 64M White Sands | H-5 |
| 65M Wright Brothers | F-13 |
| 66M Wupatki | F-4 |

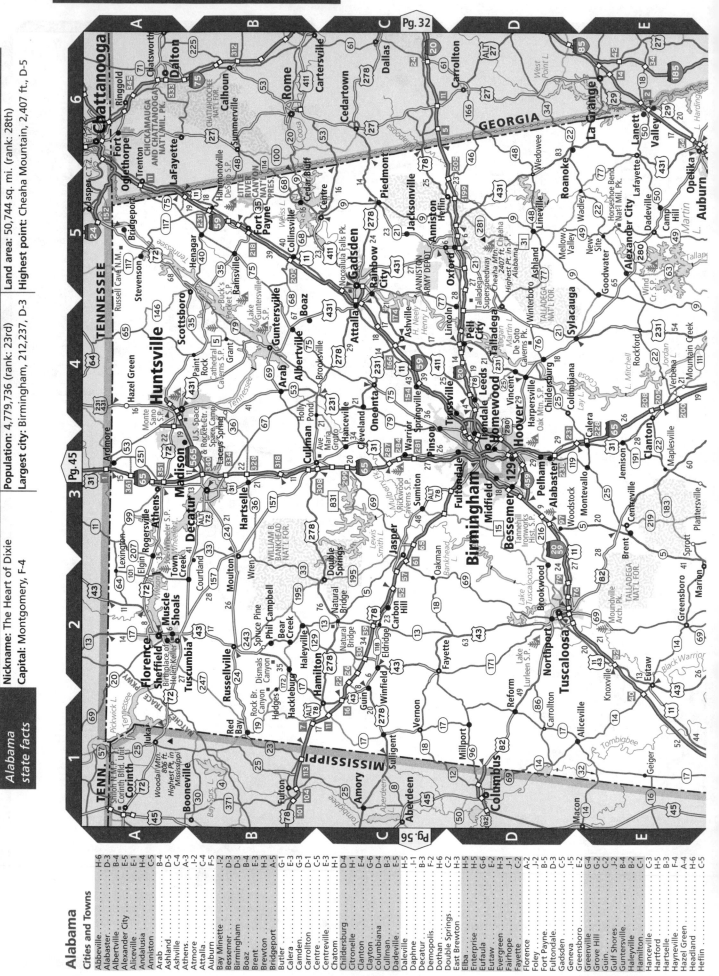

## Alabama
### state facts

**Nickname:** The Heart of Dixie
**Capital:** Montgomery, F-4

**Population:** 4,779,736 (rank: 23rd)
**Largest city:** Birmingham, 212,237, D-3

**Land area:** 50,744 sq. mi. (rank: 28th)
**Highest point:** Cheaha Mountain, 2,407 ft., D-5

## Alabama
### Cities and Towns

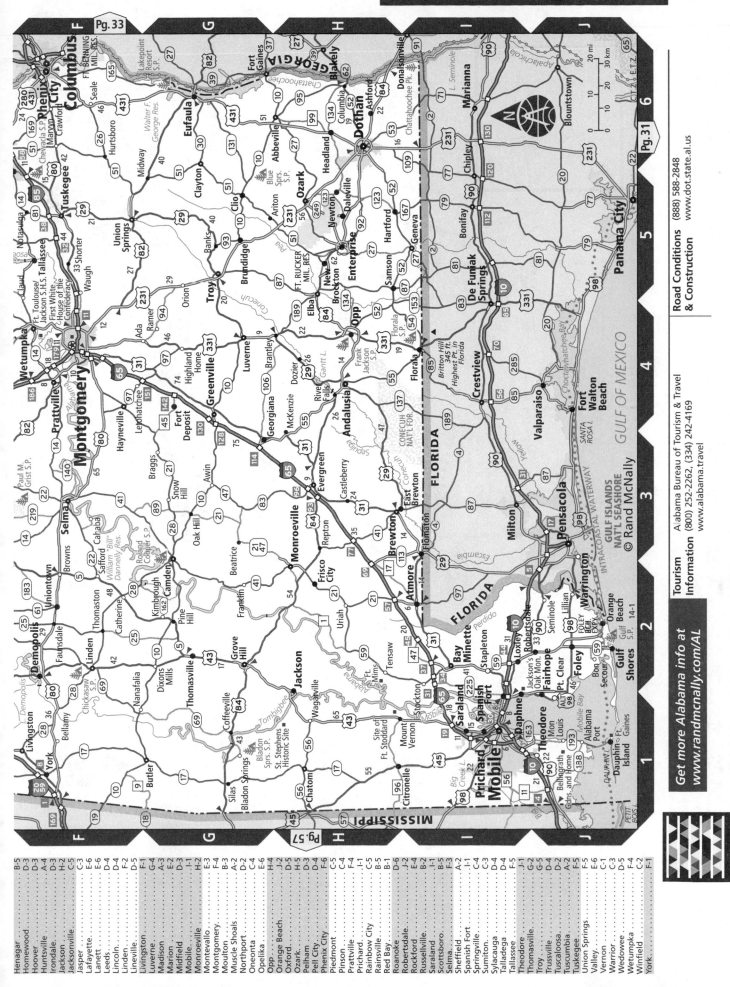

**Tourism** Alabama Bureau of Tourism & Travel
**Information** (800) 252-2262, (334) 242-4169
www.alabama.travel

**Road Conditions** (888) 588-2848
**& Construction** www.dot.state.al.us

*Get more Alabama info at*
**www.randmcnally.com/AL**

© Rand McNally

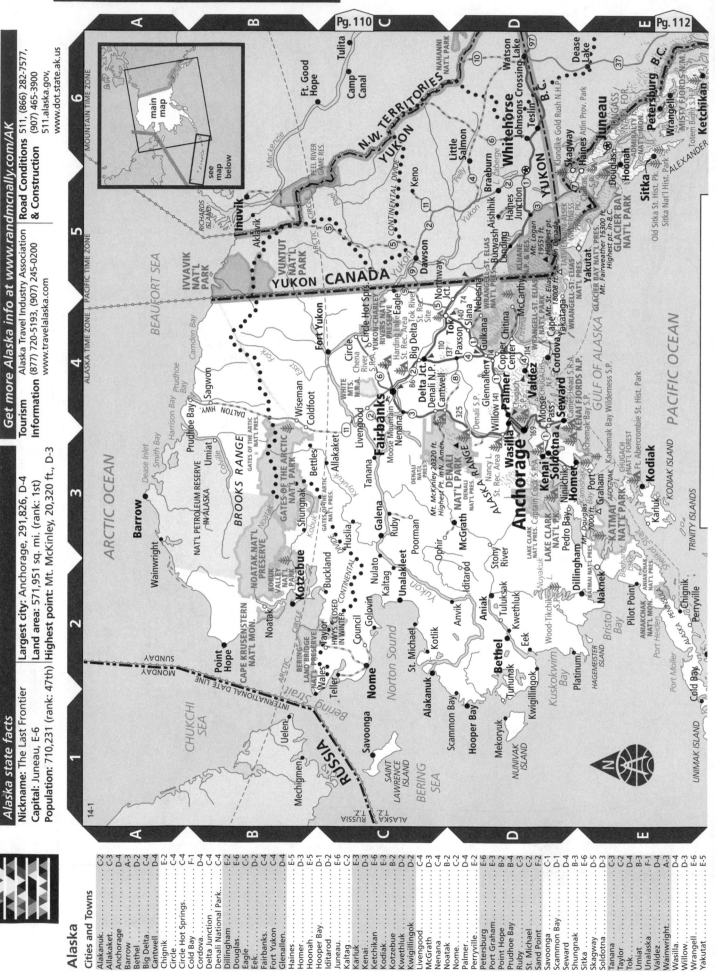

## Alaska state facts

**Nickname:** The Last Frontier
**Capital:** Juneau, E-6
**Population:** 710,231 (rank: 47th)

**Largest city:** Anchorage, 291,826, D-4
**Land area:** 571,951 sq. mi. (rank: 1st)
**Highest point:** Mt. McKinley, 20,320 ft., D-3

## Get more Alaska info at www.randmcnally.com/AK

| | |
|---|---|
| **Tourism** | Alaska Travel Industry Association |
| **Information** | (877) 720-5193, (907) 245-0200 |
| | www.travelalaska.com |
| **Road Conditions** | 511, (866) 282-7577, |
| **& Construction** | (907) 465-3900 |
| | 511.alaska.gov, |
| | www.dot.state.ak.us |

## Alaska

### Cities and Towns

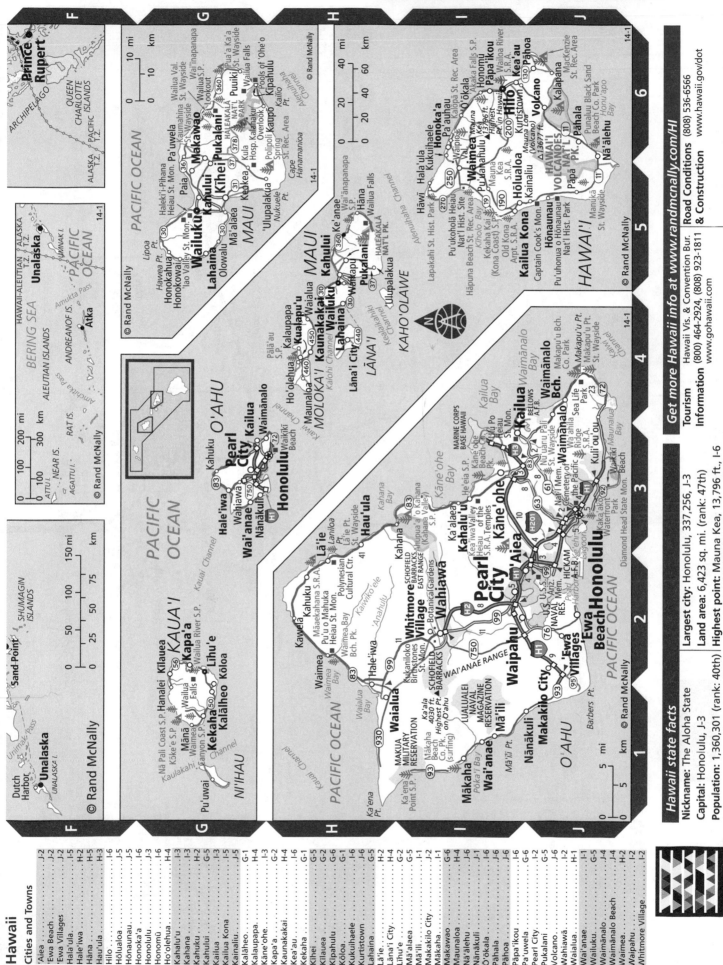

## Hawaii

### Cities and Towns

---

## Hawaii state facts

Nickname: The Aloha State
Capital: Honolulu, J-3
Population: 1,360,301 (rank: 40th)
Largest city: Honolulu, 337,256, J-3
Land area: 6,423 sq. mi. (rank: 47th)
Highest point: Mauna Kea, 13,796 ft., I-6

Get more Hawaii info at www.randmcnally.com/HI

Tourism  Hawaii Vis. & Convention Bur. (800) 464-2924, (808) 923-1811
Information  www.gohawaii.com

Road Conditions  (808) 536-6566
& Construction  www.hawaii.gov/dot

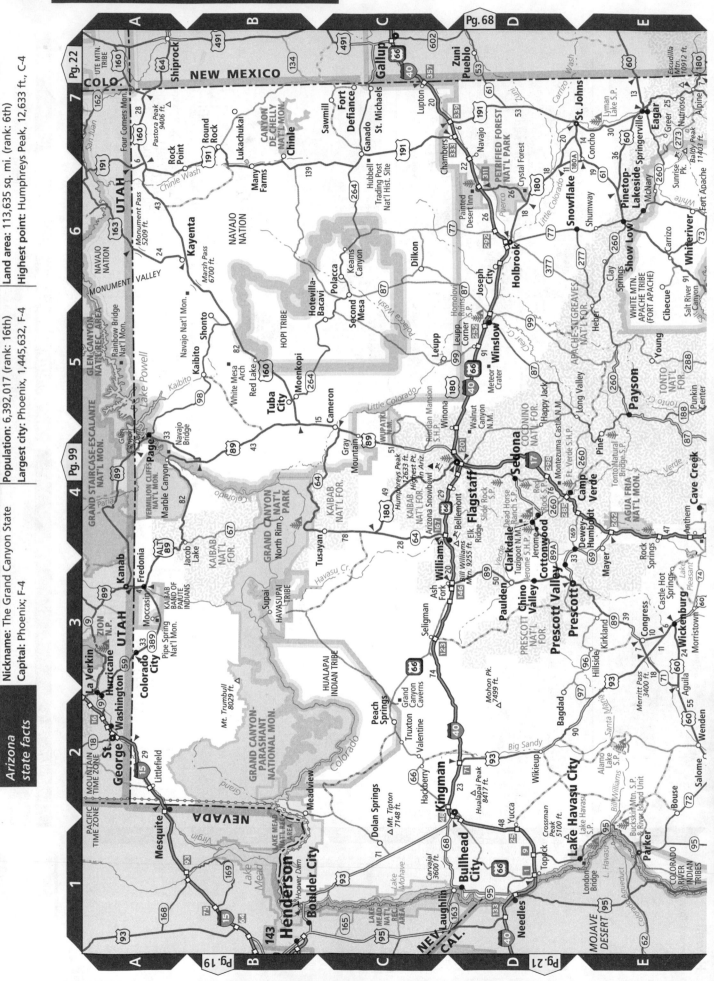

*Arizona*
*state facts*

Nickname: The Grand Canyon State

Capital: Phoenix; F-4

Population: 6,392,017 (rank: 16th)

Largest city: Phoenix; 1,445,632, F-4

Land area: 113,635 sq. mi. (rank: 6th)

Highest point: Humphreys Peak, 12,633 ft., C-4

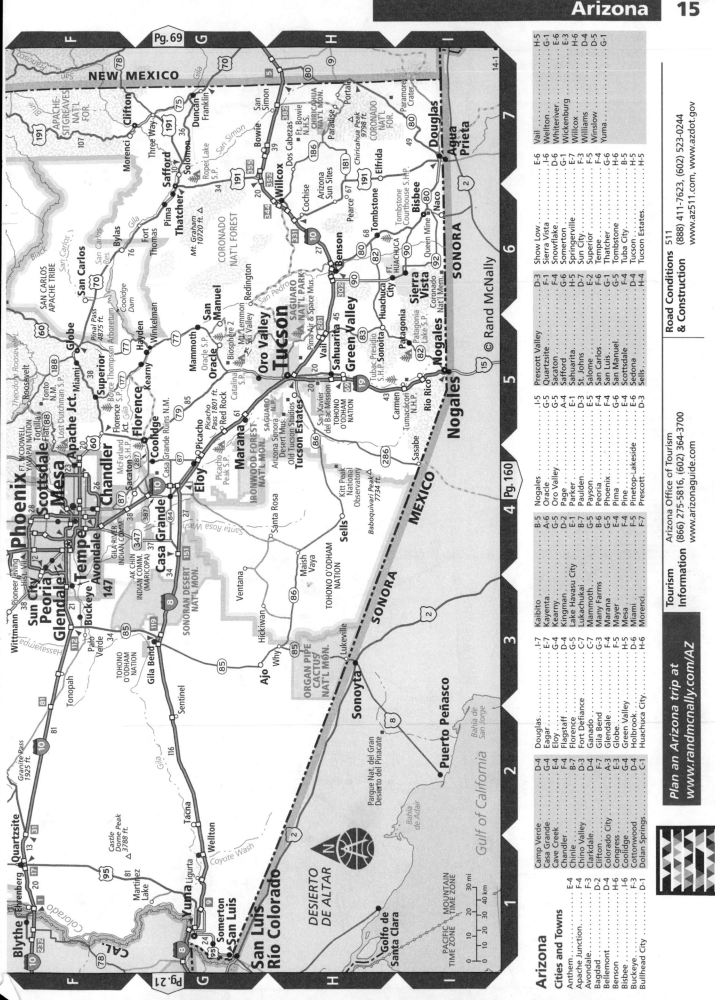

**Tourism Information**
Arizona Office of Tourism
(866) 275-5816, (602) 364-3700
www.arizonaguide.com

**Road Conditions & Construction**
511
(888) 411-7623, (602) 523-0244
www.az511.com, www.azdot.gov

*Plan an Arizona trip at*
www.randmcnally.com/AZ

© Rand McNally

## Arkansas

### Cities and Towns

**Arkansas state facts**

Nickname: The Natural State
Capital: Little Rock, D-4

Population: 2,915,918 (rank: 32nd)
Largest city: Little Rock, 193,524, D-4

Land area: 52,068 sq. mi. (rank: 27th)
Highest point: Magazine Mtn., 2753 ft., C-2

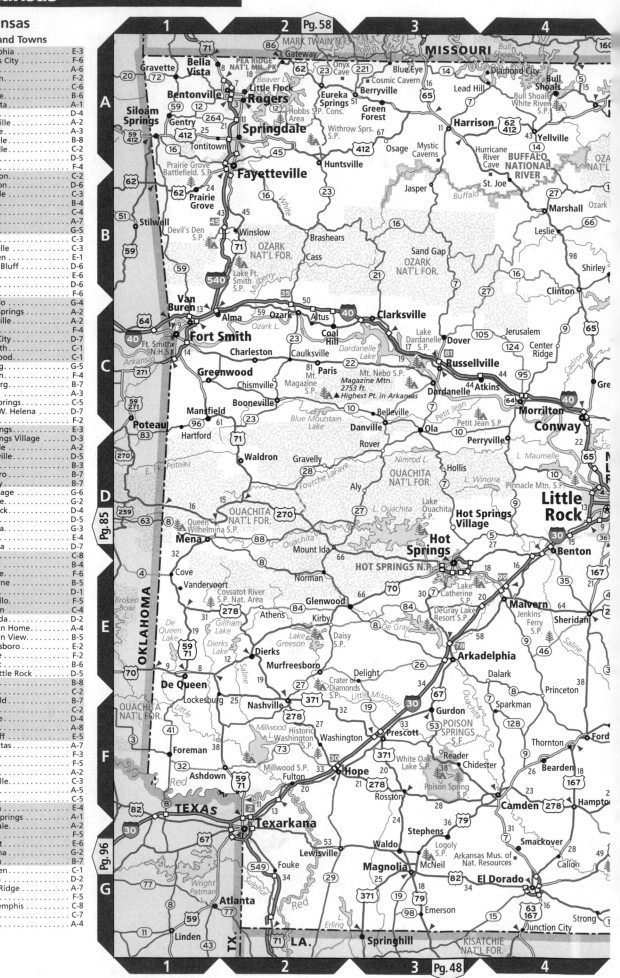

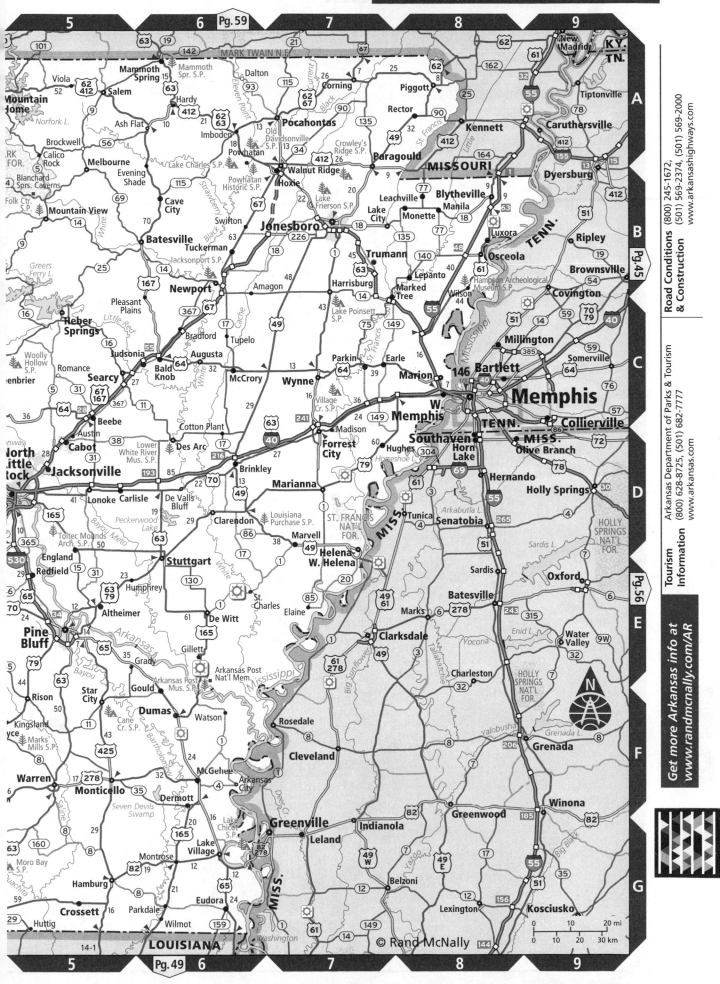

© Rand McNally

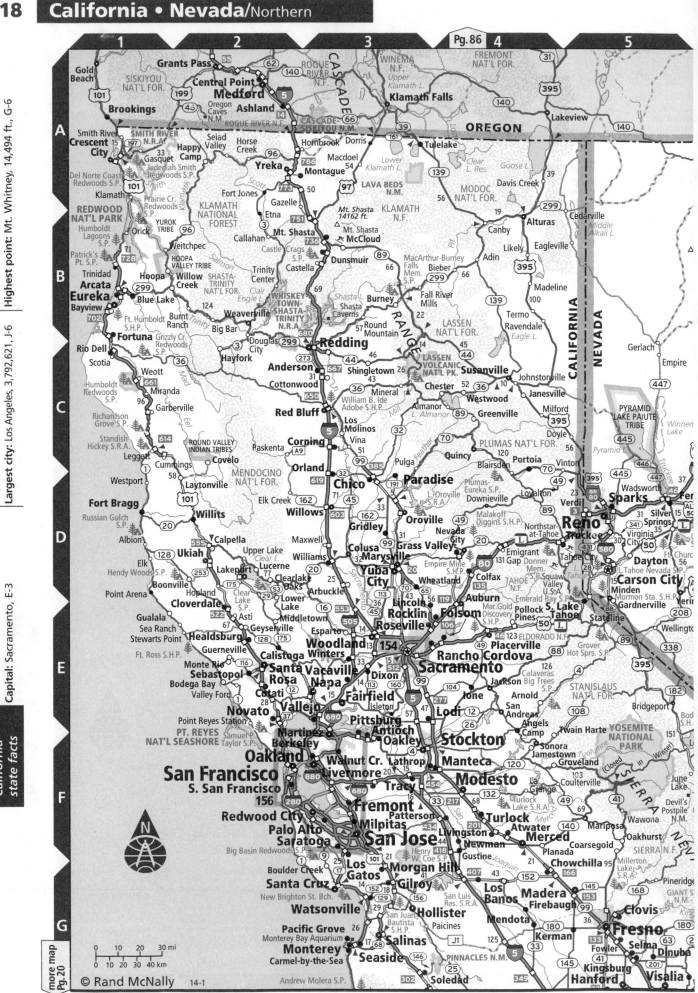

**California state facts**

Nickname: The Golden State
Capital: Sacramento, E-3
Population: 37,253,956 (rank: 1st)
Largest city: Los Angeles, 3,792,621, J-6
Land area: 155,959 sq. mi. (rank: 3rd)
Highest point: Mt. Whitney, 14,494 ft., G-6

more map Pg. 20

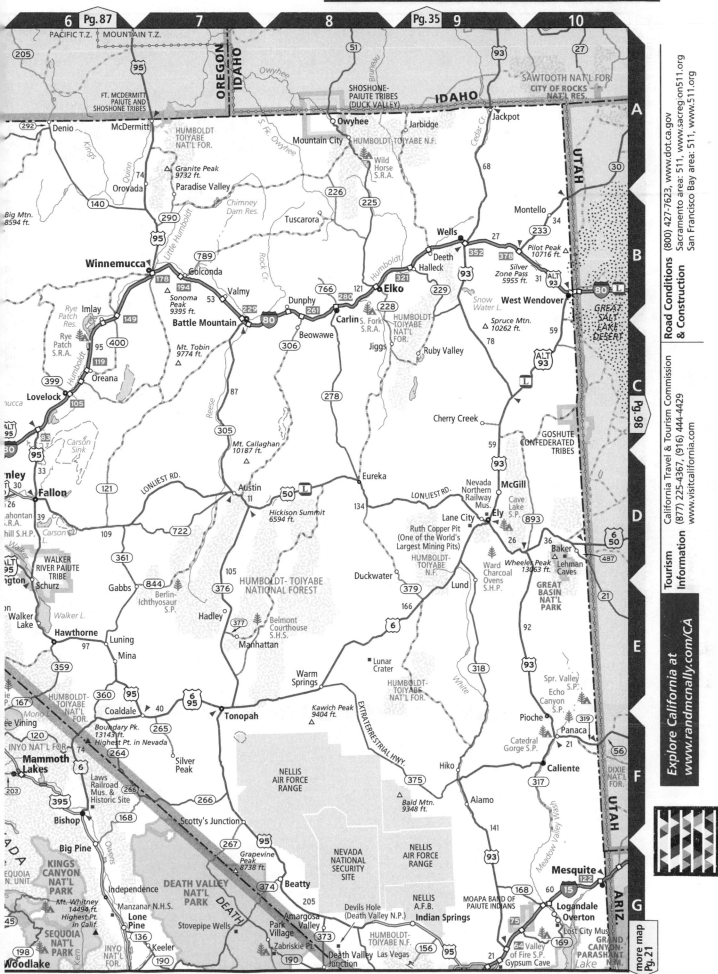

PACIFIC T.Z. | MOUNTAIN T.Z.

OREGON
IDAHO
UTAH
ARIZ.

205
95
292  Denio  McDermitt
FT. McDERMITT PAIUTE AND SHOSHONE TRIBES
HUMBOLDT-TOIYABE NAT'L FOR.
SHOSHONE-PAIUTE TRIBES (DUCK VALLEY)
51
Owyhee  Jarbidge  Jackpot
27
SAWTOOTH NAT'L FOR.
CITY OF ROCKS NAT'L RES.
30
Mountain City  HUMBOLDT-TOIYABE N.F.
Granite Peak 9732 ft.
74  Orovada
Paradise Valley
226  225
Wild Horse S.R.A.
68
Montello  34
233
Pilot Peak 10716 ft.
140
Chimney Dam Res.
Tuscarora
95
Big Mtn. 8594 ft.
290  789
Little Humboldt
Rock Cr.
Wells  27  352  378
Silver Zone Pass 5955 ft.  31  ALT 93
Winnemucca  Golconda  178  194
Valmy  53
766  121
Deeth  Halleck
Humboldt
321  Elko  229
Snow Water L.
West Wendover  80  L
GREAT SALT LAKE DESERT
Sonoma Peak 9395 ft.
Dunphy  261  280
228
Spruce Mtn. 10262 ft.  59
229  80  Carlin
Battle Mountain  149
Beowawe
S. Fork S.R.A.
HUMBOLDT-TOIYABE NAT'L FOR.
Rye Patch Res.
Imlay  Mt. Tobin 9774 ft.
306  Jiggs  Ruby Valley  78
Rye Patch S.R.A.  95  400
119  87
278
ALT 93
399  Oreana
Lovelock  105
Reese
305  Mt. Callaghan 10187 ft.
Cherry Creek  59
L
GOSHUTE CONFEDERATED TRIBES
ALT 95  83
Carson Sink
95
33
30  Fallon  121  LONLIEST RD.
722
Austin  50  L  11
Eureka  134
LONLIEST RD.
93  McGill
Nevada Northern Railway Mus.
Cave Lake S.P.
Pg. 98
Lahontan S.R.A.  39
Carson L.
Hickison Summit 6594 ft.
Ely  893
hill S.H.P.
109
Lane City
Ruth Copper Pit (One of the World's Largest Mining Pits)
26  36  Baker  487
6 50
WALKER RIVER PAIUTE TRIBE
361
Duckwater
HUMBOLDT-TOIYABE N.F.
379  Lund
Ward Charcoal Ovens S.H.P.
Wheeler Peak 13063 ft.  Lehman Caves
GREAT BASIN NAT'L PARK
21
Schurz  Gabbs  844
105
376
HUMBOLDT-TOIYABE NATIONAL FOREST
166
92
Walker L.
Hadley  377
6
Belmont Courthouse S.H.S.
Spr. Valley S.P.
Echo Canyon S.P.
Hawthorne  97  Luning
Manhattan
Lunar Crater
318
93  Pioche  319
Panaca  56
Mina
Warm Springs
EXTRATERRESTRIAL HWY.
White
HUMBOLDT-TOIYABE NAT'L FOR.
Catedral Gorge S.P.  21
359
360  95
Kawich Peak 9404 ft.
Coaldale  40  6 95
265  Tonopah
Boundary Pk. 13143 ft. Highest Pt. in Nevada
264
Silver Peak
375
Hiko
Caliente  317
DIXIE NAT'L FOR.
Mammoth Lakes  74
INYO NAT'L FOR.
Laws Railroad Mus. & Historic Site
266
NELLIS AIR FORCE RANGE
Bald Mtn. 9348 ft.
Alamo  141
UTAH
120  395  203
Bishop  168
Scotty's Junction
NEVADA NATIONAL SECURITY SITE
NELLIS AIR FORCE RANGE
93
Mesquite  122
15
Big Pine  267  95
Grapevine Peak 8738 ft.
374  Beatty
168  60
KINGS CANYON NAT'L PARK
Owens
266
DEATH VALLEY NAT'L PARK
205
Devils Hole (Death Valley N.P.)
NELLIS A.F.B.
MOAPA BAND OF PAIUTE INDIANS
Logandale  75  Overton
GRAND CANYON-PARASHANT N.M.
Mt. Whitney 14494 ft. Highest Pt. in Calif.
Manzanar N.H.S.
Independence
Lone Pine  136
Stovepipe Wells
Amargosa Valley
Park Village  373
Zabriskie Pt.
Death Valley Junction
Indian Springs
156  95
HUMBOLDT-TOIYABE N.F.
64  Valley of Fire S.P.
Gypsum Cave
169  Lost City Mus.
Lake
45  SEQUOIA NAT'L PARK  198
Woodlake  190  Keeler  190  21

A  B  C  D  E  F  G

more map Pg. 21

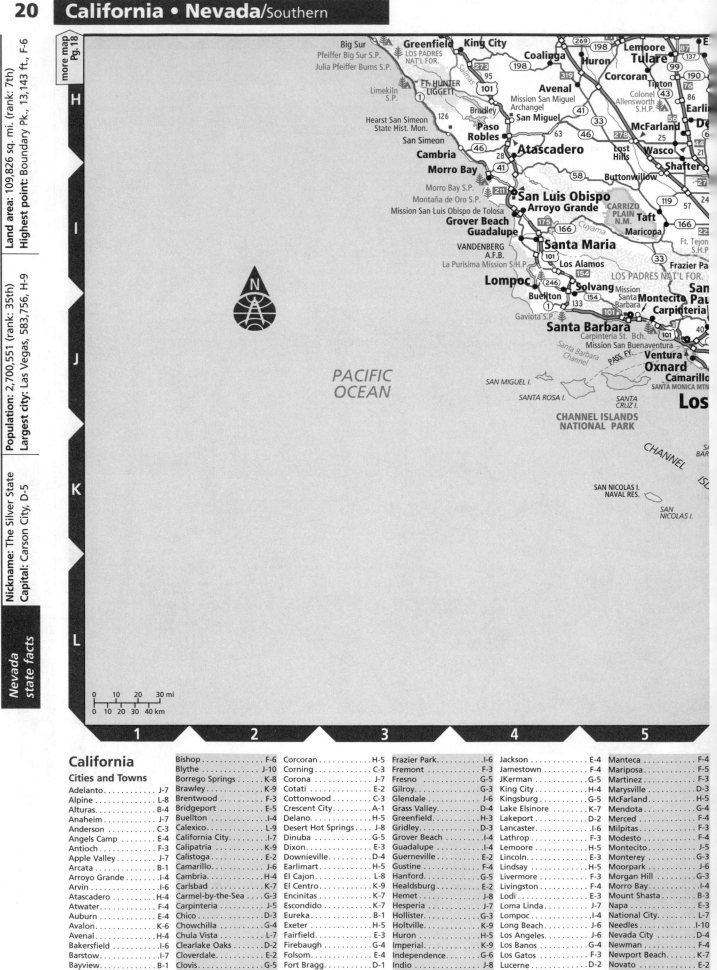

**Nevada state facts**

Nickname: The Silver State
Capital: Carson City, D-5

Population: 2,700,551 (rank: 35th)
Largest city: Las Vegas, 583,756, H-9

Land area: 109,826 sq. mi. (rank: 7th)
Highest point: Boundary Pk., 13,143 ft., F-6

more map Pg. 18

## California

### Cities and Towns

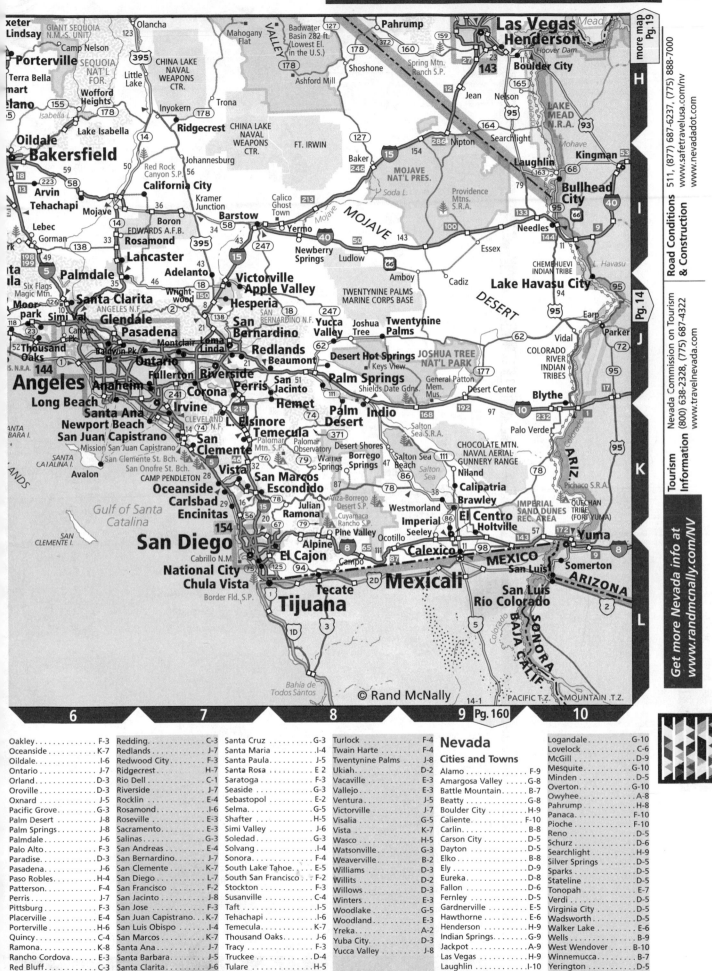

## Colorado

### Cities and Towns

**Colorado state facts**

Nickname: The Centennial State
Capital: Denver, C-6

Population: 5,029,196 (rank: 22nd)
Largest city: Denver, 600,158, C-6

Land area: 103,718 sq. mi. (rank: 8th)
Highest point: Mt. Elbert, 14,433 ft., D-4

© Rand McNally

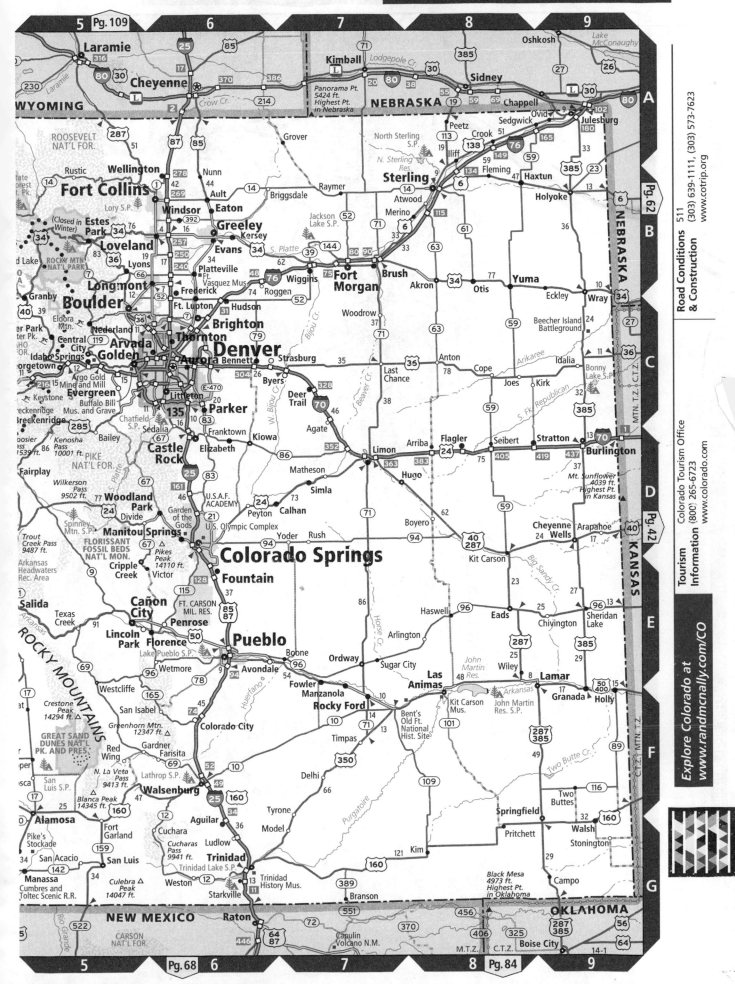

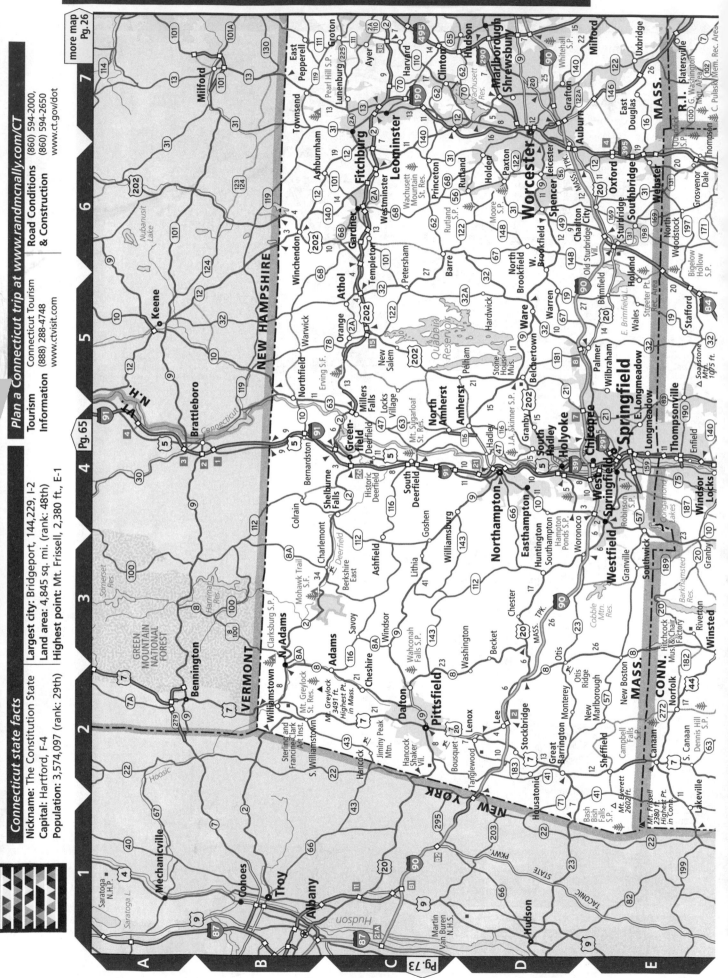

more map Pg. 26

Plan a Connecticut trip at www.randmcnally.com/CT

| Tourism | Connecticut Tourism | (860) 594-2000, |
| Information | (888) 288-4748 | (860) 594-2650 |
| | www.ctvisit.com | www.ct.gov/dot |
| | Road Conditions | |
| | & Construction | |

**Connecticut state facts**

Nickname: The Constitution State
Capital: Hartford, F-4
Population: 3,574,097 (rank: 29th)

Largest city: Bridgeport, 144,229, I-2
Land area: 4,845 sq. mi. (rank: 48th)
Highest point: Mt. Frissell, 2,380 ft., E-1

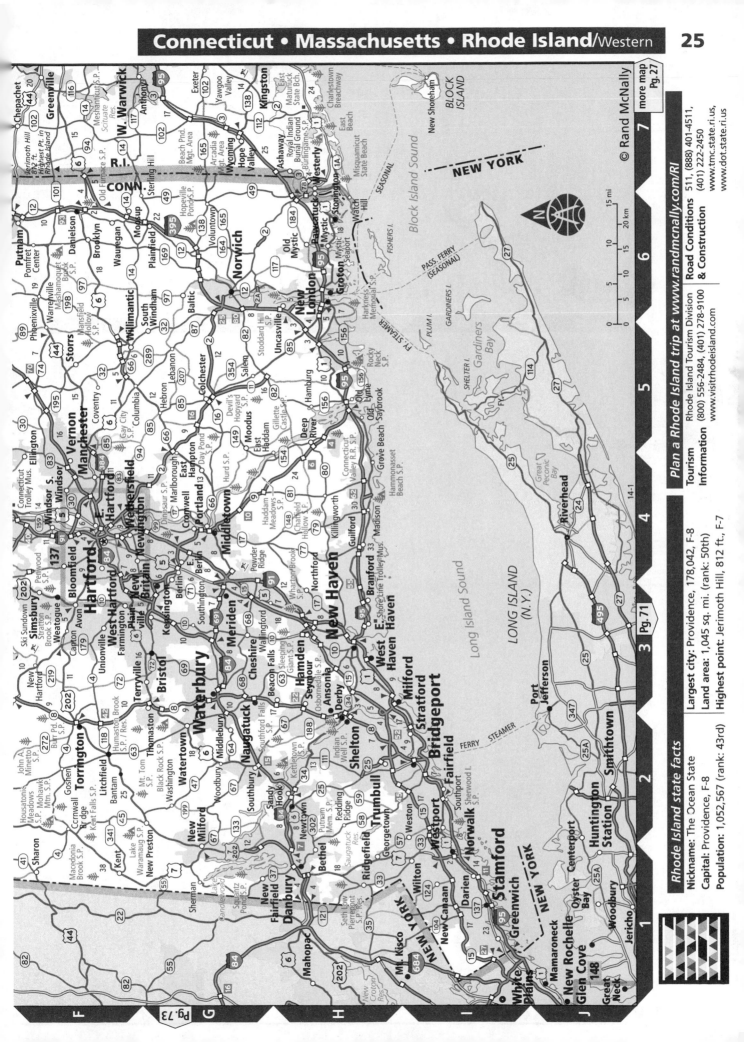

© Rand McNally

more map Pg. 27

**NEW YORK**

---

**Plan a Rhode Island trip at www.randmcnally.com/RI**

| | |
|---|---|
| **Tourism** | Rhode Island Tourism Division |
| **Information** | (800) 556-2484, (401) 278-9100 |
| | www.visitrhodeisland.com |
| **Road Conditions** | 511, (888) 401-4511, |
| **& Construction** | (401) 222-2450 |
| | www.tmc.state.ri.us, |
| | www.dot.state.ri.us |

**Rhode Island state facts**

**Nickname:** The Ocean State
**Capital:** Providence, F-8
**Population:** 1,052,567 (rank: 43rd)
**Largest city:** Providence, 178,042, F-8
**Land area:** 1,045 sq. mi. (rank: 50th)
**Highest point:** Jerimoth Hill, 812 ft., F-7

## Connecticut

### Cities and Towns

## Massachusetts state facts

Nickname: The Bay State
Capital: Boston, D-9

Population: 6,547,629 (rank: 14th)
Largest city: Boston, 617,594, D-9

Land area: 7,840 sq. mi. (rank: 45th)
Highest point: Mt. Greylock, 3,491 ft., B-2

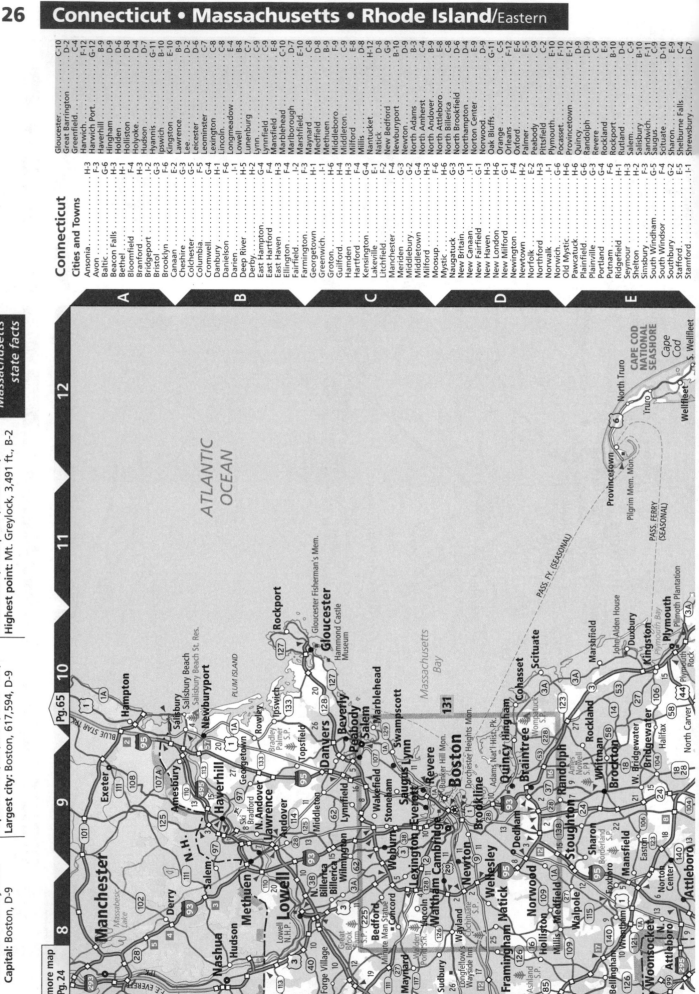

more map Pg. 24

| | |
|---|---|
| Smith Mills | G-9 |
| Somerset | F-9 |
| South Deerfield | C-4 |
| South Hadley | D-4 |
| South Yarmouth | G-12 |
| Southampton | D-4 |
| Southbridge | E-6 |
| Spencer | E-6 |
| Springfield | E-4 |
| Stoneham | C-9 |
| Sturbridge | E-6 |
| Sudbury Center | D-8 |
| Swampscott | C-9 |
| Taunton | F-9 |
| Topsfield | B-9 |
| Uxbridge | E-7 |
| Vineyard Haven | G-10 |
| Wakefield | E-8 |
| Walpole | D-8 |
| Waltham | D-8 |
| Ware | D-5 |
| Wareham Center | F-10 |
| Wayland | D-8 |
| Webster | E-6 |
| Wellesley | D-8 |
| West Bridgewater | E-9 |
| West Springfield | E-4 |
| West Yarmouth | G-12 |
| Westfield | E-4 |
| Westport | E-9 |
| Whitman | D-7 |
| Wilbraham | E-5 |
| Williamstown | B-2 |
| Wilmington | C-9 |
| Winchendon | D-5 |
| Woburn | C-8 |
| Worcester | D-7 |
| Wrentham | E-8 |

| | |
|---|---|
| Storrs | F-5 |
| Stratford | I-2 |
| Terryville | G-3 |
| Thomaston | G-3 |
| Thompsonville | E-4 |
| Torrington | F-2 |
| Trumbull | H-2 |
| Uncasville | H-6 |
| Unionville | F-3 |
| Vernon | F-4 |
| Waterbury | G-3 |
| Watertown | G-2 |
| Weatogue | F-3 |
| West Hartford | F-4 |
| West Haven | H-3 |
| Weston | I-2 |
| Westport | J-2 |
| Wethersfield | F-4 |
| Willimantic | F-5 |
| Wilton | I-1 |
| Windsor | G-4 |
| Windsor Locks | E-4 |
| Winsted | E-3 |

## Massachusetts
### Cities and Towns

| | |
|---|---|
| Adams | C-2 |
| Amesbury | B-9 |
| Amherst | D-4 |
| Andover | C-5 |
| Athol | C-5 |
| Attleboro | E-8 |
| Auburn | D-7 |
| Ayer | C-7 |
| Barnstable | F-11 |
| Bedford | C-8 |
| Belchertown | D-5 |
| Bellingham | E-8 |
| Beverly | C-9 |
| Billerica | C-8 |
| Boston | D-9 |
| Braintree | D-9 |
| Brewster | F-12 |
| Bridgewater | E-9 |
| Brockton | E-9 |
| Brookline | D-9 |
| Buzzards Bay | F-10 |
| Cambridge | D-9 |
| Chicopee | E-4 |
| Clinton | C-7 |
| Cohasset | D-10 |
| Concord | C-8 |
| Dalton | C-2 |
| Danvers | C-9 |
| Dartmouth | F-9 |
| Dedham | D-9 |
| Dennis | F-12 |
| East Douglas | E-7 |
| East Falmouth | G-11 |
| East Longmeadow | E-4 |
| East Pepperell | B-7 |
| Easthampton | D-4 |
| Edgartown | H-11 |
| Everett | C-9 |
| Fairhaven | F-9 |
| Fall River | F-9 |
| Falmouth | G-10 |
| Fitchburg | C-7 |
| Foxboro | E-8 |
| Framingham | D-8 |
| Gardner | C-6 |
| Georgetown | B-9 |

## Rhode Island
### Cities and Towns

| | |
|---|---|
| Anthony | F-7 |
| Bristol | G-8 |
| Central Falls | F-8 |
| Cranston | G-8 |
| East Greenwich | F-8 |
| East Providence | F-8 |
| Exeter | F-7 |
| Greenville | F-8 |
| Jamestown | G-8 |
| Kingston | G-8 |
| Middletown | H-8 |
| Narragansett Pier | G-8 |
| Newport | H-8 |
| North Kingstown | G-8 |
| Pawtucket | F-8 |
| Portsmouth | G-9 |
| Providence | F-8 |
| Tiverton | G-9 |
| Warwick | F-8 |
| West Warwick | F-8 |
| Westerly | H-7 |
| Woonsocket | E-8 |

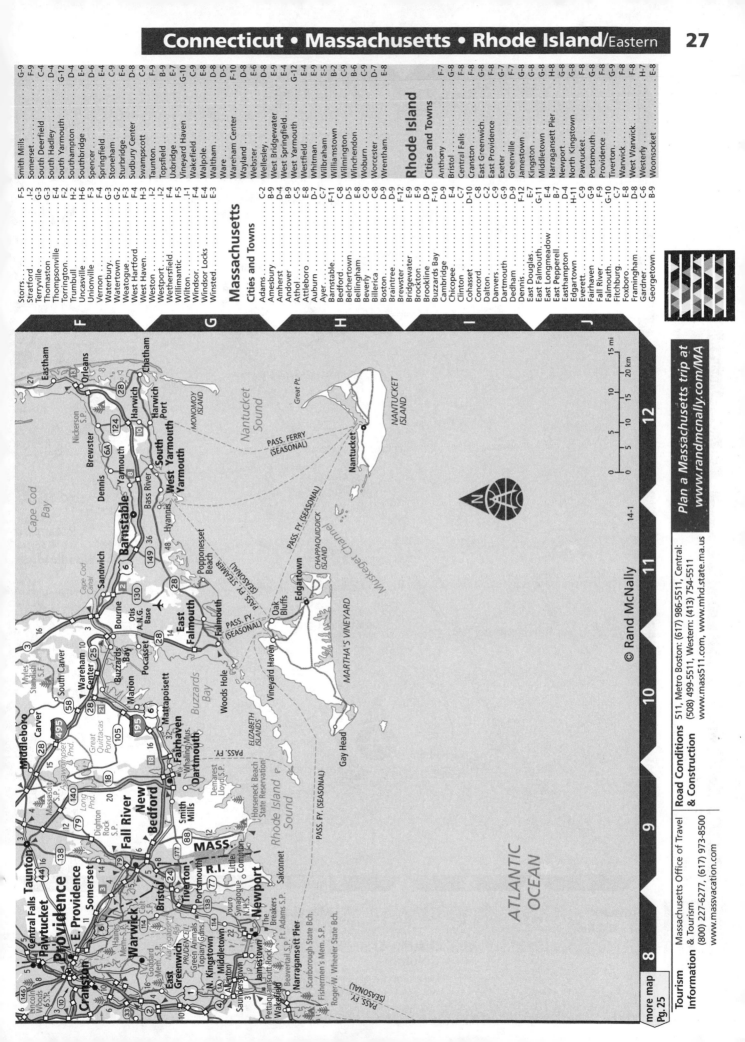

© Rand McNally

**Tourism Information** — Massachusetts Office of Travel & Tourism (800) 227-6277, (617) 973-8500 www.massvacation.com

**Road Conditions & Construction** — 511, Metro Boston: (617) 986-5511, Central: (508) 499-5511, Western: (413) 754-5511 www.mass511.com, www.mhd.state.ma.us

**Plan a Massachusetts trip at www.randmcnally.com/MA**

more map Pg. 25

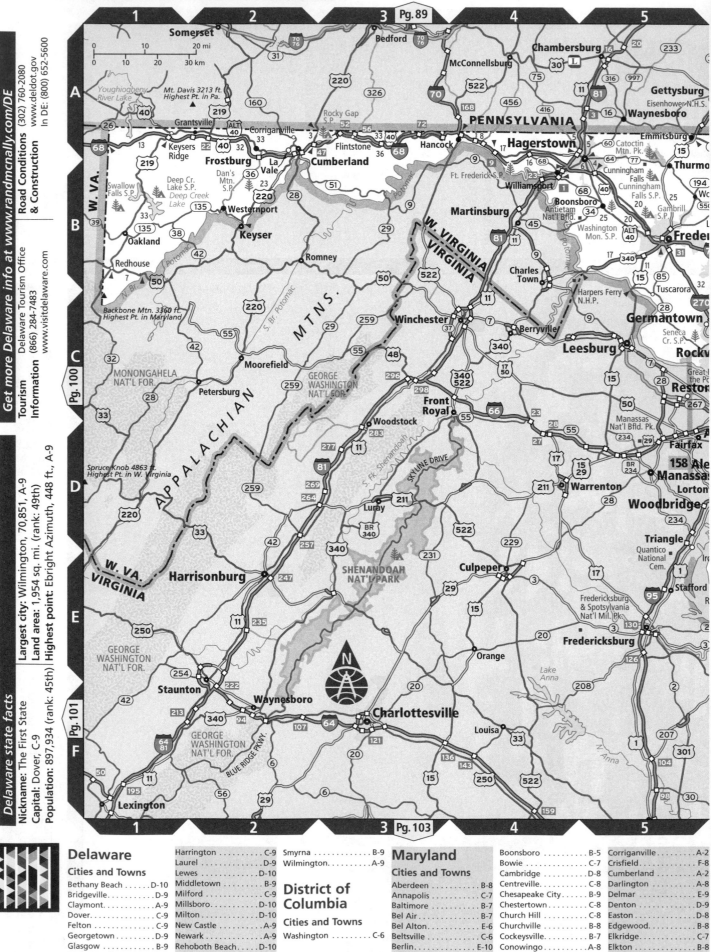

Get more Delaware info at www.randmcnally.com/DE

**Road Conditions & Construction**
(302) 760-2080
www.deldot.gov
In DE: (800) 652-5600

**Tourism Information**
Delaware Tourism Office
(866) 284-7483
www.visitdelaware.com

**Delaware state facts**
Nickname: The First State
Capital: Dover, C-9
Population: 897,934 (rank: 45th)
Highest point: Ebright Azimuth, 448 ft., A-9
Land area: 1,954 sq. mi. (rank: 49th)
Largest city: Wilmington, 70,851, A-9

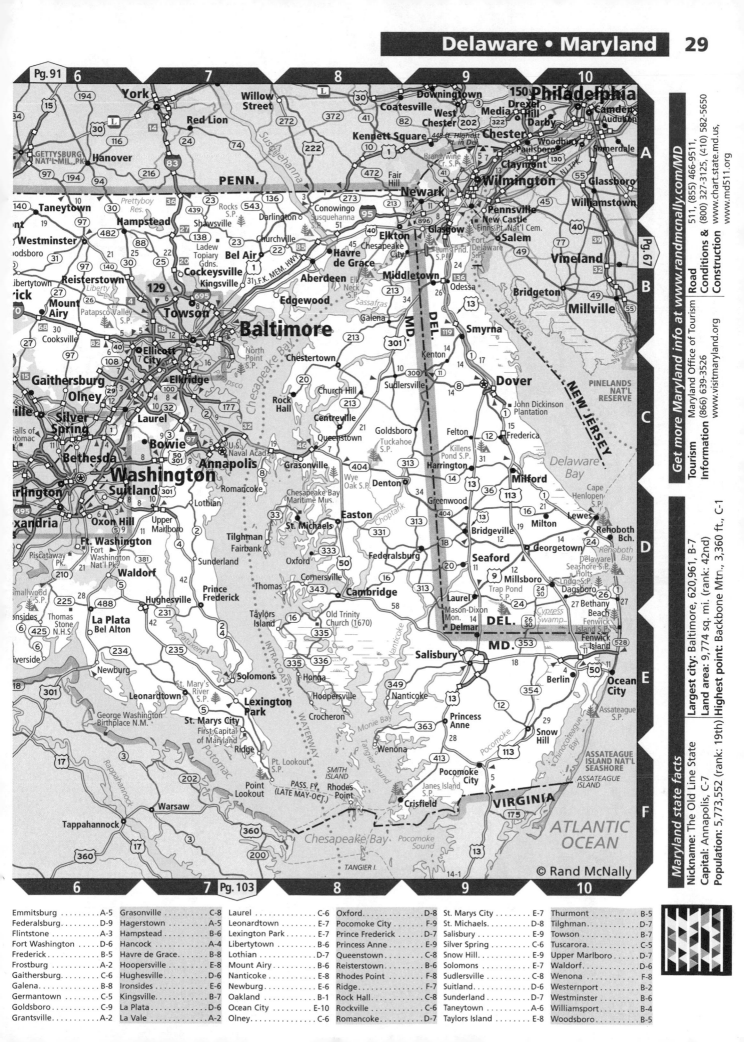

Get more Maryland info at www.randmcnally.com/MD

**Tourism** Maryland Office of Tourism
**Information** (866) 639-3526
www.visitmaryland.org

**Road** 511, (855) 466-9511,
**Conditions &** (800) 327-3125, (410) 582-5650
**Construction** www.chart.state.md.us,
www.md511.org

## Maryland state facts

**Nickname:** The Old Line State
**Capital:** Annapolis, C-7
**Population:** 5,773,552 (rank: 19th)

**Largest city:** Baltimore, 620,961, B-7
**Land area:** 9,774 sq. mi. (rank: 42nd)
**Highest point:** Backbone Mtn., 3,360 ft., C-1

© Rand McNally

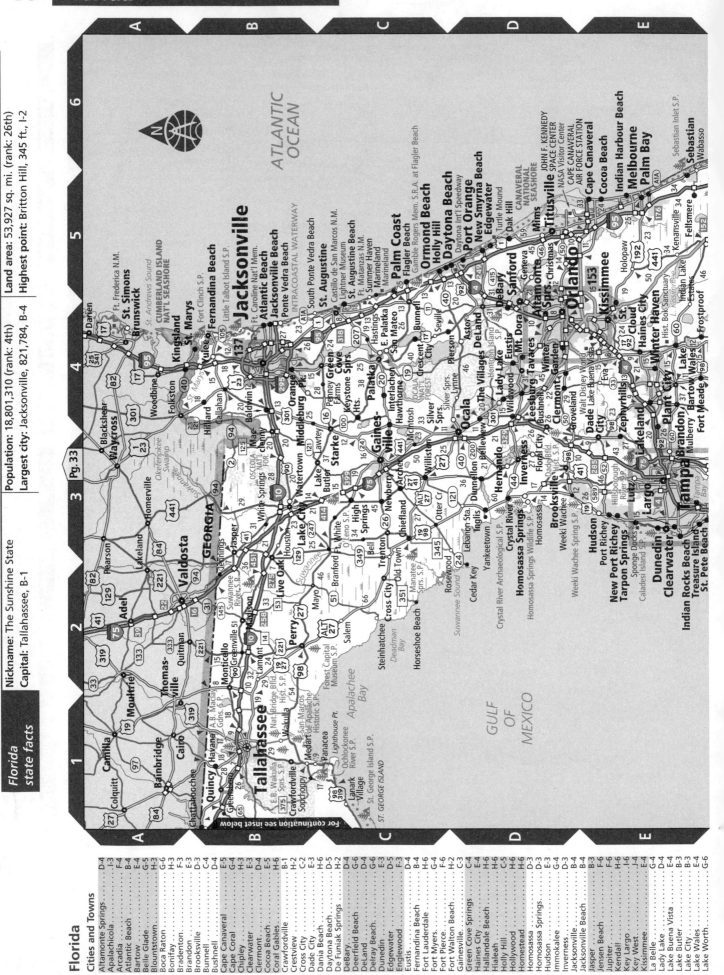

*Florida*
state facts

**Nickname:** The Sunshine State
**Capital:** Tallahassee, B-1

**Population:** 18,801,310 (rank: 4th)
**Largest city:** Jacksonville, 821,784, B-4

**Land area:** 53,927 sq. mi. (rank: 26th)
**Highest point:** Britton Hill, 345 ft, I-2

## Florida

### Cities and Towns

| | | | | | |
|---|---|---|---|---|---|
| **Tourism Information** | Visit Florida (888) 735-2872, (850) 488-5607 www.visitflorida.com | | **Road Conditions & Construction** | 511 (866) 374-3368 www.fl511.com, www.dot.state.fl.us | |

*Plan a Florida trip at*
**www.randmcnally.com/FL**

**Georgia**
*state facts*

**Nickname:** The Peach State
**Capital:** Atlanta, C-2

**Population:** 9,687,653 (rank: 9th)
**Largest city:** Atlanta, 420,003, C-2

**Land area:** 57,906 sq. mi. (rank: 21st)
**Highest point:** Brasstown Bald, 4,784 ft., A-3

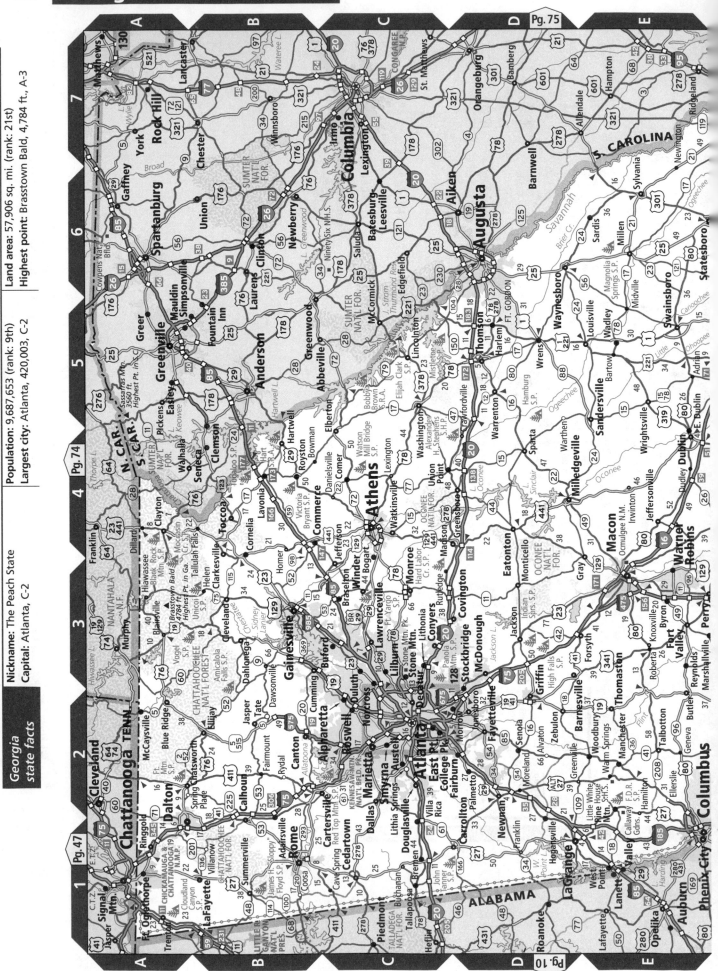

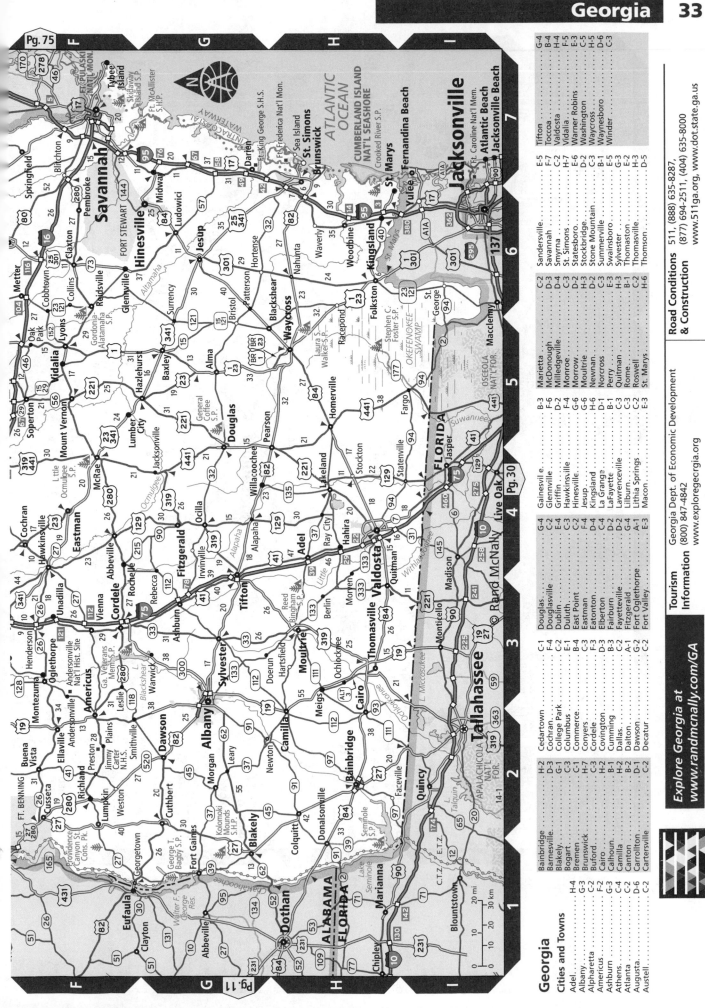

**Tourism** Georgia Dept. of Economic Development
**Information** (800) 847-4842
www.exploregeorgia.org

**Road Conditions** 511, (888) 635-8287,
**& Construction** (877) 694-2511, (404) 635-8000
www.511ga.org, www.dot.state.ga.us

*Explore Georgia at*
*www.randmcnally.com/GA*

# Idaho

**Idaho**
**state facts**

Nickname: The Gem State
Capital: Boise, H-2

Population: 1,567,582 (rank: 39th)
Largest city: Boise, 205,671, H-2

Land area: 82,747 sq. mi. (rank: 11th)
Highest point: Borah Peak, 12,662 ft., G-4

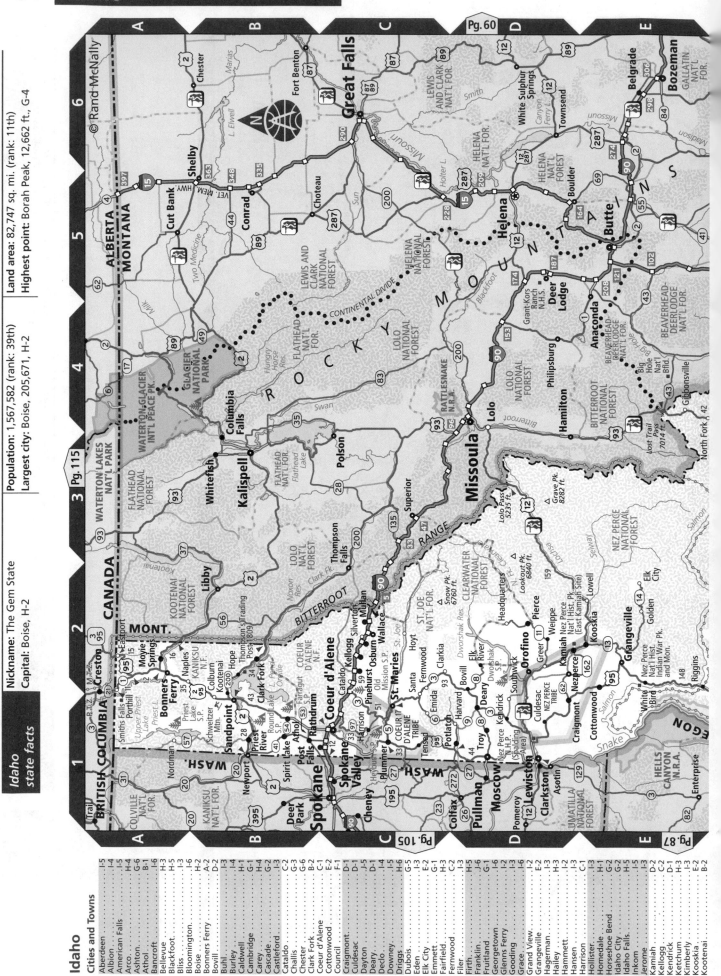

## Cities and Towns

Pg. 60   Pg. 108   Pg. 87   Pg. 19   Pg. 98

WYO.   MONT.   NEVADA   UTAH   OREGON   ID.

**Road Conditions & Construction**  511  (888) 432-7623  www.511.idaho.gov, www.itd.idaho.gov

**Tourism Information**  Idaho Division of Tourism Development  (800) 847-4843, (208) 334-2470  www.visitidaho.org

*Get more Idaho travel info at* **www.randmcnally.com/ID**

*Illinois*
*state facts*

**Nickname:** Land of Lincoln
**Capital:** Springfield, E-3

**Population:** 12,830,632 (rank: 5th)
**Largest city:** Chicago, 2,695,598, B-6

**Land area:** 55,584 sq. mi. (rank: 24th)
**Highest point:** Charles Mound, 1,235 ft., A-2

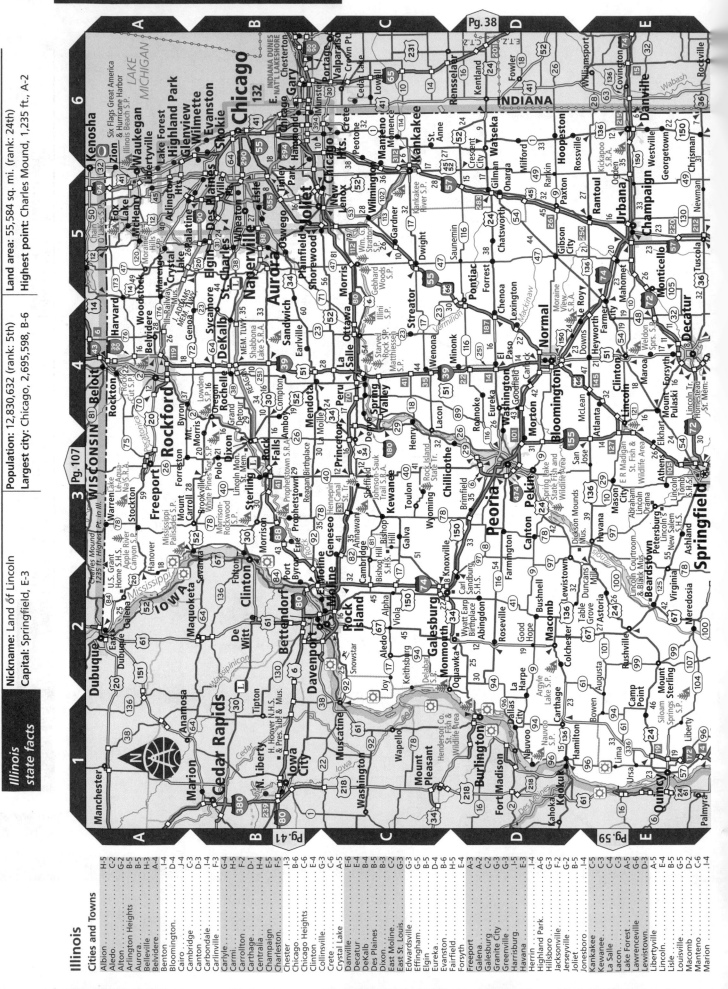

## Illinois
### Cities and Towns

**Road Conditions & Construction** (800) 452-4368, (312) 368-4636
www.gettingaroundillinois.com
www.dot.il.gov

**Tourism Information** Illinois Bureau of Tourism
(800) 226-6632
www.enjoyillinois.com

*Plan an Illinois trip at*
**www.randmcnally.com/IL**

*Indiana*
*state facts*

Nickname: The Hoosier State
Capital: Indianapolis, F-4

Land area: 35,867 sq. mi. (rank: 38th)
Highest point: Hoosier Hill, 1,257 ft, E-6

Population: 6,483,802 (rank: 15th)
Largest city: Indianapolis, 820,445, F-4

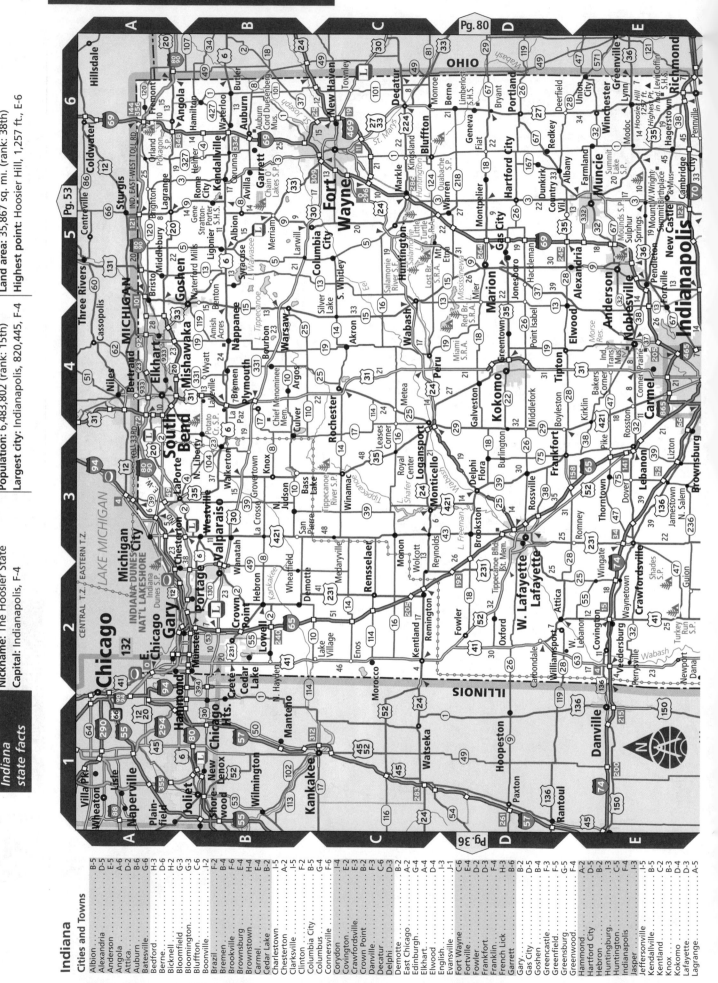

## Indiana
### Cities and Towns

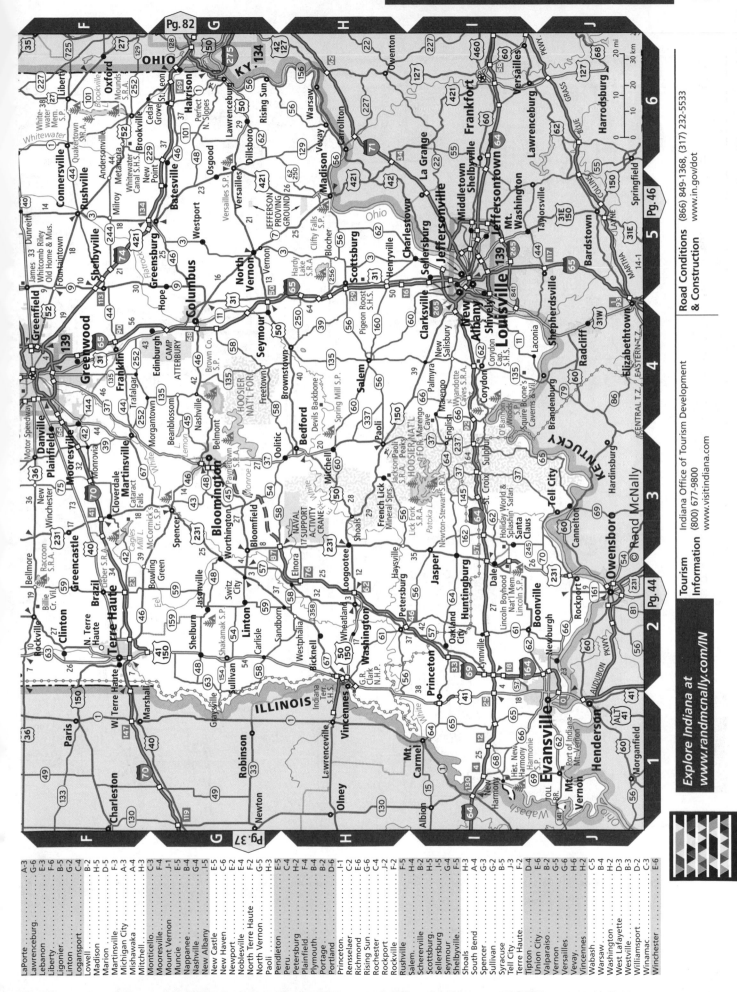

**Road Conditions** (866) 849-1368, (317) 232-5533
**& Construction** www.in.gov/dot

**Tourism** Indiana Office of Tourism Development
**Information** (800) 677-9800
www.visitindiana.com

*Explore Indiana at*
*www.randmcnally.com/IN*

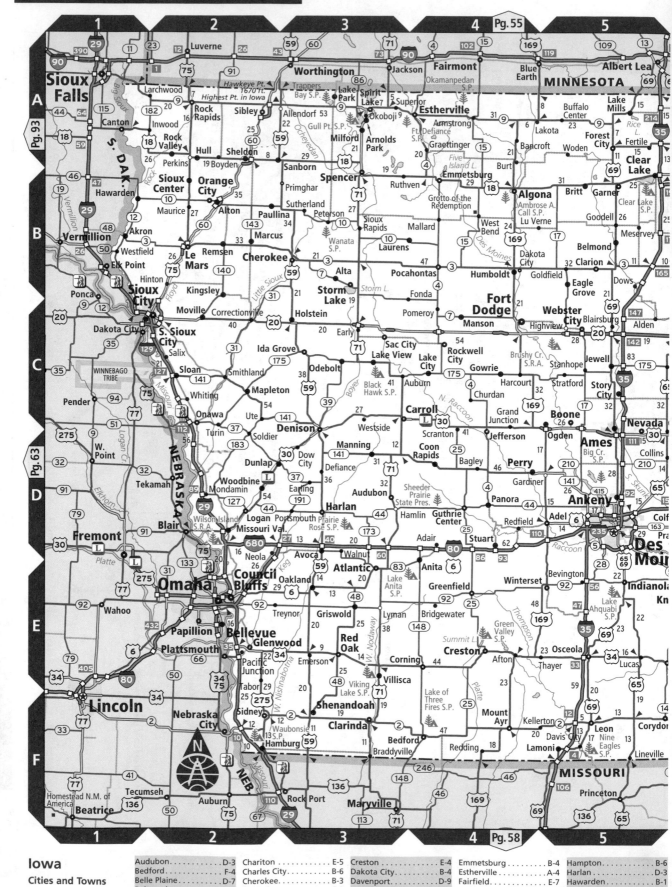

**Iowa**
**state facts**

Nickname: The Hawkeye State
Capital: Des Moines, D-5

Population: 3,046,355 (rank: 30th)
Largest city: Des Moines, 203,433, D-5

Land area: 55,869 sq. mi. (rank: 23rd)
Highest point: Hawkeye Point, 1,670 ft., A-2

## Iowa

### Cities and Towns

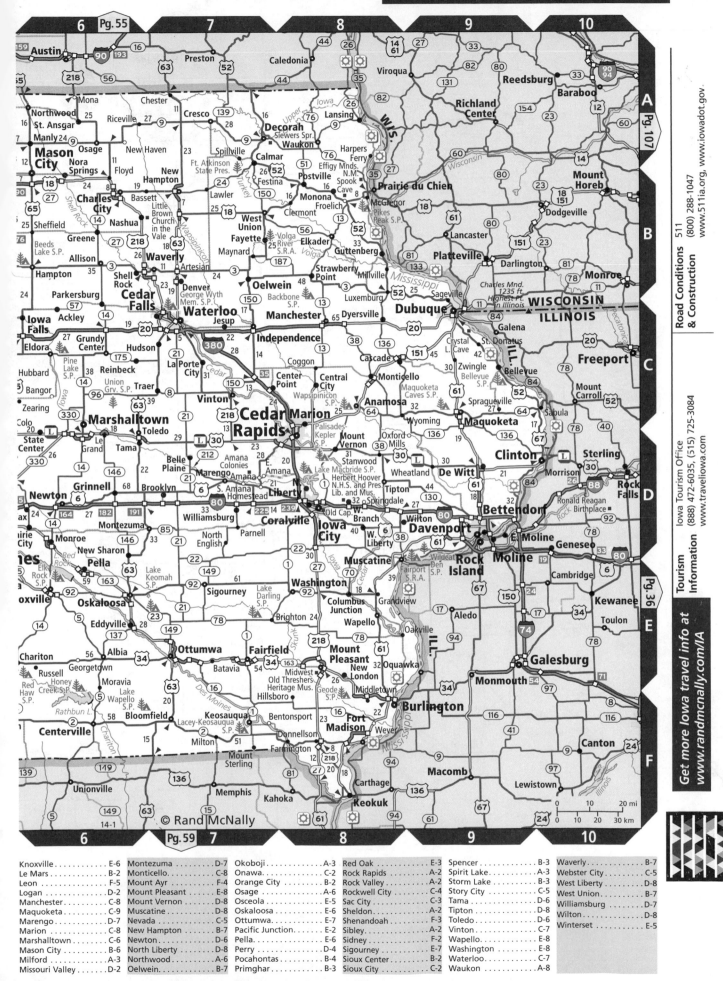

Road Conditions
& Construction

511
(800) 288-1047
www.511ia.org, www.iowadot.gov.

Tourism
Information

Iowa Tourism Office
(888) 472-6035, (515) 725-3084
www.traveliowa.com

Get more Iowa travel info at
www.randmcnally.com/IA

Pg. 107
Pg. 36

© Rand McNally

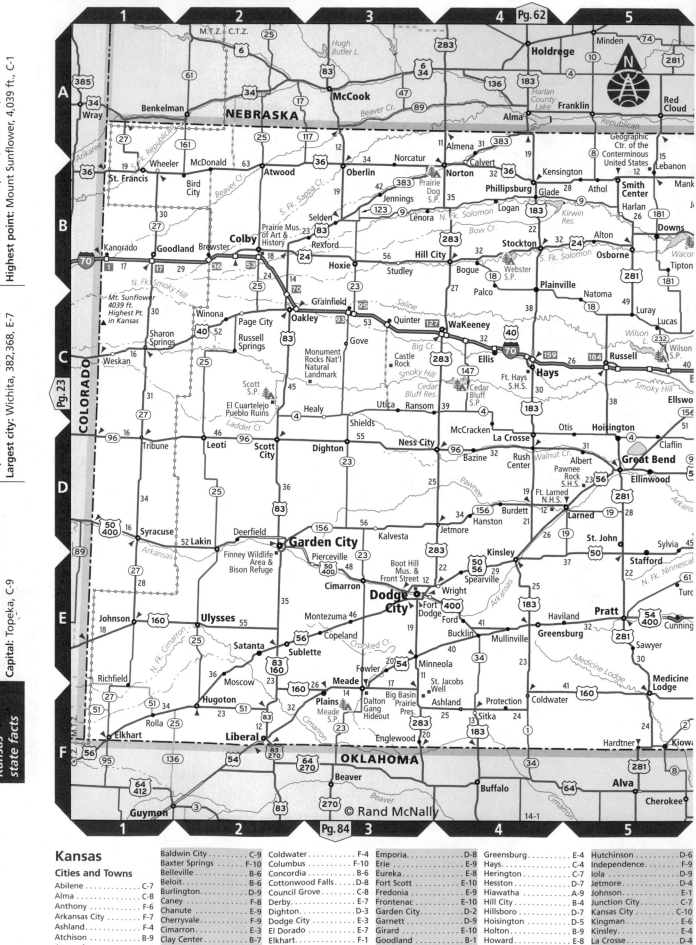

**Kansas state facts**

Land area: 81,815 sq. mi. (rank: 13th)
Highest point: Mount Sunflower, 4,039 ft., C-1

Population: 2,853,118 (rank: 33rd)
Largest city: Wichita, 382,368, E-7

Nickname: The Sunflower State
Capital: Topeka, C-9

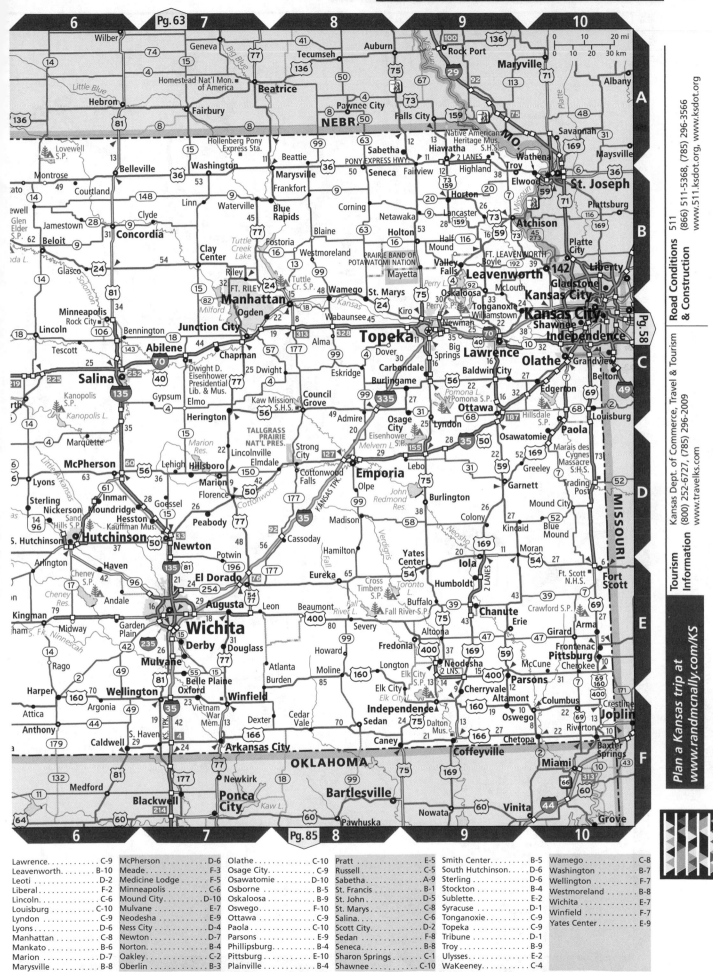

Tourism Information
Kansas Dept. of Commerce, Travel & Tourism
(800) 252-6727, (785) 296-2009
www.travelks.com

Road Conditions & Construction
511
(866) 511-5368, (785) 296-3566
www.511.ksdot.org, www.ksdot.org

Plan a Kansas trip at www.randmcnally.com/KS

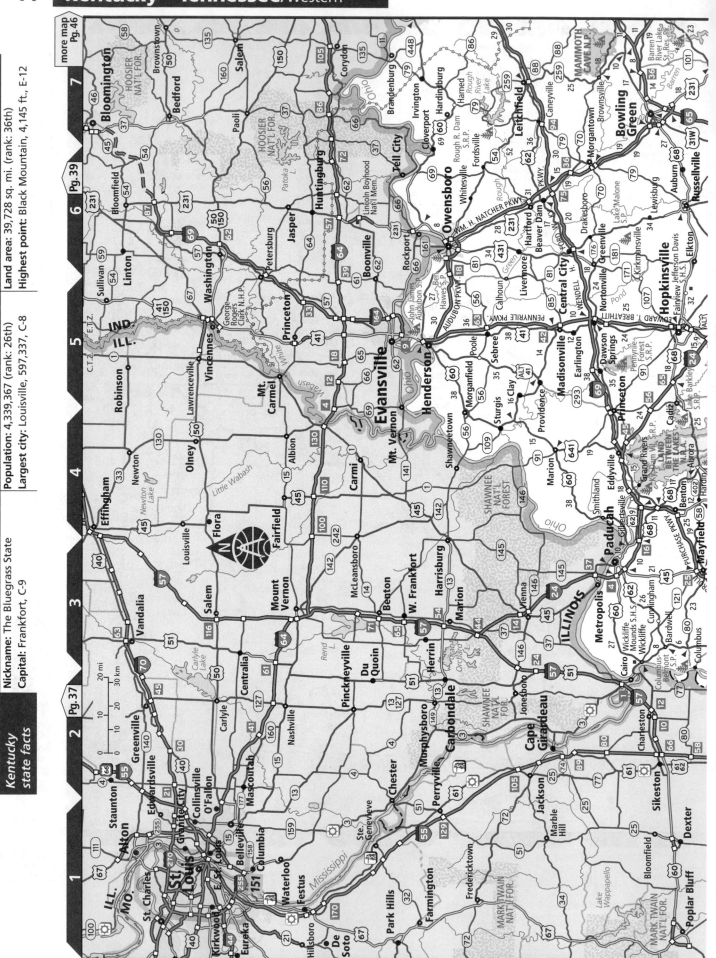

more map Pg.46
Pg. 39
Pg. 37
Pg.59

## Kentucky state facts

**Nickname:** The Bluegrass State
**Capital:** Frankfort, C-9

**Population:** 4,339,367 (rank: 26th)
**Largest city:** Louisville, 597,337, C-8

**Land area:** 39,728 sq. mi. (rank: 36th)
**Highest point:** Black Mountain, 4,145 ft., E-12

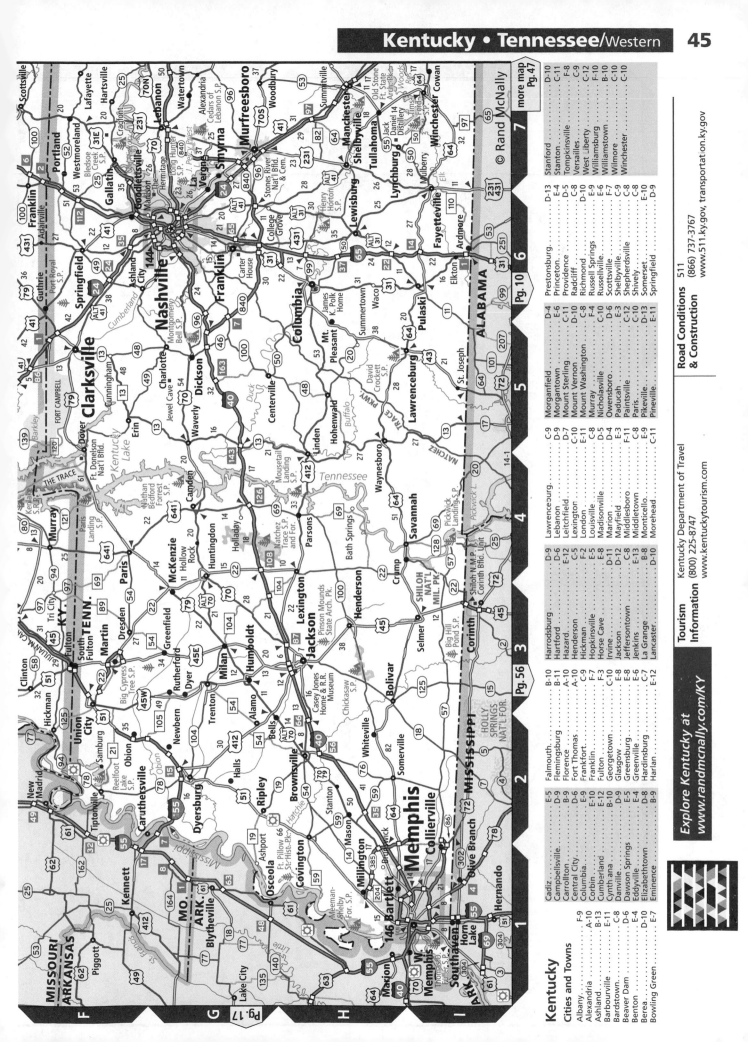

© Rand McNally

more map Pg.47

## Kentucky

### Cities and Towns

Albany............F-9
Alexandria.........A-10
Ashland..........B-13
Barbourville........E-11
Bardstown.........C-8
Beaver Dam........D-6
Benton...........E-4
Berea............D-10
Bowling Green......E-7

Cadiz............E-5
Campbellsville.....D-9
Carrollton.........B-9
Central City.......D-6
Columbia..........D-9
Corbin............E-10
Cynthiana.........B-10
Danville..........D-9
Dawson Springs.....E-5
Eddyville.........E-4
Elizabethtown......D-8
Eminence..........B-9

Falmouth..........B-10
Flemingsburg......C-11
Florence..........A-10
Fort Thomas.......A-10
Frankfort.........C-9
Franklin..........E-7
Fulton............F-3
Georgetown........C-10
Glasgow...........D-9
Greensburg........D-9
Greenville........E-5
Hardinsburg.......D-7
Harlan............E-12

Harrodsburg.......C-9
Hartford..........D-6
Hazard...........E-12
Henderson.........C-5
Hickman...........F-2
Hopkinsville......E-5
Irvine...........D-11
Jackson..........D-12
Jenkins..........D-13
La Grange.........B-8
Lancaster.........D-10

Lawrenceburg......C-9
Lebanon..........D-9
Leitchfield.......D-7
Lexington.........C-10
London............E-11
Louisville........C-8
Madisonville......D-5
Marion...........D-4
Mayfield.........E-3
Middlesboro.......F-11
Middletown........C-8
Monticello........E-9
Morehead.........C-11

Morganfield.......D-4
Morgantown........D-6
Mount Sterling....C-11
Mount Vernon......D-10
Mount Washington..C-8
Murray...........E-4
Nicholasville.....C-10
Owensboro.........D-6
Paducah..........D-4
Paris............C-10
Paintsville.......C-12
Pikeville.........D-13
Pineville.........E-11

Prestonsburg.......D-12
Princeton.........E-4
Providence........D-5
Radcliff..........C-8
Richmond.........D-10
Russell Springs....E-9
Russellville......E-6
Scottsville.......F-7
Shelbyville.......C-9
Shepherdsville.....C-8
Shively...........C-8
Somerset.........E-10
Springfield.......D-9

Stanford.........D-10
Stanton..........E-4
Tompkinsville.....D-5
Versailles........C-8
West Liberty......D-10
Williamsburg......F-10
Williamstown......B-10
Wilmore..........C-9
Winchester.......C-10

### Road Conditions & Construction
511
(866) 737-3767
www.511.ky.gov, transportation.ky.gov

### Tourism Information
Kentucky Department of Travel
(800) 225-8747
www.kentuckytourism.com

Kentucky Tourism
511
www.511.ky.gov

**Explore Kentucky at**
**www.randmcnally.com/KY**

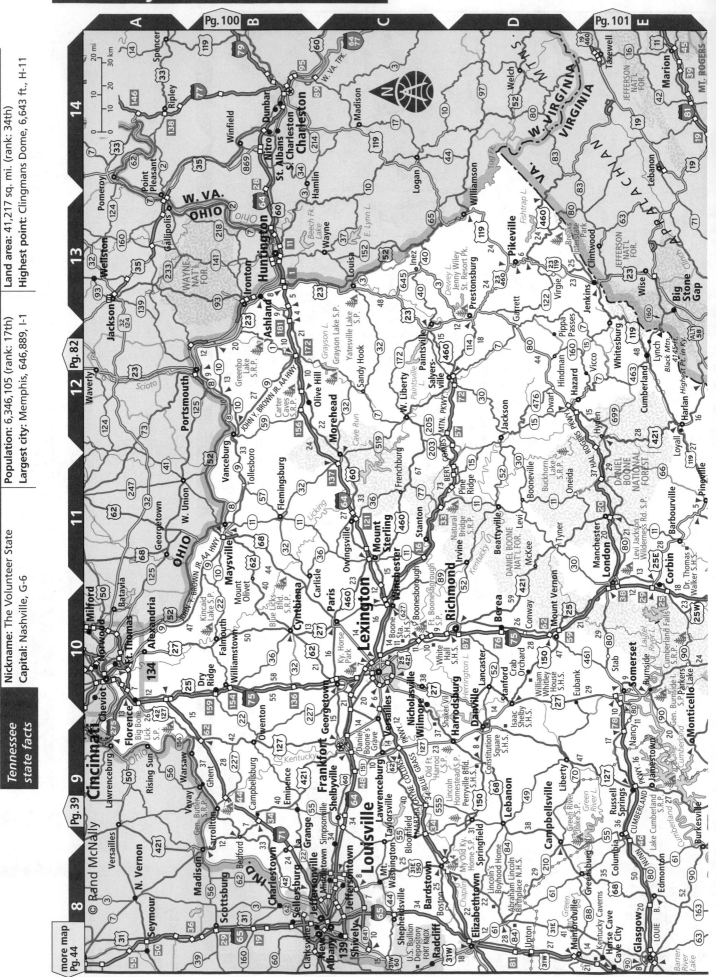

*Tennessee state facts*

Nickname: The Volunteer State
Capital: Nashville, G-6

Population: 6,346,105 (rank: 17th)
Land area: 41,217 sq. mi. (rank: 34th)
Largest city: Memphis, 646,889, I-1
Highest point: Clingmans Dome, 6,643 ft., H-11

Pg. 100
Pg. 101
Pg. 82
Pg. 39
more map Pg. 44

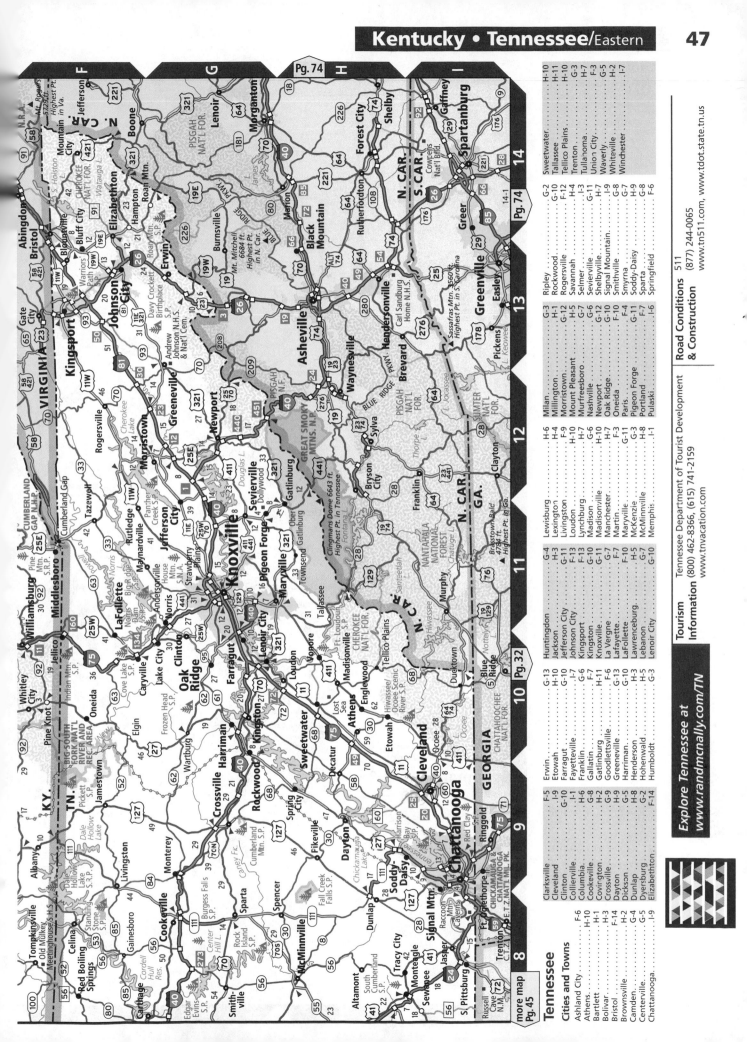

## Louisiana

### Cities and Towns

**Louisiana state facts**

Nickname: The Pelican State
Capital: Baton Rouge, E-6

Population: 4,533,372 (rank: 25th)
Largest city: New Orleans, 343,829, F-7

Land area: 43,562 sq. mi. (rank: 33rd)
Highest point: Driskill Mountain, 535 ft., B-3

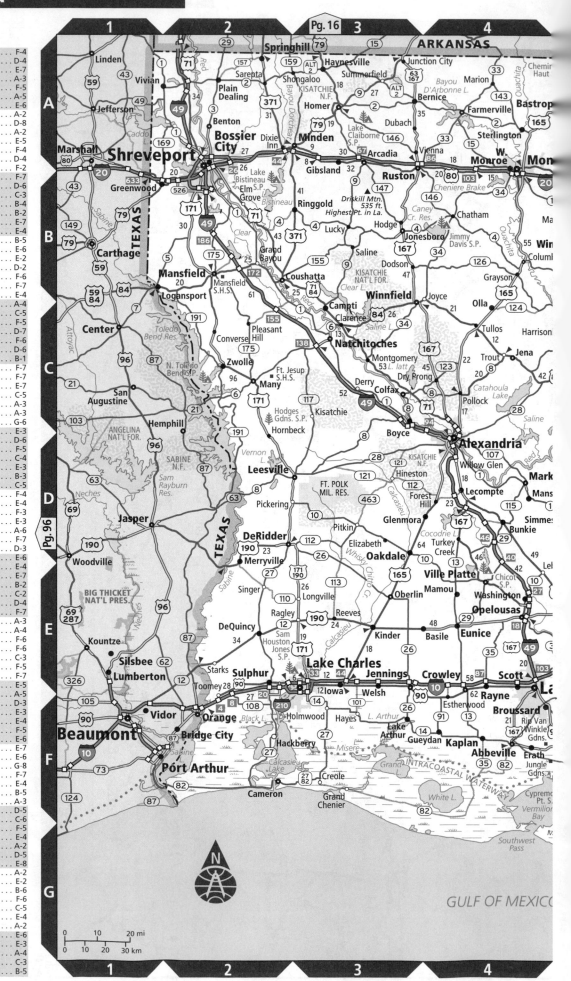

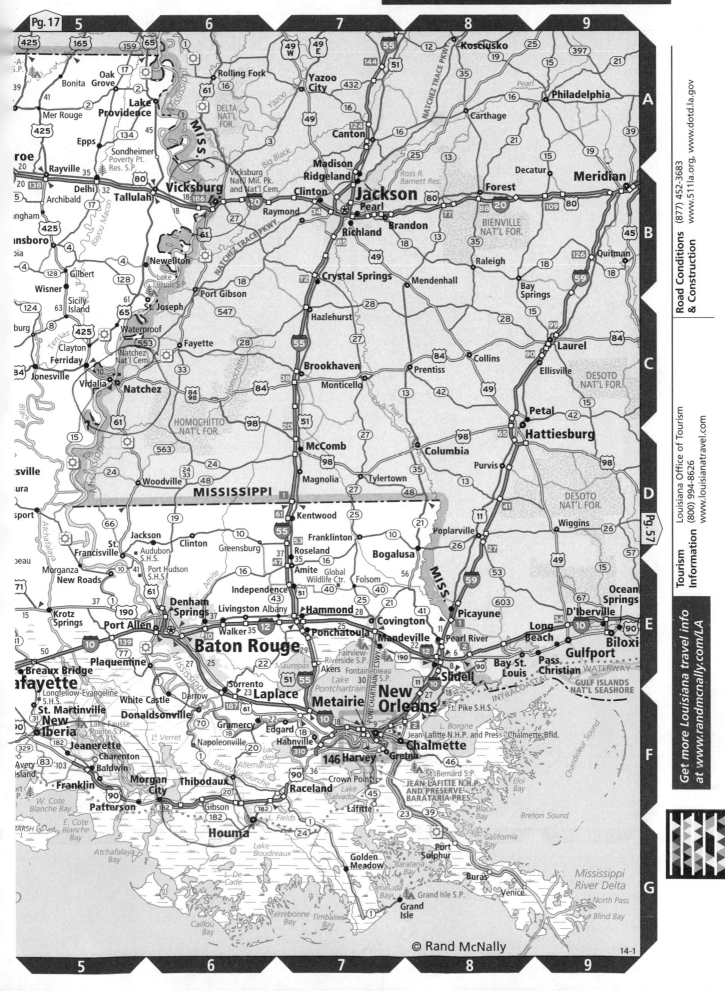

Road Conditions & Construction (877) 452-3683 www.511la.org, www.dotd.la.gov

Tourism Information Louisiana Office of Tourism (800) 994-8626 www.louisianatravel.com

Get more Louisiana travel info at www.randmcnally.com/LA

© Rand McNally

14-1

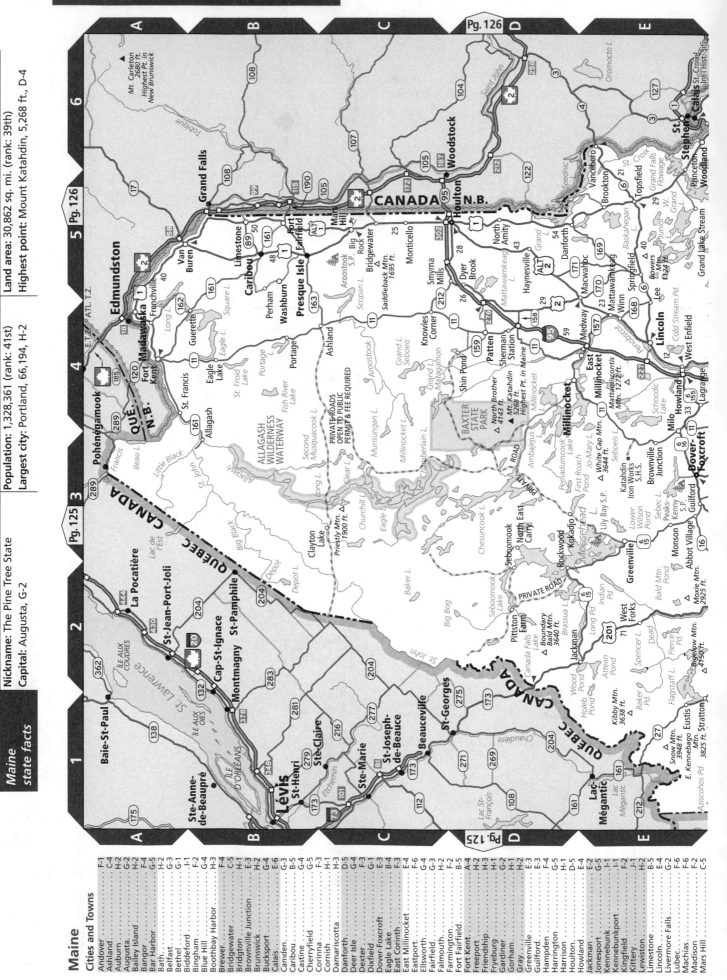

Pg. 126

Pg. 126
Pg. 125
Pg. 125

*Maine*
*state facts*

| | |
|---|---|
| **Nickname:** The Pine Tree State | **Land area:** 30,862 sq. mi. (rank: 39th) |
| **Capital:** Augusta, G-2 | **Highest point:** Mount Katahdin, 5,268 ft, D-4 |
| **Population:** 1,328,361 (rank: 41st) | |
| **Largest city:** Portland, 66,194, H-2 | |

## Maine
### Cities and Towns

| | |
|---|---|
| Andover | F-1 |
| Ashland | C-4 |
| Auburn | H-2 |
| Augusta | G-2 |
| Bailey Island | H-2 |
| Bangor | F-4 |
| Bar Harbor | G-5 |
| Bath | H-2 |
| Belfast | G-3 |
| Bethel | G-1 |
| Biddeford | I-1 |
| Bingham | F-2 |
| Blue Hill | G-4 |
| Boothbay Harbor | H-3 |
| Brewer | F-4 |
| Bridgewater | C-5 |
| Bridgton | H-1 |
| Brownville Junction | E-3 |
| Brunswick | H-2 |
| Bucksport | G-4 |
| Calais | E-6 |
| Camden | G-3 |
| Caribou | B-5 |
| Castine | G-4 |
| Cherryfield | F-5 |
| Corinna | F-3 |
| Cornish | H-1 |
| Damariscotta | H-3 |
| Danforth | D-5 |
| Deer Isle | G-4 |
| Dexter | F-3 |
| Dixfield | G-1 |
| Dover-Foxcroft | E-3 |
| Eagle Lake | B-4 |
| East Corinth | F-3 |
| East Millinocket | E-4 |
| Eastport | F-6 |
| Ellsworth | G-4 |
| Fairfield | G-3 |
| Falmouth | H-2 |
| Farmington | G-2 |
| Fort Fairfield | B-5 |
| Fort Kent | A-4 |
| Freeport | H-2 |
| Friendship | H-3 |
| Fryeburg | H-1 |
| Gardiner | G-2 |
| Gorham | H-1 |
| Gray | H-2 |
| Greenville | E-3 |
| Guilford | E-3 |
| Hampden | F-4 |
| Harrington | F-5 |
| Harrison | H-1 |
| Houlton | D-5 |
| Howland | E-4 |
| Jackman | D-2 |
| Jonesport | G-5 |
| Kennebunk | I-1 |
| Kennebunkport | I-1 |
| Kingfield | F-2 |
| Kittery | J-1 |
| Lewiston | H-2 |
| Lincoln | E-4 |
| Limestone | B-5 |
| Livermore Falls | G-2 |
| Lubec | F-6 |
| Machias | F-6 |
| Madison | F-2 |
| Mars Hill | C-5 |

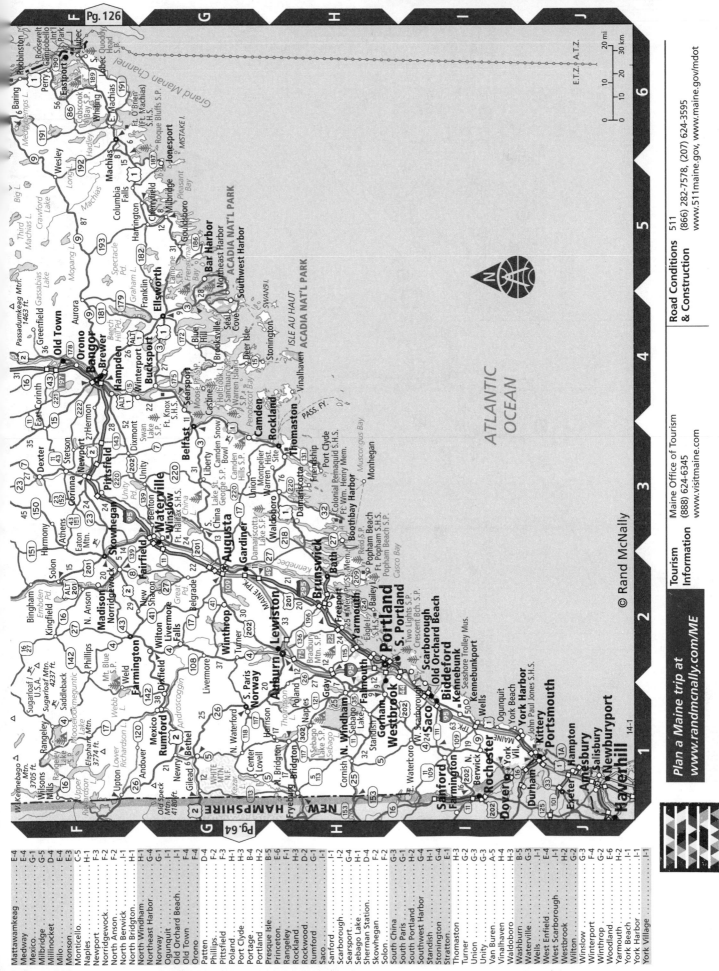

## Michigan

### *Michigan state facts*

**Nickname:** The Great Lake State
**Capital:** Lansing, H-4

**Population:** 9,883,640 (rank: 8th)
**Largest city:** Detroit, 713,777, I-6

**Land area:** 56,804 sq. mi. (rank: 22nd)
**Highest point:** Mount Arvon, 1,979 ft., B-6

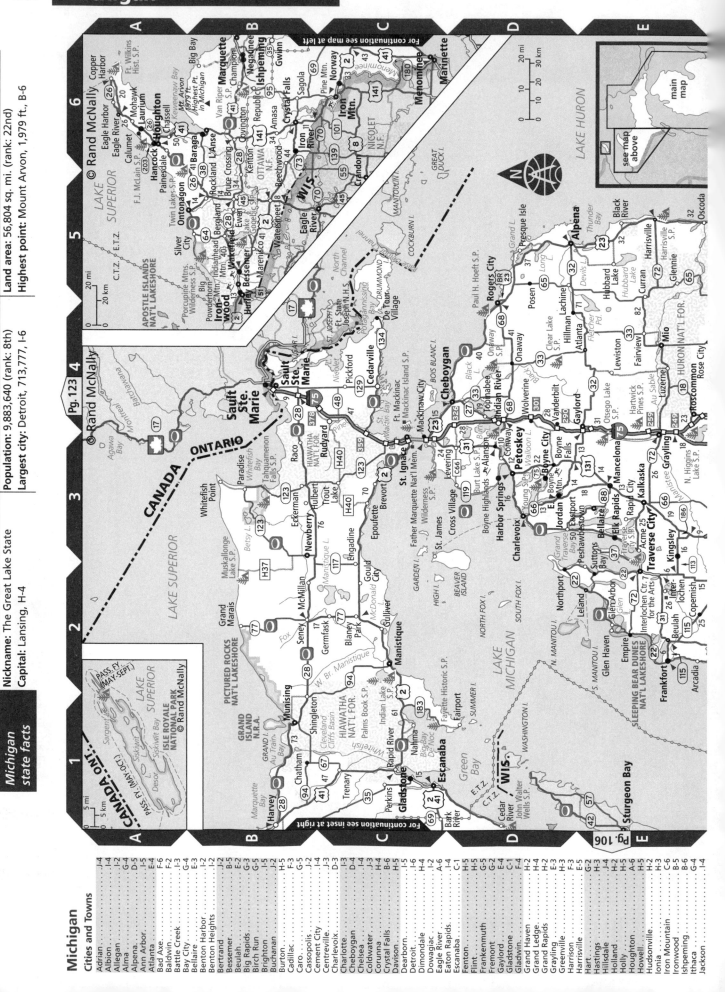

### Michigan
### Cities and Towns

For continuation see map at left

For continuation see inset at right

Pg. 123

Pg. 106

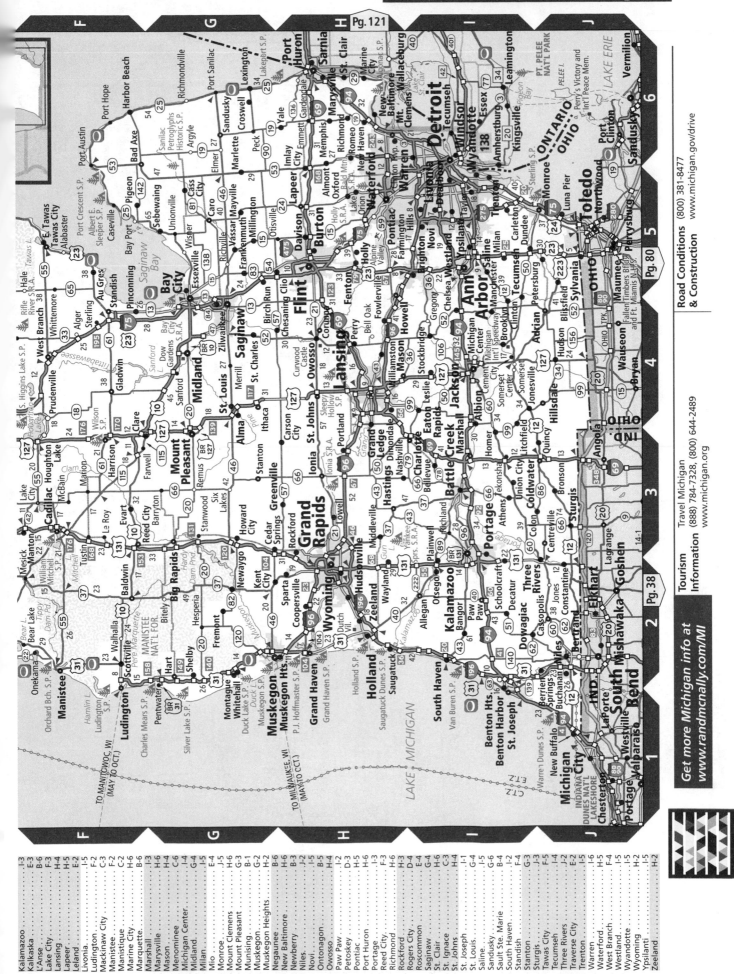

**Road Conditions** (800) 381-8477
**& Construction** www.michigan.gov/drive

**Tourism** Travel Michigan
**Information** (888) 784-7328, (800) 644-2489
www.michigan.org

*Get more Michigan info at*
*www.randmcnally.com/MI*

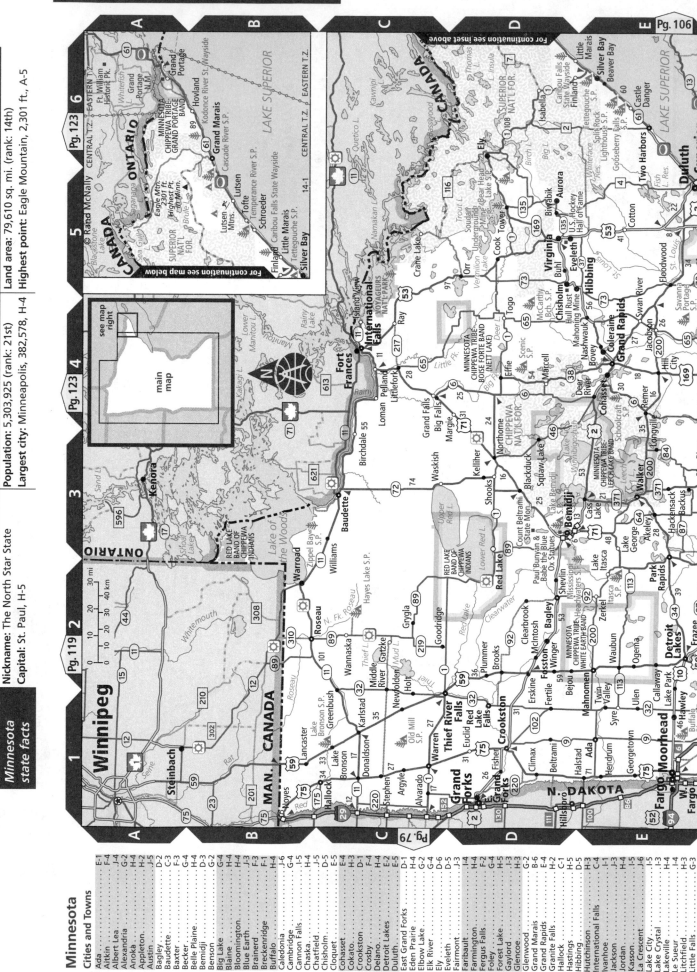

**Minnesota state facts**

Nickname: The North Star State
Capital: St. Paul, H-5

Population: 5,303,925 (rank: 21st)
Largest city: Minneapolis, 382,578, H-4

Land area: 79,610 sq. mi. (rank: 14th)
Highest point: Eagle Mountain, 2,301 ft., A-5

Pg. 106
Pg. 123
Pg. 123
Pg. 119
Pg. 79

© Rand McNally

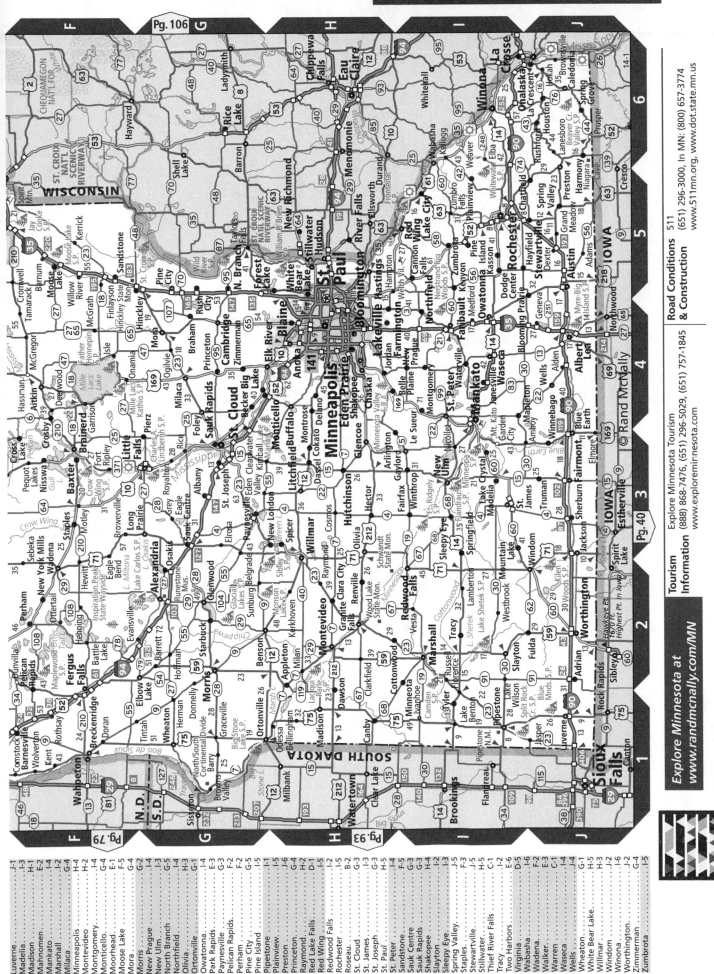

**Tourism Information**
Explore Minnesota Tourism
(888) 868-7476, (651) 296-5029, (651) 757-1845
www.exploreminnesota.com

**Road Conditions & Construction**
511
(651) 296-3000, In MN: (800) 657-3774
www.511mn.org, www.dot.state.mn.us

© Rand McNally

*Explore Minnesota at*
*www.randmcnally.com/MN*

*Mississippi state facts*

Nickname: The Magnolia State
Capital: Jackson, F-3

Population: 2,967,297 (rank: 31st)
Largest city: Jackson, 173,514, F-3

Land area: 46,907 sq. mi. (rank: 31st)
Highest point: Woodall Mountain, 806 ft., B-6

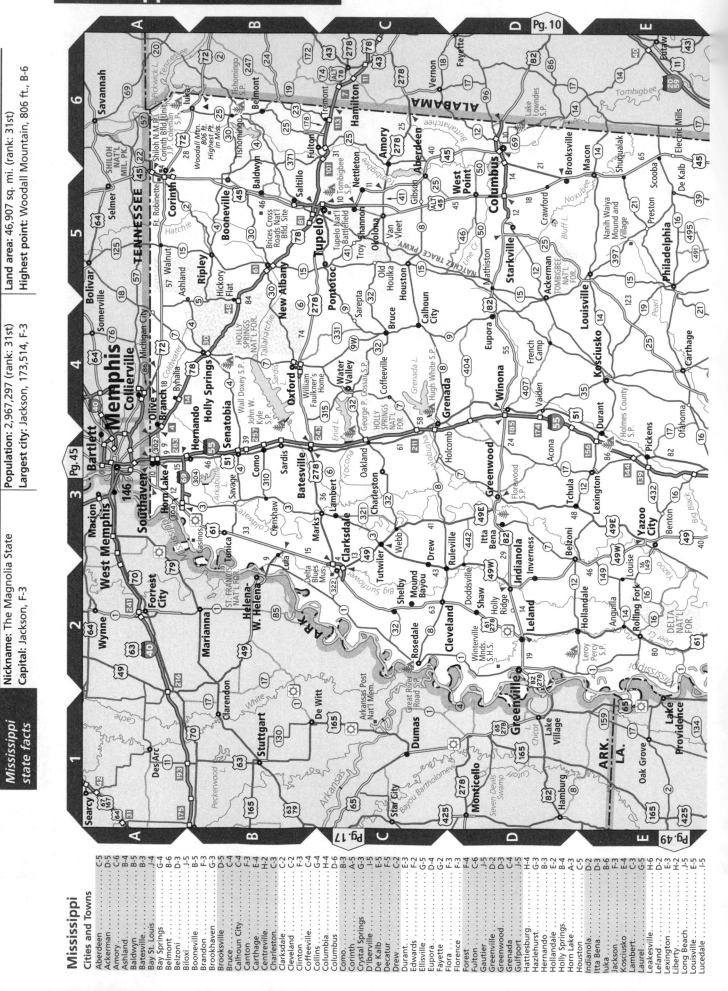

## Mississippi

### Cities and Towns

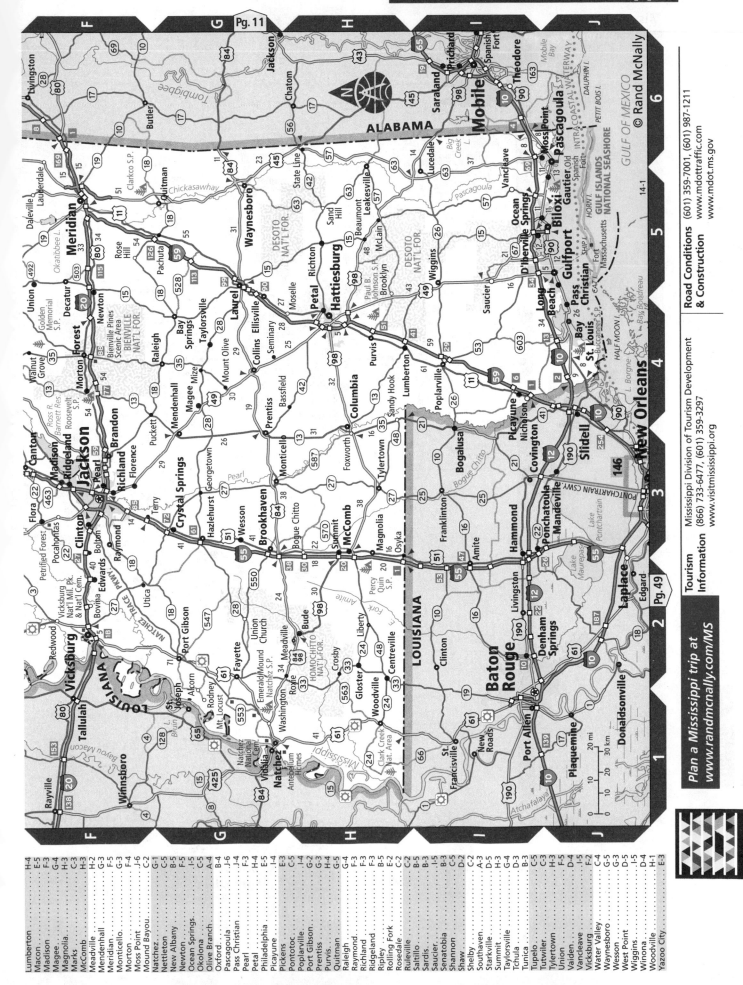

© Rand McNally

**Road Conditions** (601) 359-7001, (601) 987-1211
**& Construction** www.mdottraffic.com
www.mdot.ms.gov

**Tourism** Mississippi Division of Tourism Development
**Information** (866) 733-6477, (601) 359-3297
www.visitmississippi.org

*Plan a Mississippi trip at*
**www.randmcnally.com/MS**

## Missouri

### Cities and Towns

*Missouri* state facts

**Nickname:** The Show Me State
**Capital:** Jefferson City, D-5

**Population:** 5,988,927 (rank: 18th)
**Largest city:** Kansas City, 459,787, C-2

**Land area:** 68,886 sq. mi. (rank: 18th)
**Highest point:** Taum Sauk Mtn., 1,772 ft., E-7

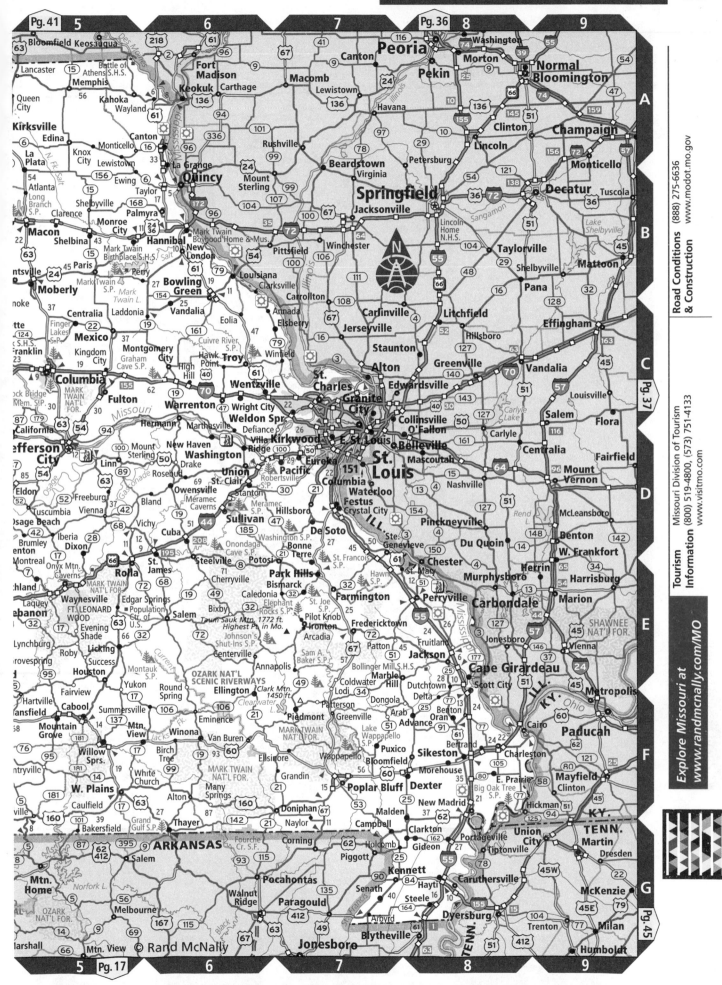

**Road Conditions & Construction** (888) 275-6636 www.modot.mo.gov

**Tourism** Missouri Division of Tourism **Information** (800) 519-4800, (573) 751-4133 www.visitmo.com

*Explore Missouri at* www.randmcnally.com/MO

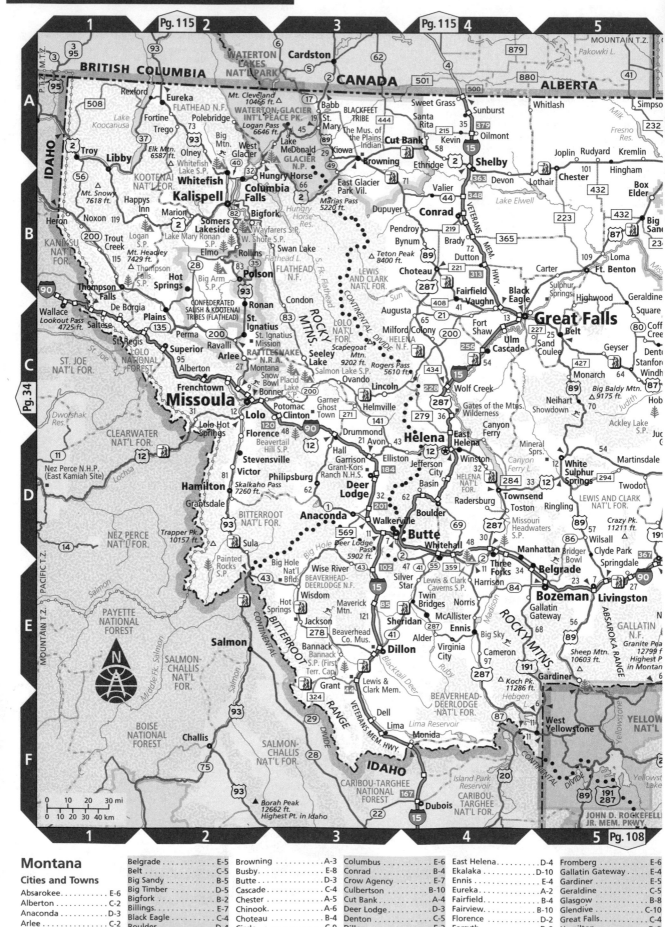

Pg. 115
Pg. 115
Pg. 34
Pg. 108

Montana state facts

**Nickname:** The Treasure State
**Capital:** Helena, D-4

**Population:** 989,415 (rank: 44th)
**Largest city:** Billings, 104,170, E-7

**Land area:** 145,552 sq. mi. (rank: 4th)
**Highest point:** Granite Peak, 12,799 ft., E-6

# Montana

## Cities and Towns

© Rand McNally

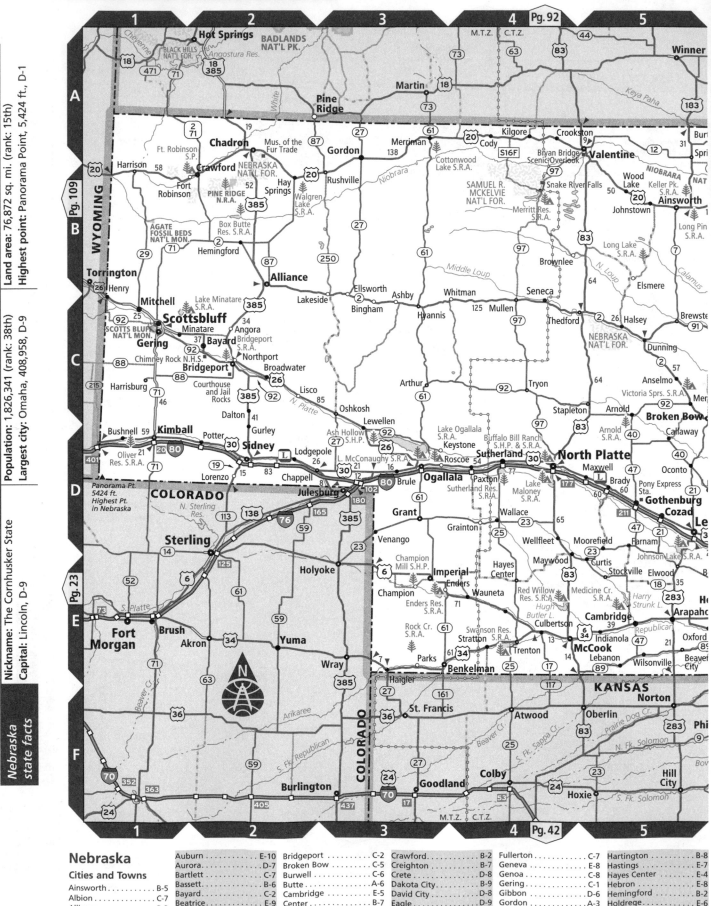

Pg. 92
Pg. 109
Pg. 23
Pg. 42

## Nebraska

### Cities and Towns

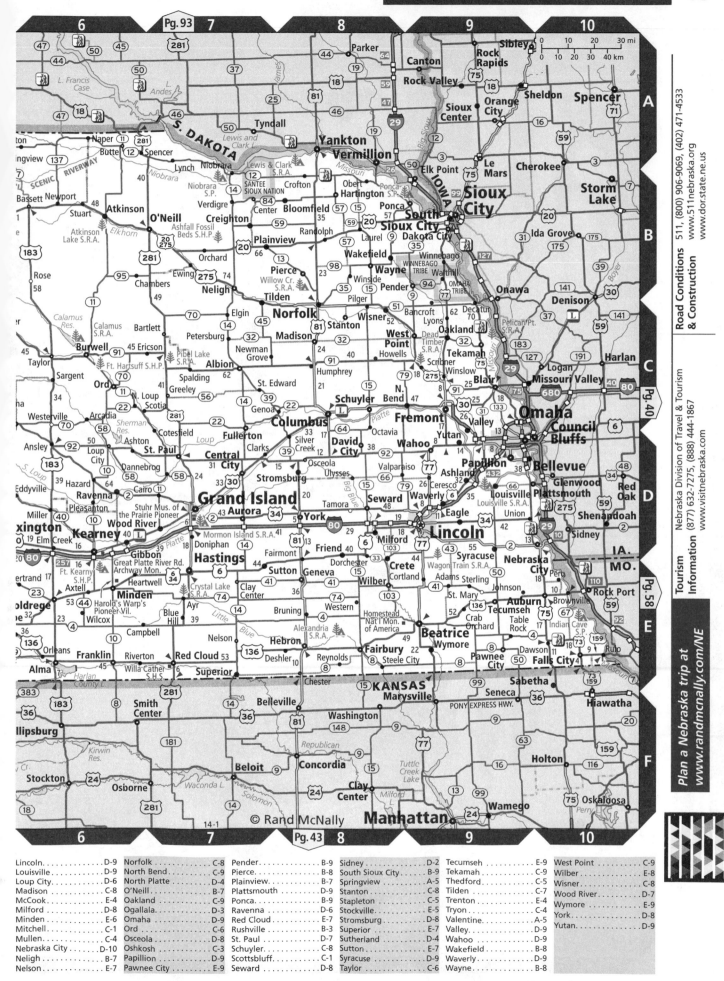

Road Conditions & Construction — 511, (800) 906-9069, (402) 471-4533 — www.511nebraska.org — www.dor.state.ne.us

Tourism Information — Nebraska Division of Travel & Tourism — (877) 632-7275, (888) 444-1867 — www.visitnebraska.com

Plan a Nebraska trip at www.randmcnally.com/NE

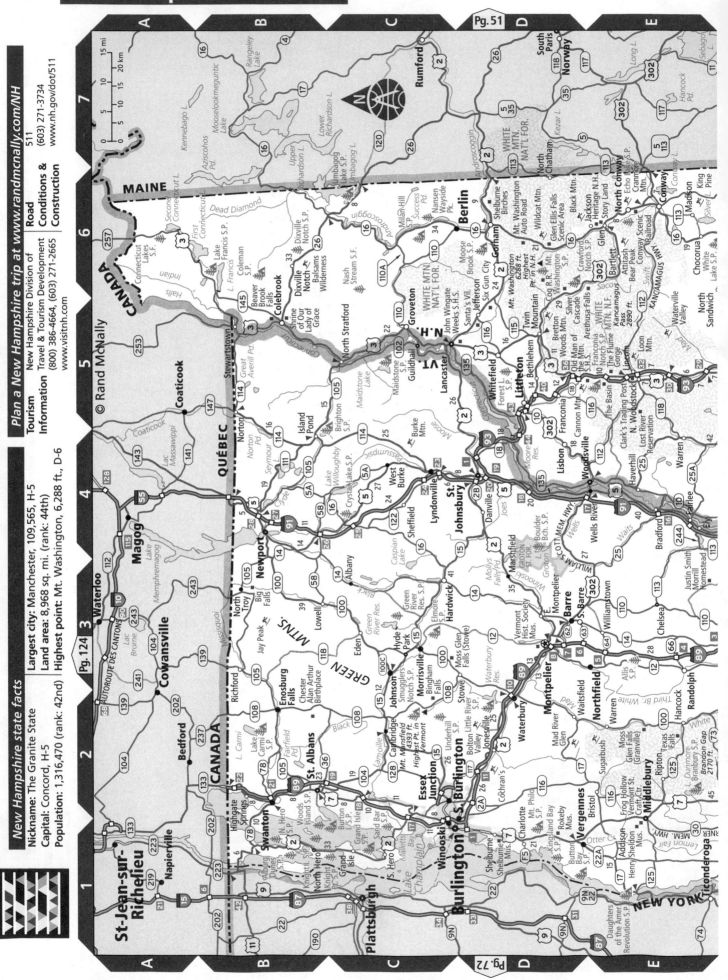

**New Hampshire state facts**

Nickname: The Granite State
Capital: Concord, H-5
Population: 1,316,470 (rank: 42nd)

Largest city: Manchester, 109,565, H-5
Land area: 8,968 sq. mi. (rank: 44th)
Highest point: Mt. Washington, 6,288 ft., D-6

**Plan a New Hampshire trip at www.randmcnally.com/NH**

Tourism     New Hampshire Division of
Information  Travel & Tourism Development
            (800) 386-4664, (603) 271-2665
            www.visitnh.com

Road         511
Conditions &  (603) 271-3734
Construction  www.nh.gov/dot/511

© Rand McNally

Pg. 51
Pg. 124
Pg. 72

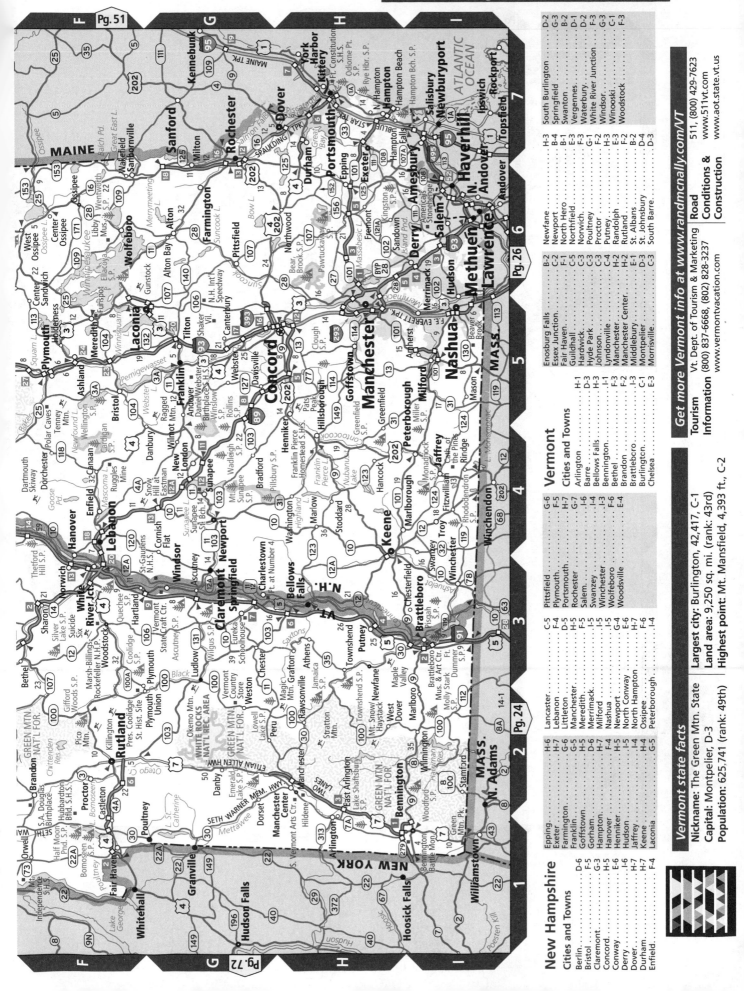

**Get more Vermont info at www.randmcnally.com/VT**

| Tourism Information | Vt. Dept. of Tourism & Marketing (800) 837-6668, (802) 828-3237 www.vermontvacation.com | 511, (800) 429-7623 www.511vt.com www.aot.state.vt.us | Road Conditions & Construction |
|---|---|---|---|

**Vermont state facts**

Nickname: The Green Mtn. State
Capital: Montpelier, D-3
Population: 625,741 (rank: 49th)

Largest city: Burlington, 42,417, C-1
Land area: 9,250 sq. mi. (rank: 43rd)
Highest point: Mt. Mansfield, 4,393 ft., C-2

**New Jersey state facts**

| | |
|---|---|
| Nickname: The Garden State | Land area: 7,417 sq. mi. (rank: 46th) |
| Capital: Trenton, E-3 | Highest point: High Point, 1,803 ft., A-4 |
| Population: 8,791,894 (rank: 11th) | |
| Largest city: Newark, 277,140, C-5 | |

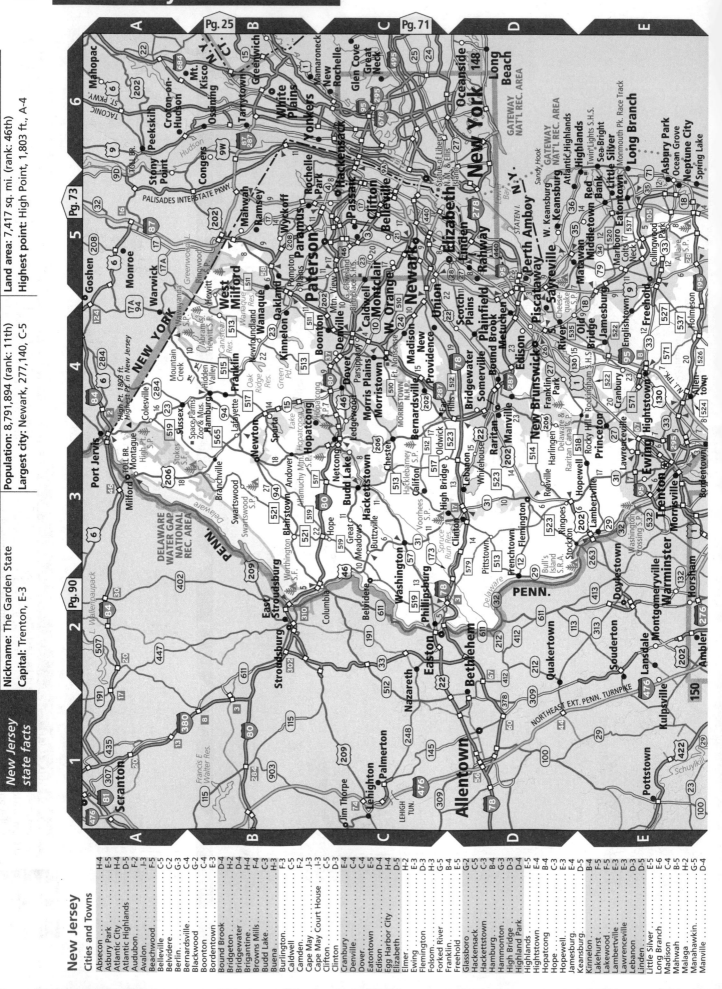

## New Jersey
### Cities and Towns

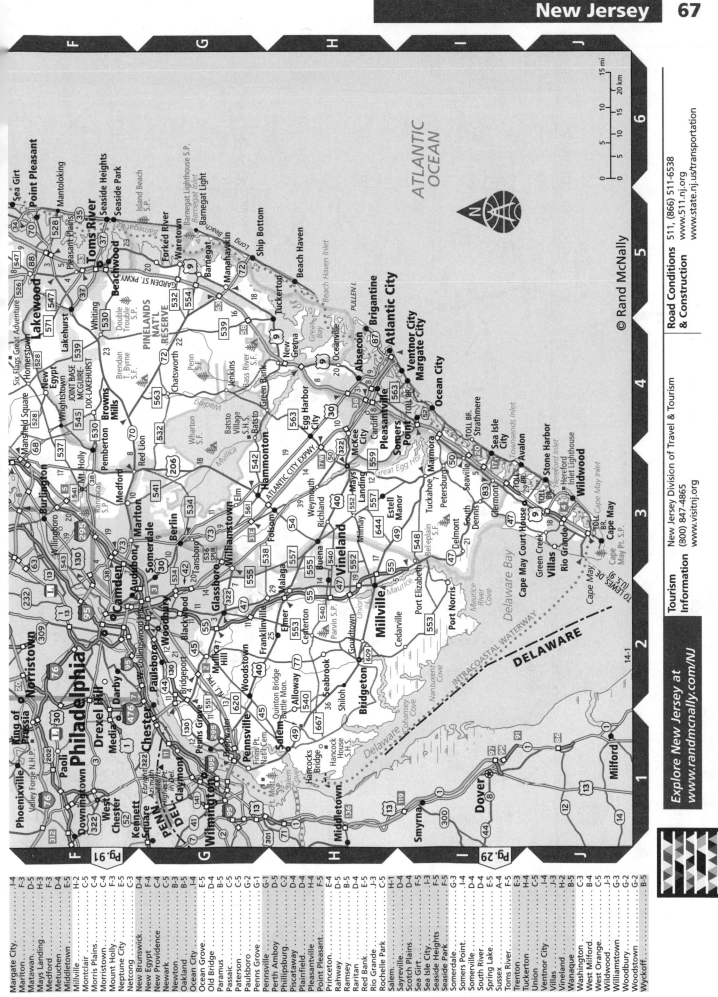

Tourism
Information   New Jersey Division of Travel & Tourism
(800) 847-4865
www.visitnj.org

Road Conditions   511, (866) 511-6538
& Construction   www.511.nj.org
www.state.nj.us/transportation

*Explore New Jersey at*
www.randmcnally.com/NJ

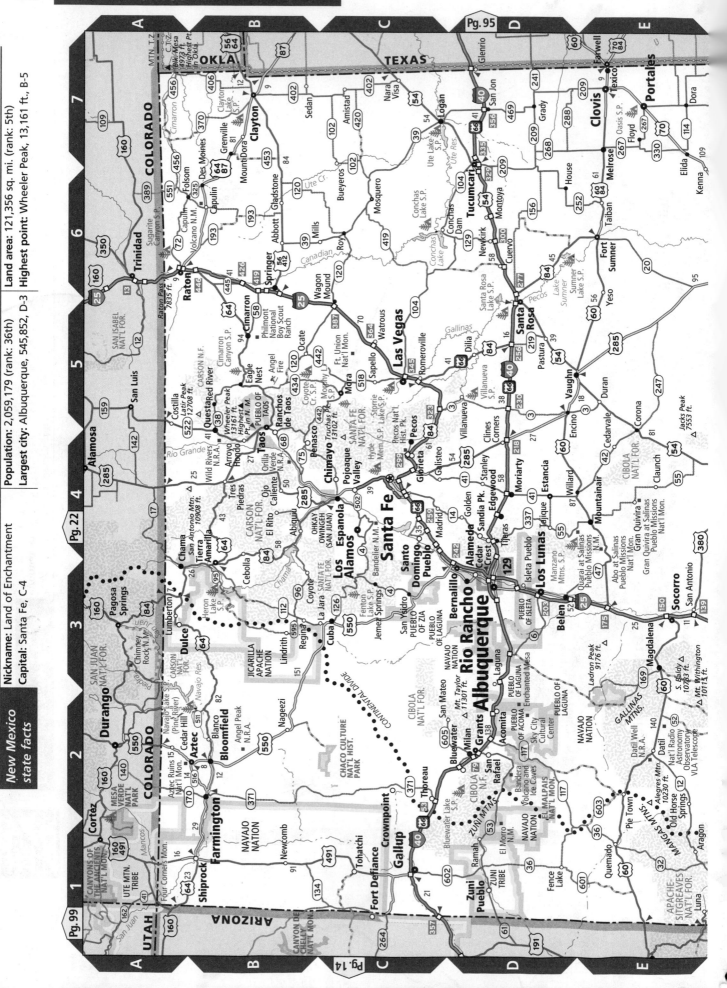

*New Mexico state facts*

**Nickname:** Land of Enchantment
**Capital:** Santa Fe, C-4

**Population:** 2,059,179 (rank: 36th)
**Land area:** 121,356 sq. mi. (rank: 5th)
**Largest city:** Albuquerque, 545,852, D-3
**Highest point:** Wheeler Peak, 13,161 ft., B-5

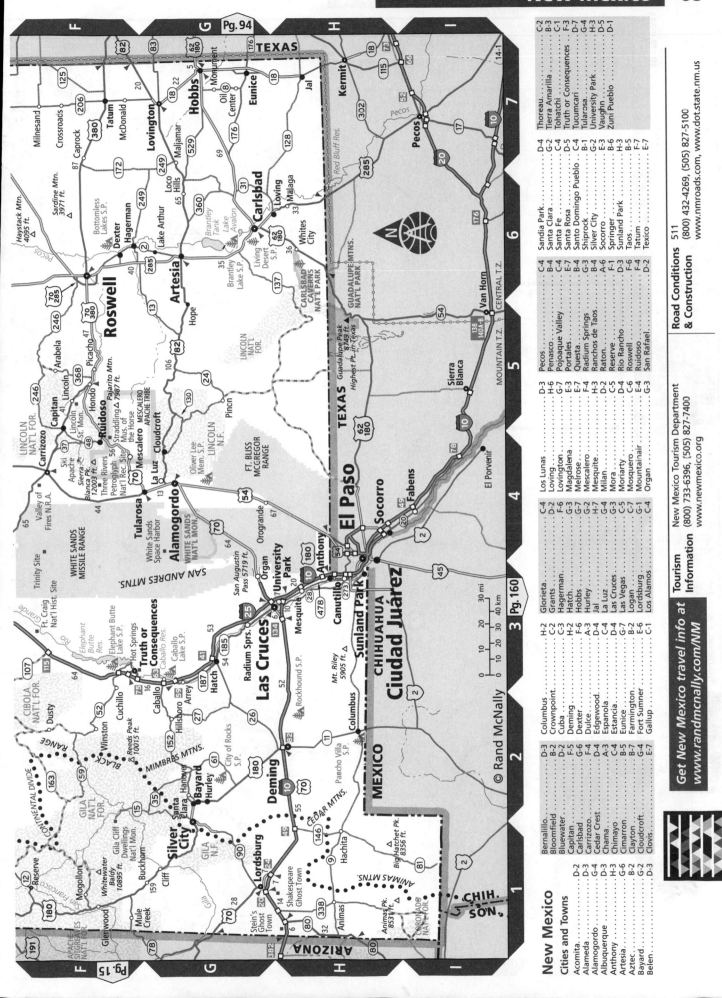

### Tourism

**New Mexico Tourism Department**
(800) 733-6396, (505) 827-7400
www.newmexico.org

### Road Conditions 511
### & Construction

(800) 432-4269, (505) 827-5100
www.nmroads.com, www.dot.state.nm.us

**Get New Mexico travel info at**
**www.randmcnally.com/NM**

© Rand McNally

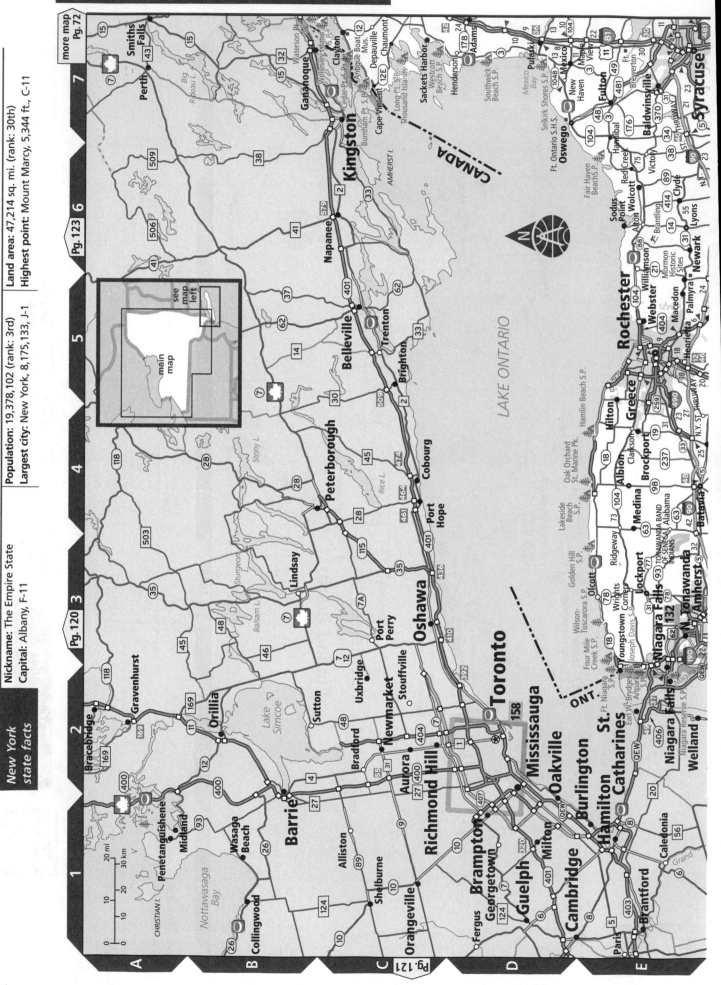

more map Pg. 72

*New York*
*state facts*

| | |
|---|---|
| Nickname: The Empire State | Population: 19,378,102 (rank: 3rd) |
| Capital: Albany, F-11 | Largest city: New York, 8,175,133, J-1 |
| | Land area: 47,214 sq. mi. (rank: 30th) |
| | Highest point: Mount Marcy, 5,344 ft., C-11 |

Pg. 123
Pg. 120
Pg. 121

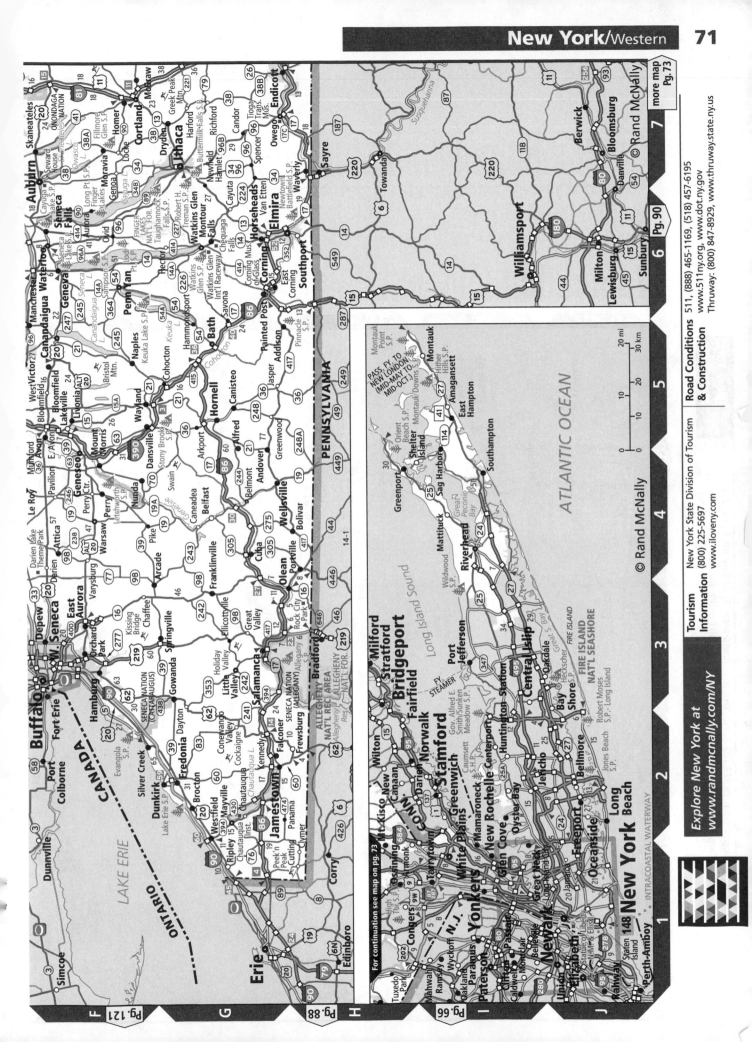

more map Pg. 73

© Rand McNally

PENNSYLVANIA

LAKE ERIE

CANADA

ONTARIO

ATLANTIC OCEAN

Long Island Sound

FIRE ISLAND NAT'L SEASHORE

© Rand McNally

For continuation see map on pg. 73

INTRACOASTAL WATERWAY

| Tourism Information | New York State Division of Tourism (800) 225-5697 www.iloveny.com | Road Conditions & Construction | 511, (888) 465-1169, (518) 457-6195 www.511ny.org, www.dot.ny.gov Thruway: (800) 847-8929, www.thruway.state.ny.us |

Explore New York at
www.randmcnally.com/NY

Pg.121   Pg.88   Pg.66

**New York state facts**

Nickname: The Empire State
Capital: Albany
Population: 19,378,102 (rank: 3rd)
Largest city: New York, 8,175,133, J-1
Land area: 47,214 sq. mi. (rank: 30th)
Highest point: Mount Marcy, 5,344 ft., C-11

## New York

### Cities and Towns

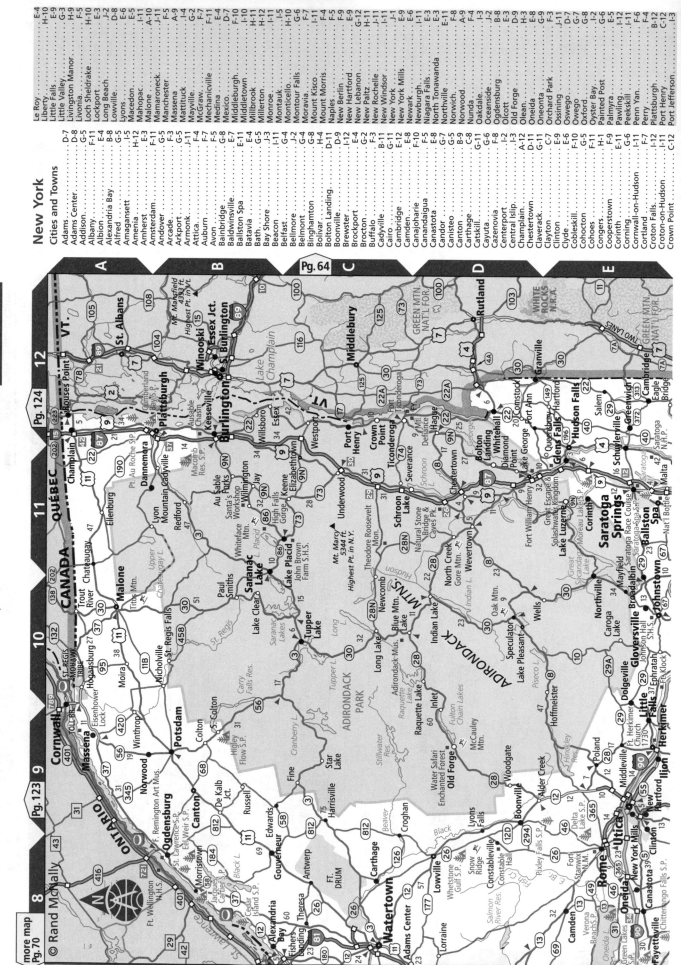

© Rand McNally

Pg. 70 — more map
Pg. 123 · Pg. 124 · Pg. 64

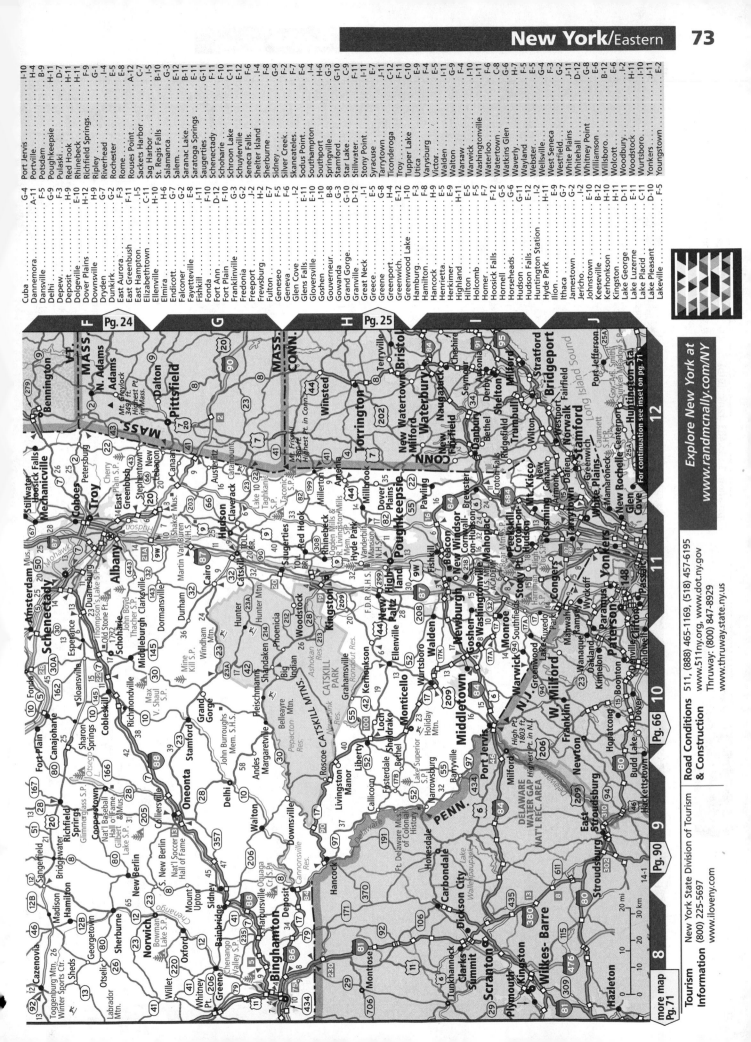

### Index (partial)

| Place | Grid | Place | Grid | Place | Grid | Place | Grid |
|---|---|---|---|---|---|---|---|
| Cuba | G-4 | Geneseo | G-10 | Port Jervis | I-10 | Sidney | G-10 |
| Dannemora | A-11 | Geneva | C-9 | Portville | H-4 | Silver Creek | C-9 |
| Dansville | F-5 | Glen Cove | I-2 | Potsdam | B-9 | Skaneateles | D-12 |
| Delhi | F-3 | Glens Falls | E-11 | Poughkeepsie | D-7 | Sodus Point | E-5 |
| Depew | H-9 | Gloversville | E-10 | Pulaski | H-11 | Southampton | G-4 |
| Deposit | E-10 | Goshen | G-3 | Red Hook | F-9 | Southport | E-12 |
| Dolgeville | D-12 | Gouverneur | B-8 | Rhinebeck | F-11 | Springville | F-11 |
| Dover Plains | H-12 | Gowanda | G-3 | Richfield Springs | G-1 | Stamford | E-9 |
| Downsville | F-3 | Grand Gorge | G-10 | Ripley | J-4 | Star Lake | I-11 |
| Dryden | G-7 | Granville | D-12 | Riverhead | E-5 | Stillwater | I-11 |
| Dunkirk | G-2 | Great Neck | I-1 | Rochester | E-8 | Stony Point | F-4 |
| East Aurora | F-3 | Greece | E-5 | Rome | A-12 | Syracuse | E-5 |
| East Greenbush | F-11 | Greene | G-4 | Rouses Point | C-7 | Tarrytown | I-6 |
| East Hampton | C-11 | Greenport | E-12 | Sackets Harbor | B-10 | Ticonderoga | C-8 |
| Elizabethtown | B-10 | Greenwich | I-10 | Sag Harbor | E-12 | Troy | G-6 |
| Ellenville | G-2 | Greenwood Lake | E-9 | St. Regis Falls | B-11 | Tupper Lake | F-5 |
| Elmira | H-6 | Hamburg | F-4 | Salamanca | G-11 | Utica | H-7 |
| Endicott | G-7 | Hamilton | E-5 | Salem | F-11 | Varysburg | F-3 |
| Falconer | G-2 | Hancock | H-9 | Saranac Lake | E-12 | Victor | H-9 |
| Fayetteville | E-8 | Henrietta | H-11 | Saratoga Springs | C-11 | Walden | H-11 |
| Fishkill | I-11 | Herkimer | I-1 | Saugerties | I-4 | Walton | E-5 |
| Fonda | F-10 | Highland | H-11 | Schenectady | F-8 | Warsaw | F-7 |
| Fort Ann | D-12 | Hilton | E-9 | Schoharie | F-2 | Warwick | F-5 |
| Fort Plain | F-10 | Holcomb | J-4 | Schroon Lake | E-6 | Washingtonville | F-12 |
| Franklinville | G-3 | Homer | H-7 | Schuylerville | I-4 | Watertown | G-5 |
| Fredonia | G-2 | Hoosick Falls | F-12 | Seneca Falls | H-6 | Watkins Glen | E-12 |
| Freeport | J-2 | Hornell | G-5 | Shelter Island | E-7 | Waverly | I-2 |
| Frewsburg | H-2 | Horseheads | H-6 | Sherburne | F-5 | Wayland | E-9 |
| Fulton | F-5 | Hudson | H-11 | | | Webster | G-7 |
| | | Hudson Falls | E-12 | | | Wellsville | I-2 |
| | | Huntington Station | I-2 | | | West Seneca | E-10 |
| | | Hyde Park | F-8 | | | Westfield | B-12 |
| | | Ilion | E-9 | | | White Plains | H-10 |
| | | Ithaca | G-7 | | | Whitehall | D-11 |
| | | Jamestown | H-2 | | | Whitney Point | E-6 |
| | | Jericho | J-2 | | | Williamson | E-6 |
| | | Johnstown | E-10 | | | Willsboro | B-12 |
| | | Keeseville | B-12 | | | Wolcott | J-2 |
| | | Kerhonkson | H-10 | | | Woodbury | I-2 |
| | | Kingston | H-11 | | | Woodstock | H-11 |
| | | Lake George | D-11 | | | Wurtsboro | I-10 |
| | | Lake Luzerne | C-11 | | | Yonkers | I-10 |
| | | Lake Placid | D-10 | | | Youngstown | E-2 |
| | | Lake Pleasant | J-1 | | | | |
| | | Lakeville | E-2 | | | | |

Pg. 24   Pg. 25   For continuation see inset on pg. 71   Pg. 71   Pg. 66   Pg. 90   more map Pg. 71

*Explore New York at*
**www.randmcnally.com/NY**

**Tourism Information** (800) 225-5697   New York State Division of Tourism (800) 225-5697   www.iloveny.com

**Road Conditions & Construction**   511, (888) 465-1169, (518) 457-6195   www.511ny.org, www.dot.ny.gov   Thruway: (800) 847-8929   www.thruway.state.ny.us

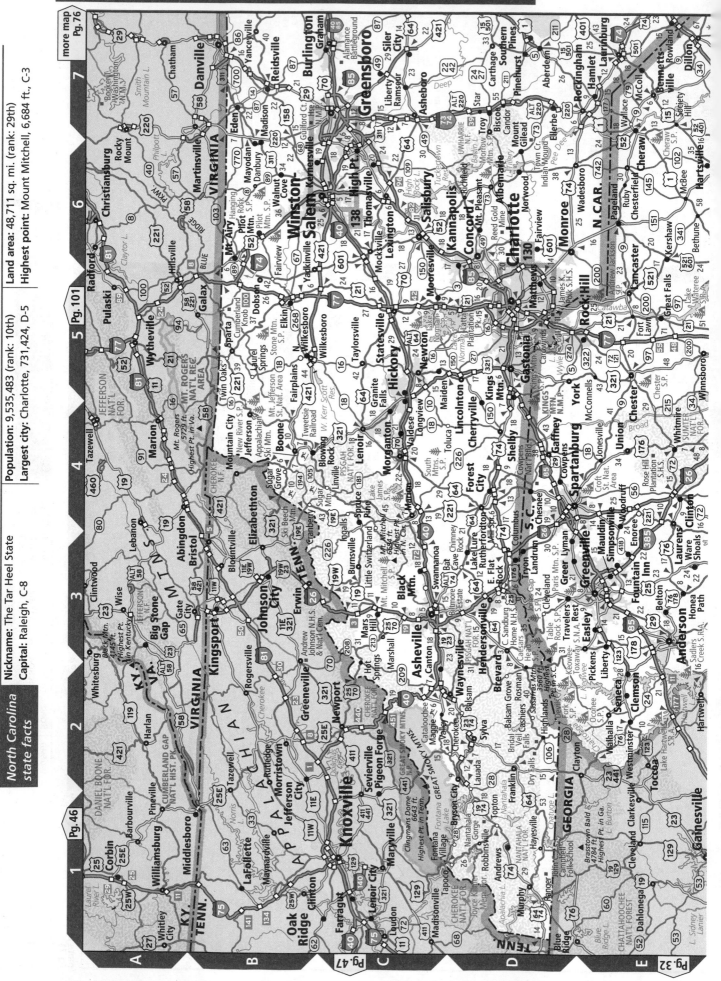

*North Carolina state facts*

**Nickname:** The Tar Heel State
**Capital:** Raleigh, C-8

**Population:** 9,535,483 (rank: 10th)
**Largest city:** Charlotte, 731,424, D-5

**Land area:** 48,711 sq. mi. (rank: 29th)
**Highest point:** Mount Mitchell, 6,684 ft., C-3

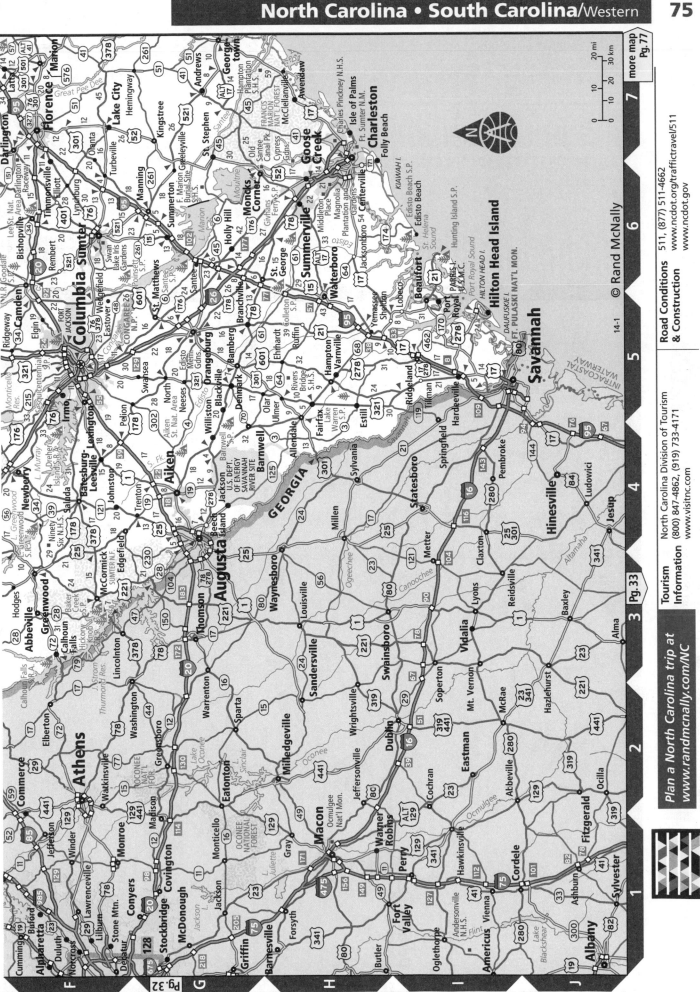

more map Pg. 77

© Rand McNally

**Road Conditions & Construction**
511, (877) 511-4662
www.ncdot.org/traffictravel/511
www.ncdot.gov

**Tourism Information**
North Carolina Division of Tourism
(800) 847-4862, (919) 733-4171
www.visitnc.com

*Plan a North Carolina trip at*
*www.randmcnally.com/NC*

Pg. 33

Pg. 32

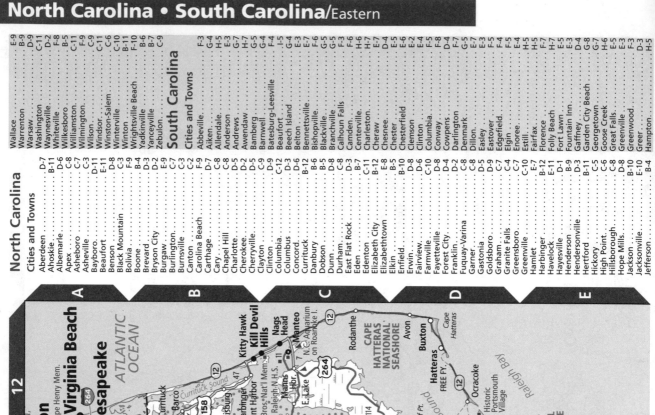

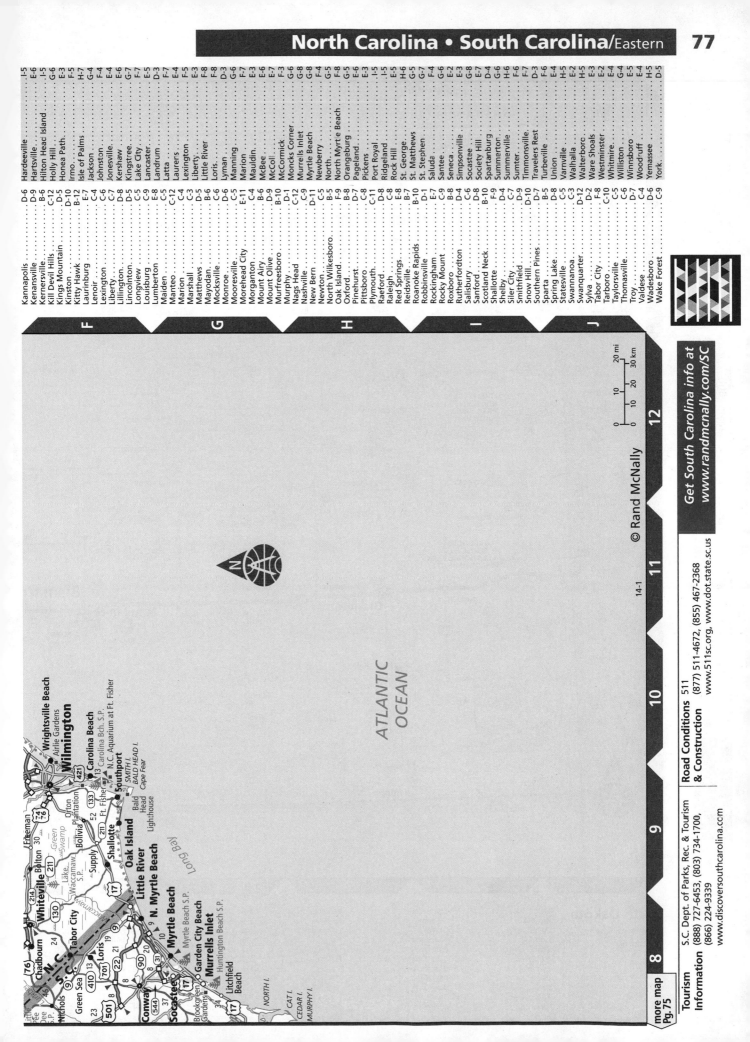

ATLANTIC OCEAN

Wrightsville Beach · Airlie Gardens · Wilmington · Carolina Beach · N.C. Aquarium at Ft. Fisher · Carolina Bch. S.P. · Ft. Fisher · SMITH I. · BALD HEAD I. · Cape Fear · Southport · Orton Plantation · Shallotte · Oak Island · Bald Head Lighthouse · Long Bay · Little River · N. Myrtle Beach · Myrtle Beach · Myrtle Beach S.P. · Garden City Beach · Murrells Inlet · Huntington Beach S.P. · Litchfield Beach · Socastee · Conway · Green Sea · Loris · Tabor City · Whiteville · Chadbourn · Nichols · Brookgreen Gardens · Bolton · Freeman · Supply · Bolivia · Green Swamp · Lake Waccamaw · NORTH I. · CAT I. · CEDAR I. · MURPHY I.

N.C. / S.C.

more map Pg. 75

0   10   20 mi
0   10   20   30 km

© Rand McNally

**Tourism Information**
S.C. Dept. of Parks, Rec. & Tourism
(888) 727-6453, (803) 734-1700,
(866) 224-9339
www.discoversouthcarolina.com

**Road Conditions & Construction**
511
(877) 511-4672, (855) 467-2368
www.511sc.org, www.dot.state.sc.us

Get South Carolina info at
www.randmcnally.com/SC

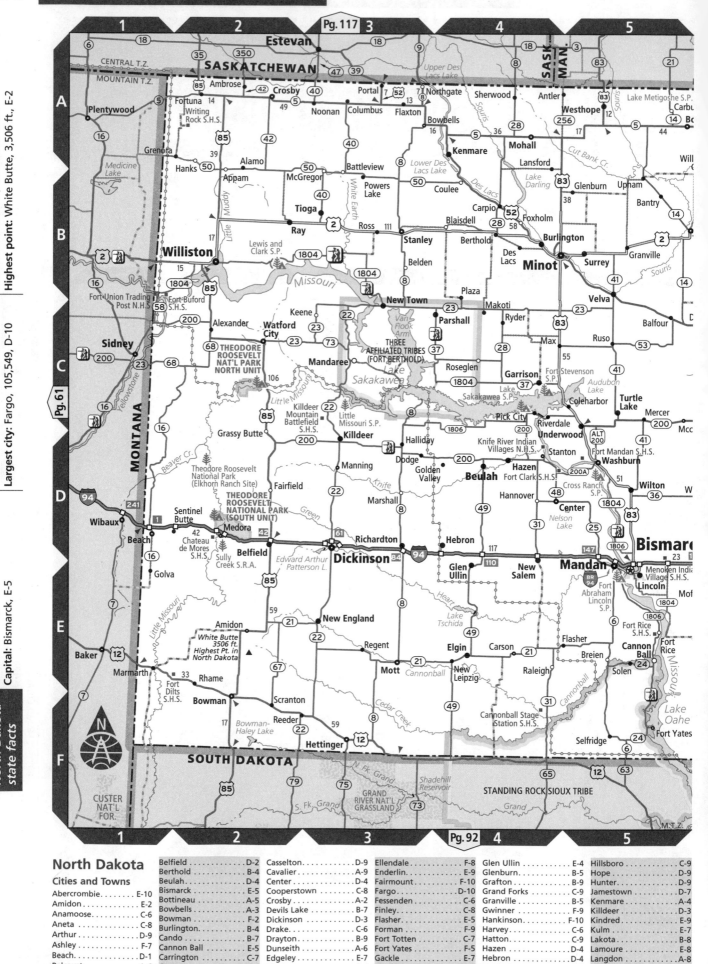

Pg. 117

Pg. 92

**North Dakota state facts**

Nickname: The Peace Garden State
Capital: Bismarck, E-5

Population: 672,591 (rank: 48th)
Largest city: Fargo, 105,549, D-10

Land area: 68,976 sq. mi. (rank: 17th)
Highest point: White Butte, 3,506 ft., E-2

## North Dakota

### Cities and Towns

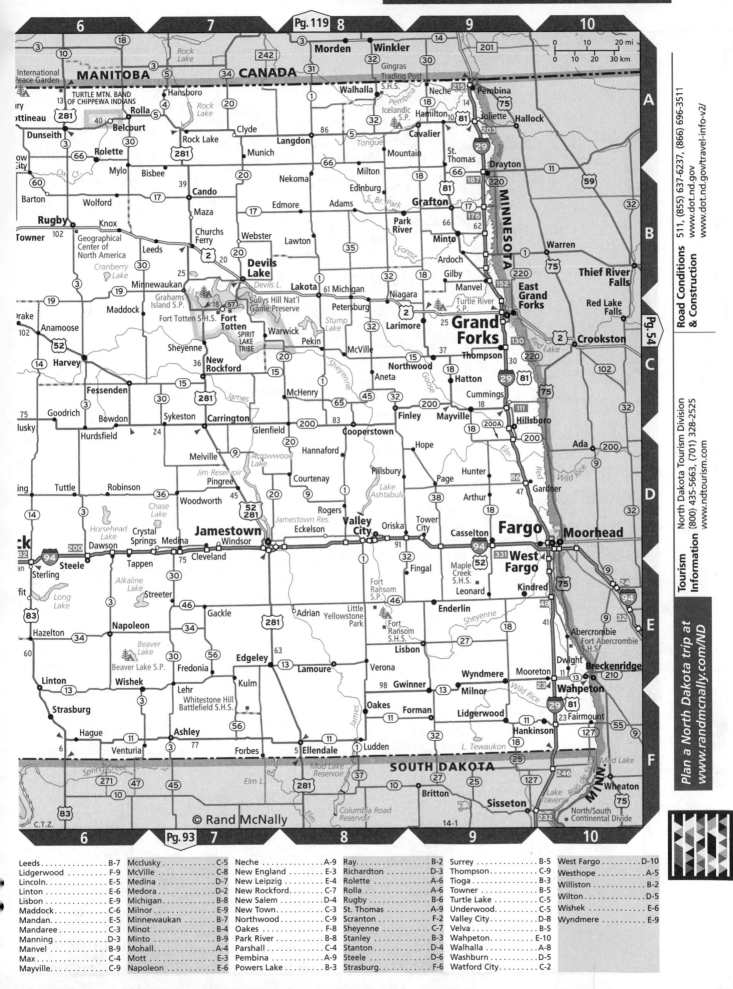

Road Conditions & Construction
511, (855) 637-6237, (866) 696-3511
www.dot.nd.gov
www.dot.nd.gov/travel-info-v2/

Tourism Information
North Dakota Tourism Division
(800) 435-5663, (701) 328-2525
www.ndtourism.com

Plan a North Dakota trip at www.randmcnally.com/ND

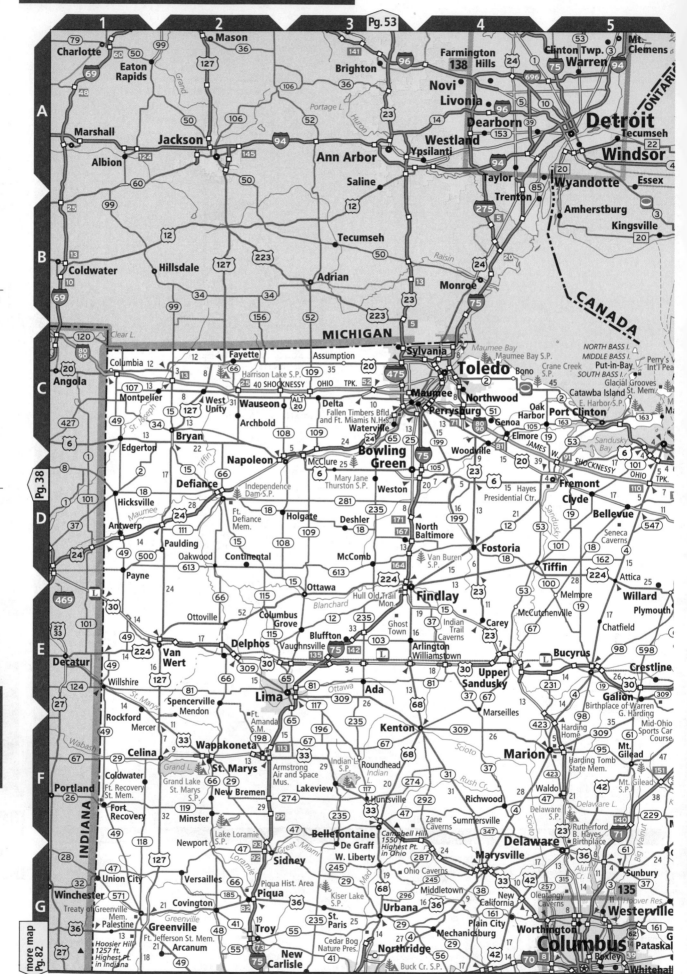

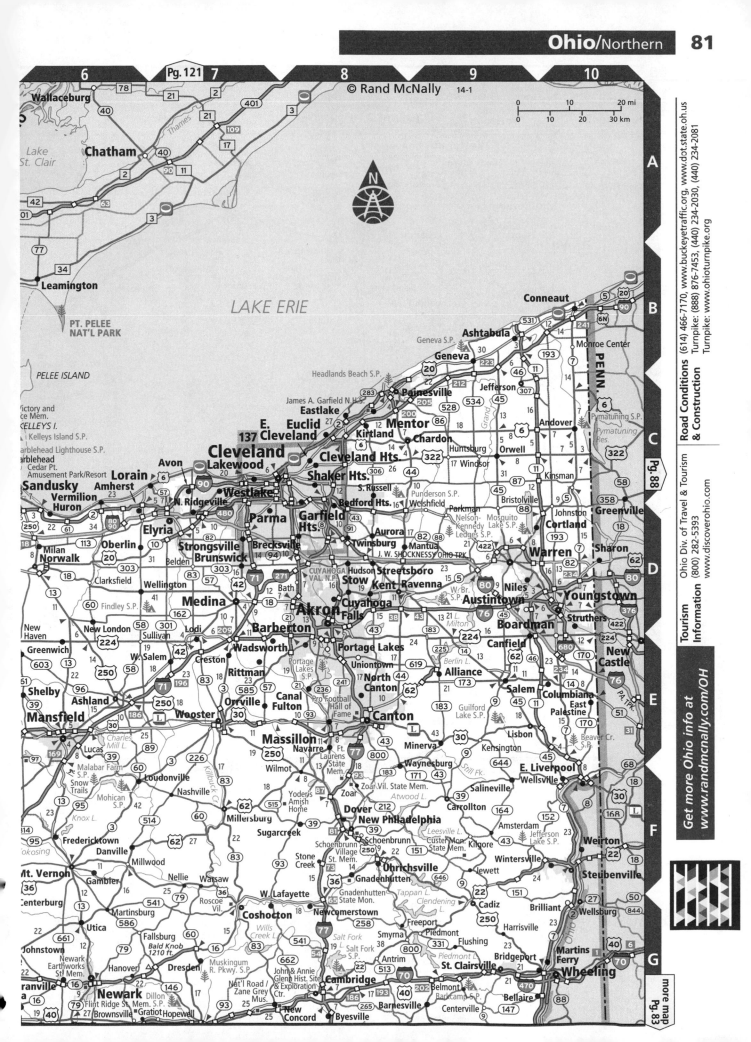

© Rand McNally  14-1

LAKE ERIE

**Ohio** state facts

Nickname: The Buckeye State | Population: 11,536,504 (rank: 7th) | Land area: 40,948 sq. mi. (rank: 35th)
Capital: Columbus, G-5 | Largest city: Columbus, G-5 | Highest point: Campbell Hill, 1,550 ft., F-3

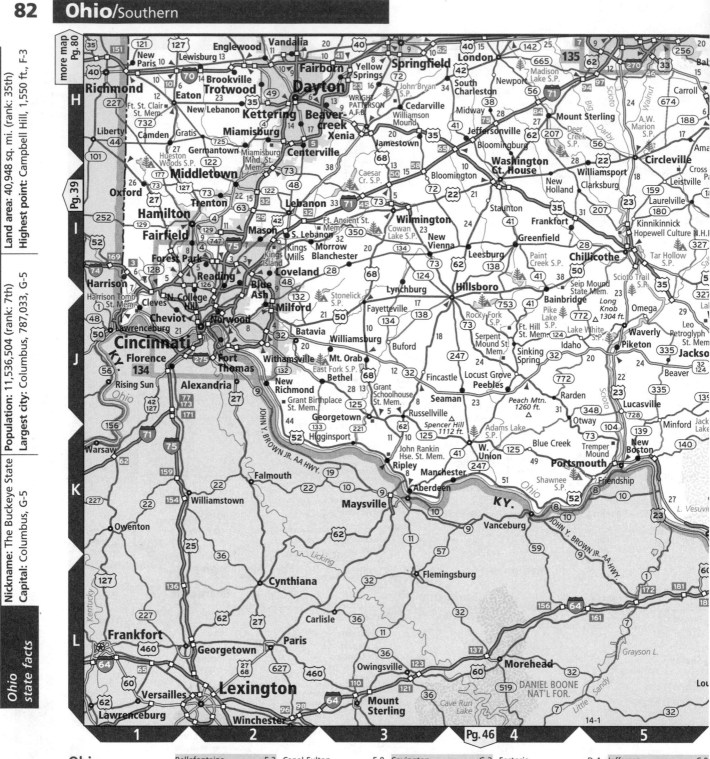

Road Conditions & Construction  (614) 466-7170
www.buckeyetraffic.org, www.dot.state.oh.us
Cincinnati metro area: 511, (513) 333-3333
www.artimis.org

Tourism Information  Ohio Div. of Travel & Tourism
(800) 282-5393
www.discoverohio.com

Get more Ohio info at
www.randmcnally.com/OH

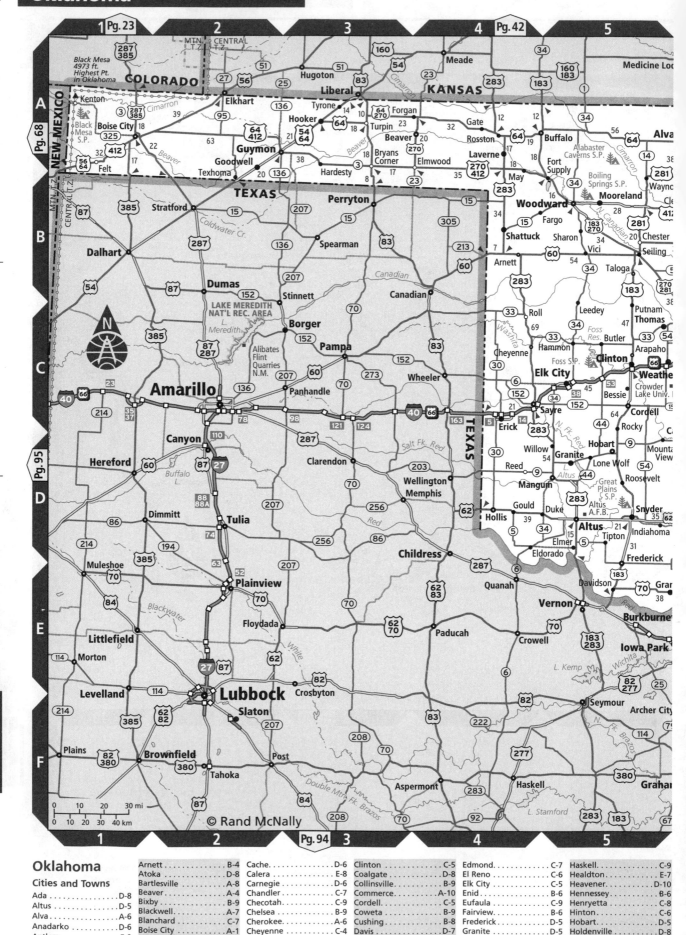

Pg. 23 | Pg. 42
Pg. 68
Pg. 95
Pg. 94

**Oklahoma state facts**

Nickname: The Sooner State
Capital: Oklahoma City, C-7

Population: 3,751,351 (rank: 28th)
Largest city: Oklahoma City, 579,999, C-7

Land area: 68,667 sq. mi. (rank: 19th)
Highest point: Black Mesa, 4,973 ft., A-1

© Rand McNally

## Oklahoma

### Cities and Towns

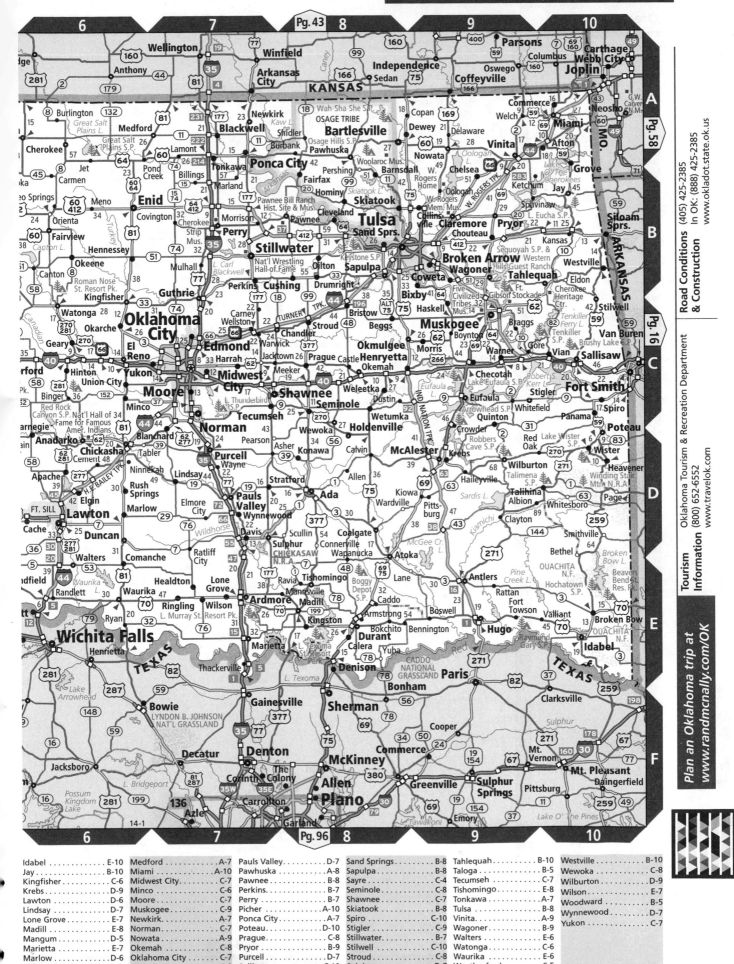

Pg. 43
Pg. 58
Pg. 16
Pg. 96

Road Conditions (405) 425-2385
& Construction In OK: (888) 425-2385
www.okladot.state.ok.us

Tourism Oklahoma Tourism & Recreation Department
Information (800) 652-6552
www.travelok.com

Plan an Oklahoma trip at
www.randmcnally.com/OK

## Oregon

### Cities and Towns

## Oregon state facts

Nickname: The Beaver State

Capital: Salem, C-2

Population: 3,831,074 (rank: 27th)

Largest city: Portland, 583,776, B-3

Land area: 95,997 sq. mi. (rank: 10th)

Highest point: Mount Hood, 11,239 ft., B-4

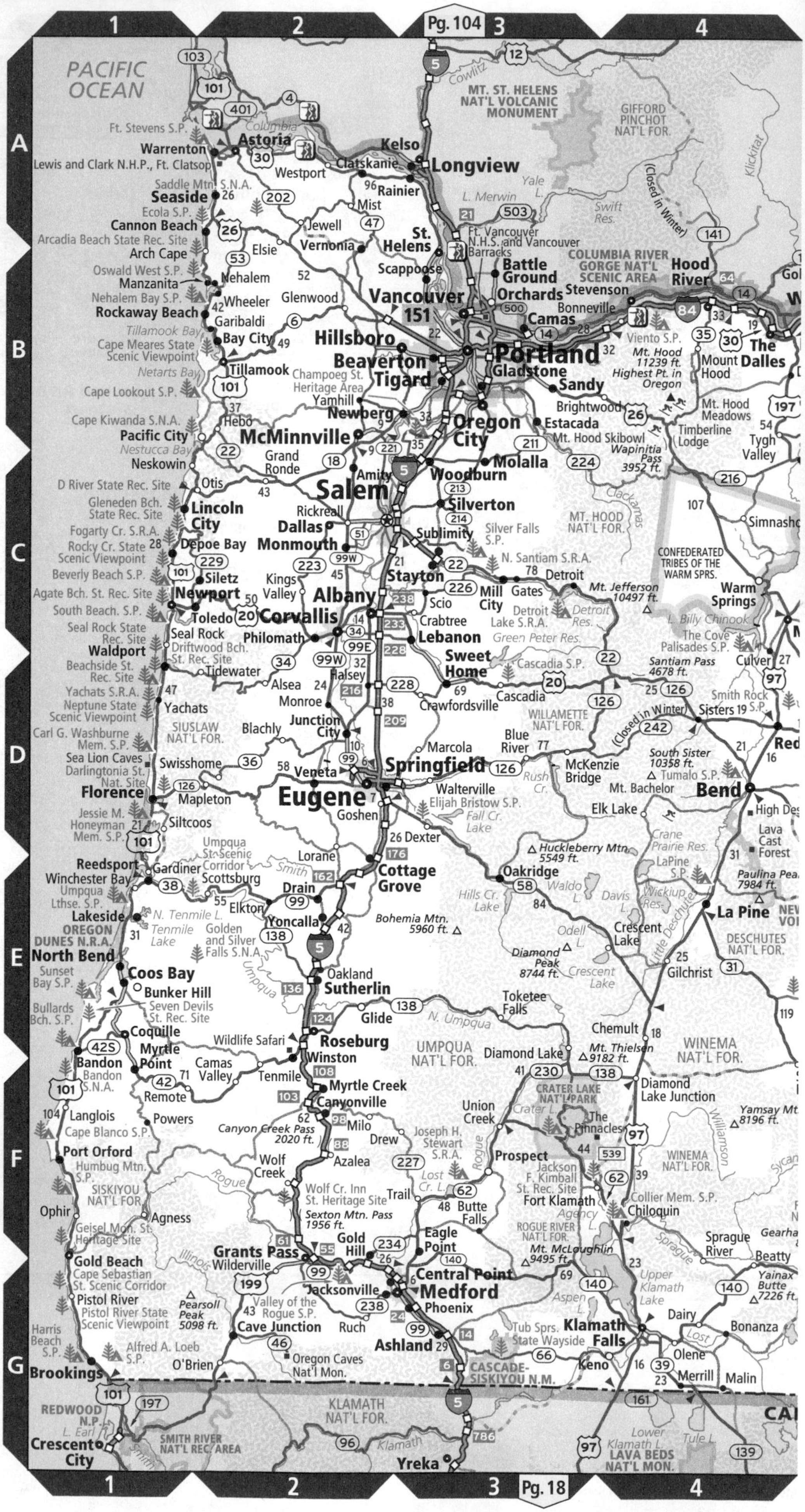

Pg. 104

Pg. 18

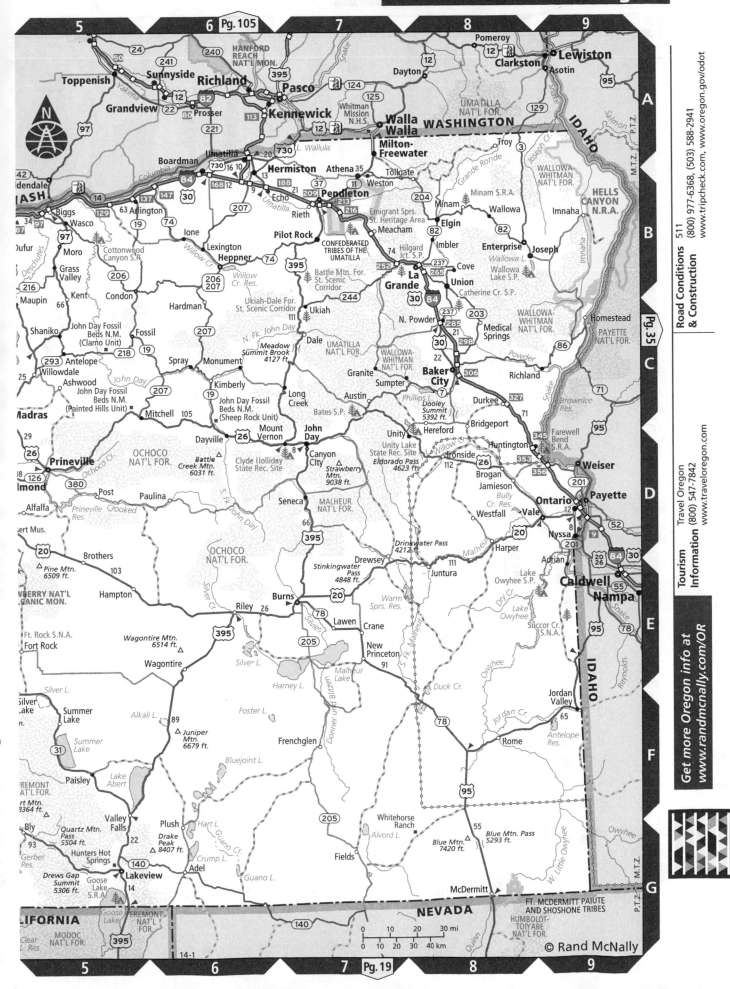

Road Conditions & Construction 511
(800) 977-6368, (503) 588-2941
www.tripcheck.com, www.oregon.gov/odot

Tourism Information Travel Oregon (800) 547-7842
www.traveloregon.com

Get more Oregon info at
www.randmcnally.com/OR

© Rand McNally

*Pennsylvania*
*state facts*

Nickname: The Keystone State
Capital: Harrisburg, G-9

Population: 12,702,379 (rank: 6th)
Largest city: Philadelphia, 1,526,006, H-13

Land area: 44,817 sq. mi. (rank: 32nd)
Highest point: Mount Davis, 3,213 ft., I-4

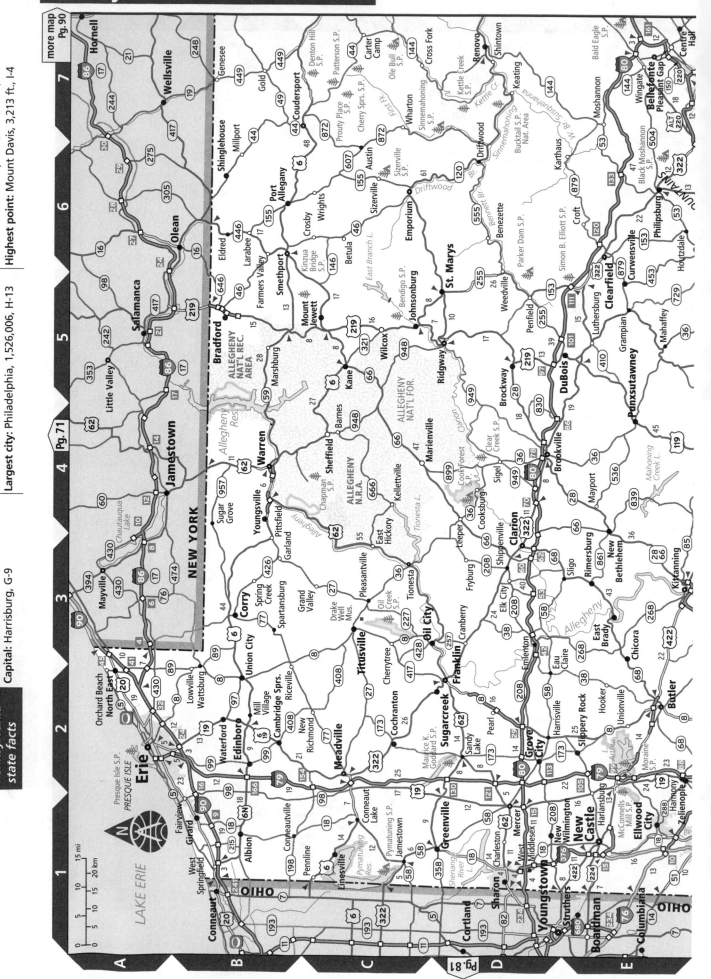

more map Pg. 90
Pg. 71
Pg. 81

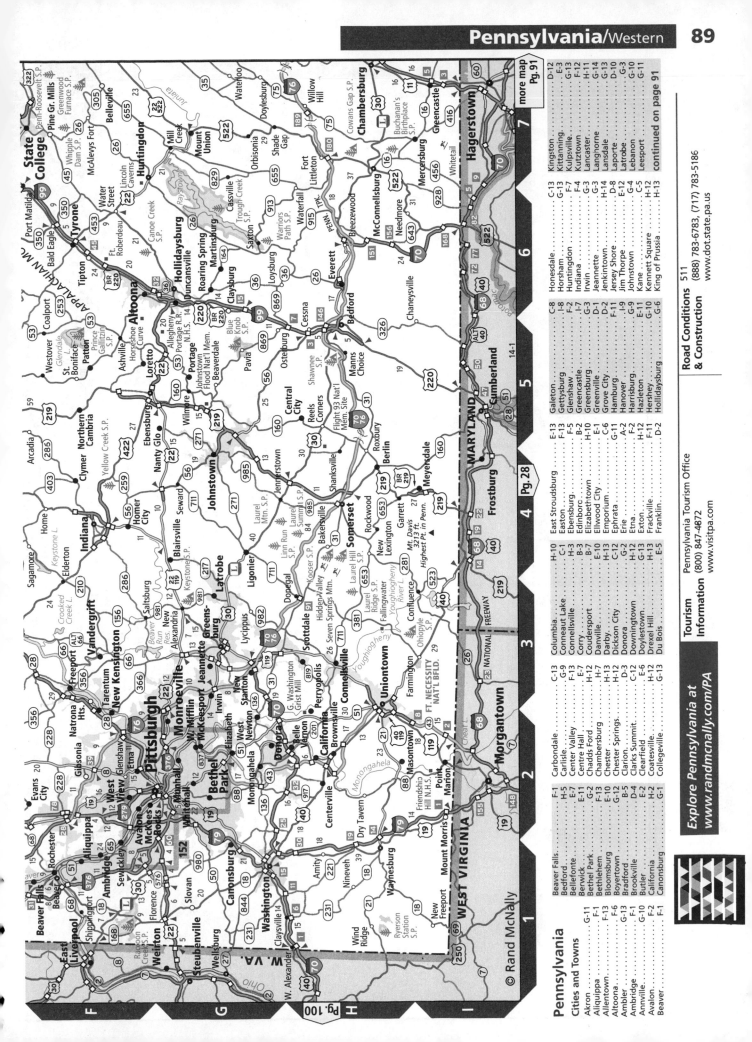

more map Pg. 91

continued on page 91

Pg. 91

Pg. 28

Pg. 100

© Rand McNally

## Pennsylvania

### Cities and Towns

**Tourism Information**
Pennsylvania Tourism Office
(800) 847-4872
www.visitpa.com

**Road Conditions & Construction**  511
(888) 783-6783, (717) 783-5186
www.dot.state.pa.us

*Explore Pennsylvania at*
www.randmcnally.com/PA

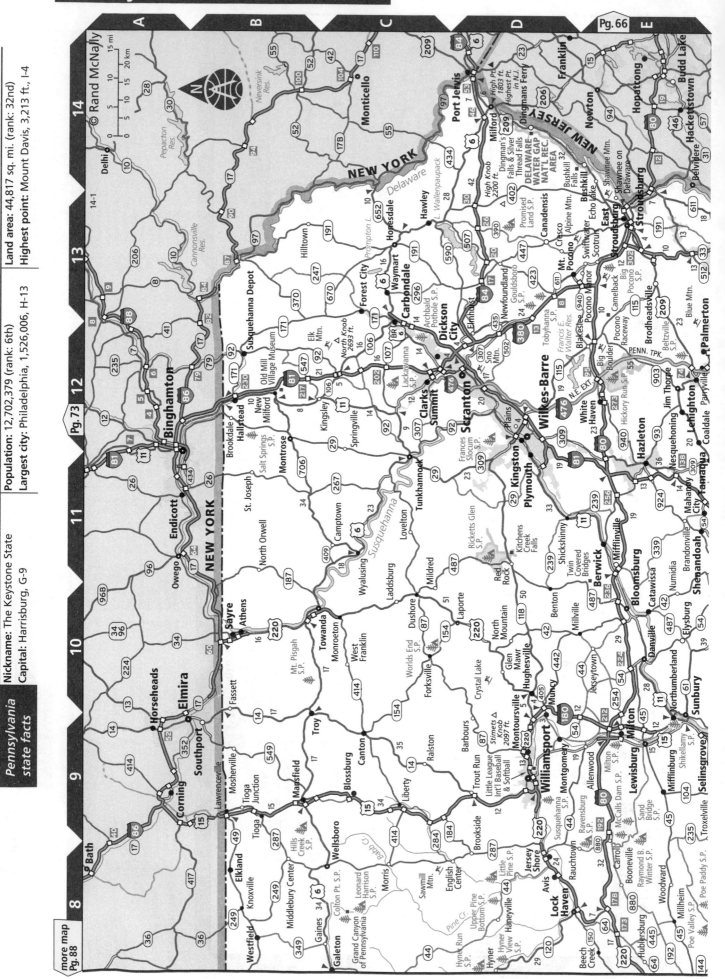

*Pennsylvania*
**state facts**

**Nickname:** The Keystone State
**Capital:** Harrisburg, G-9

**Population:** 12,702,379 (rank: 6th)
**Largest city:** Philadelphia, 1,526,006, H-13

**Land area:** 44,817 sq. mi. (rank: 32nd)
**Highest point:** Mount Davis, 3,213 ft., I-4

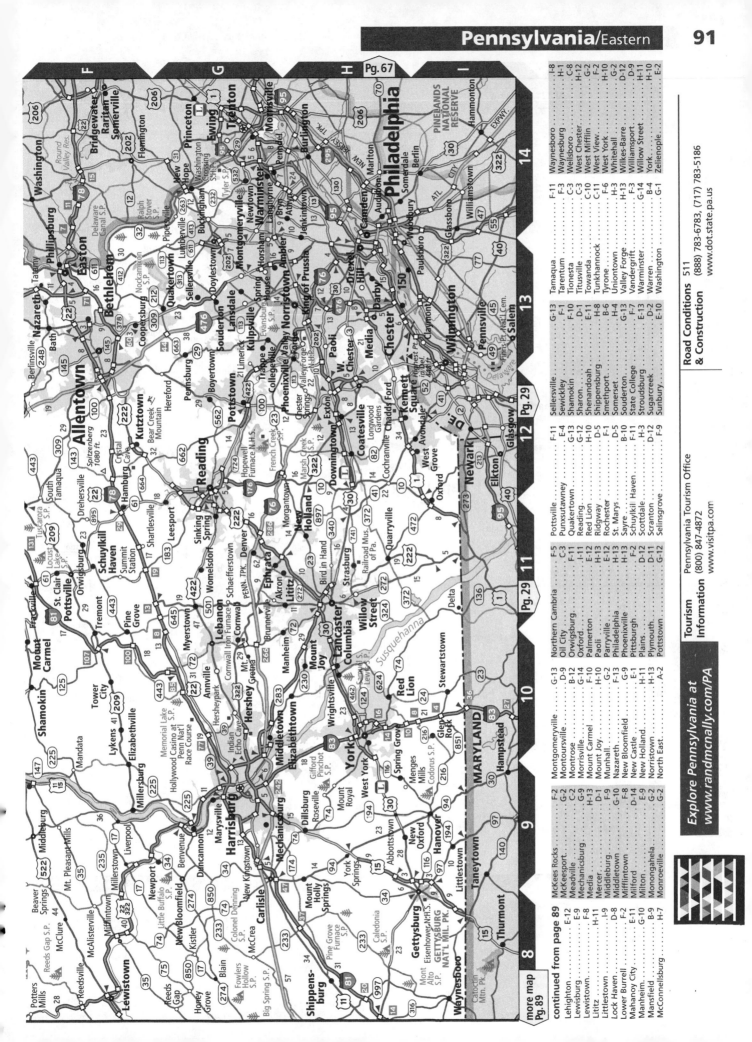

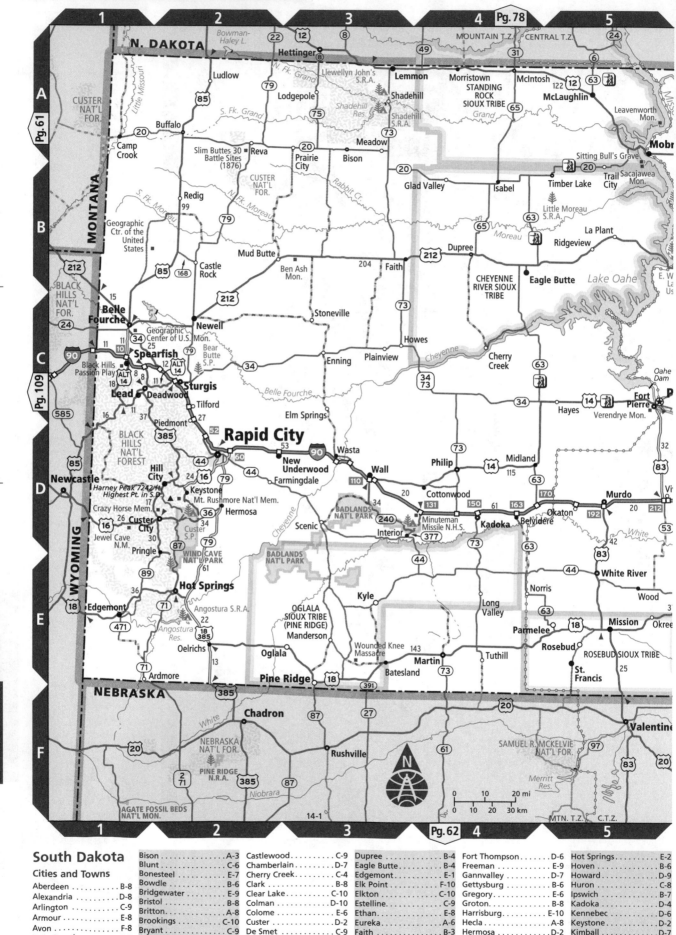

South Dakota state facts

Nickname: The Mount Rushmore State
Capital: Pierre, C-5

Population: 814,180 (rank: 46th)
Largest city: Sioux Falls, 153,888, E-10

Land area: 75,885 sq. mi. (rank: 16th)
Highest point: Harney Peak, 7,242 ft., D-2

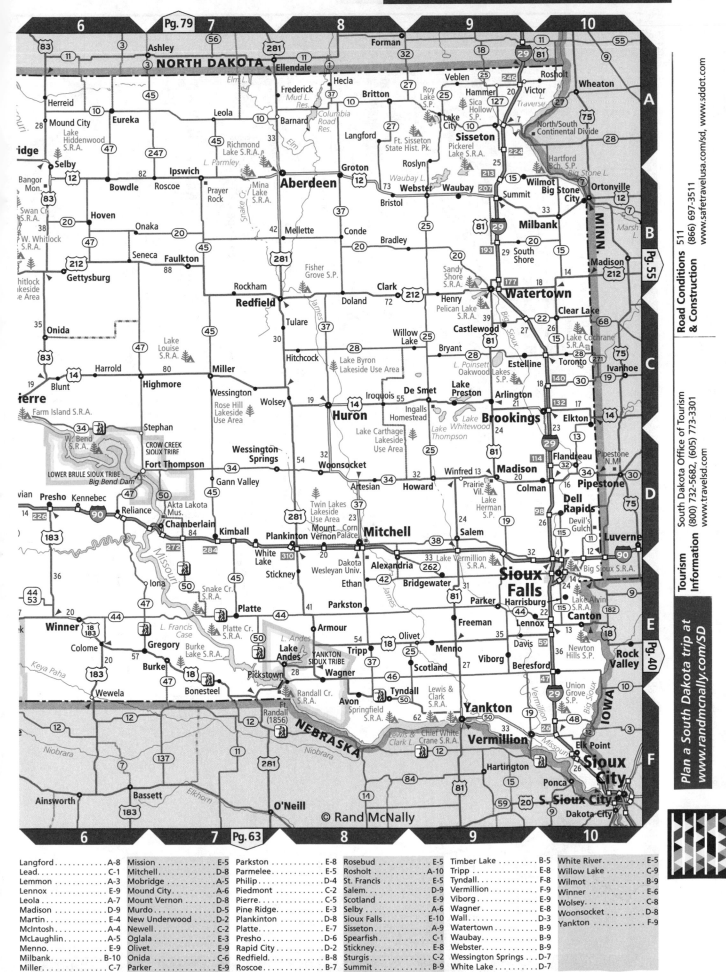

Tourism Information
South Dakota Office of Tourism
(800) 732-5682, (605) 773-3301
www.travelsd.com

Road Conditions & Construction
511
(866) 697-3511
www.safetravelusa.com/sd, www.sddot.com

Plan a South Dakota trip at
www.randmcnally.com/SD

more map
Pg. 96

For continuation see inset on pg. 95

*Texas*
state facts

Nickname: The Lone Star State
Capital: Austin, E-9

Population: 25,145,561 (rank: 2nd)
Largest city: Houston, 2,099,451, F-11

Land area: 261,797 sq. mi. (rank: 2nd)
Highest point: Guadalupe Peak, 8,749 ft., C-2

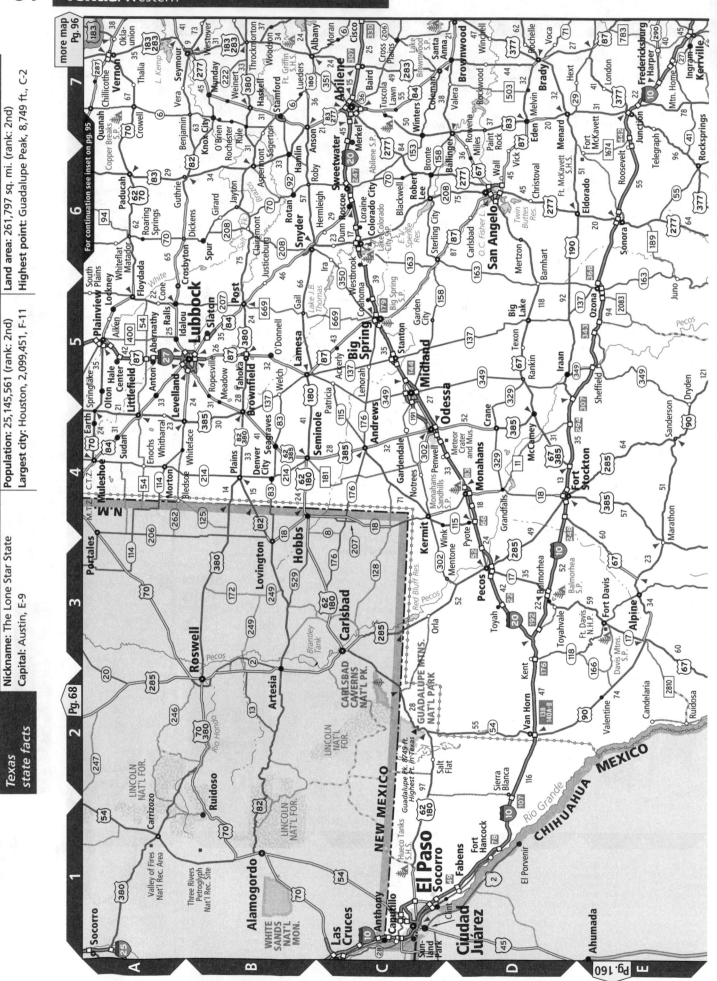

Pg. 68

Pg. 160

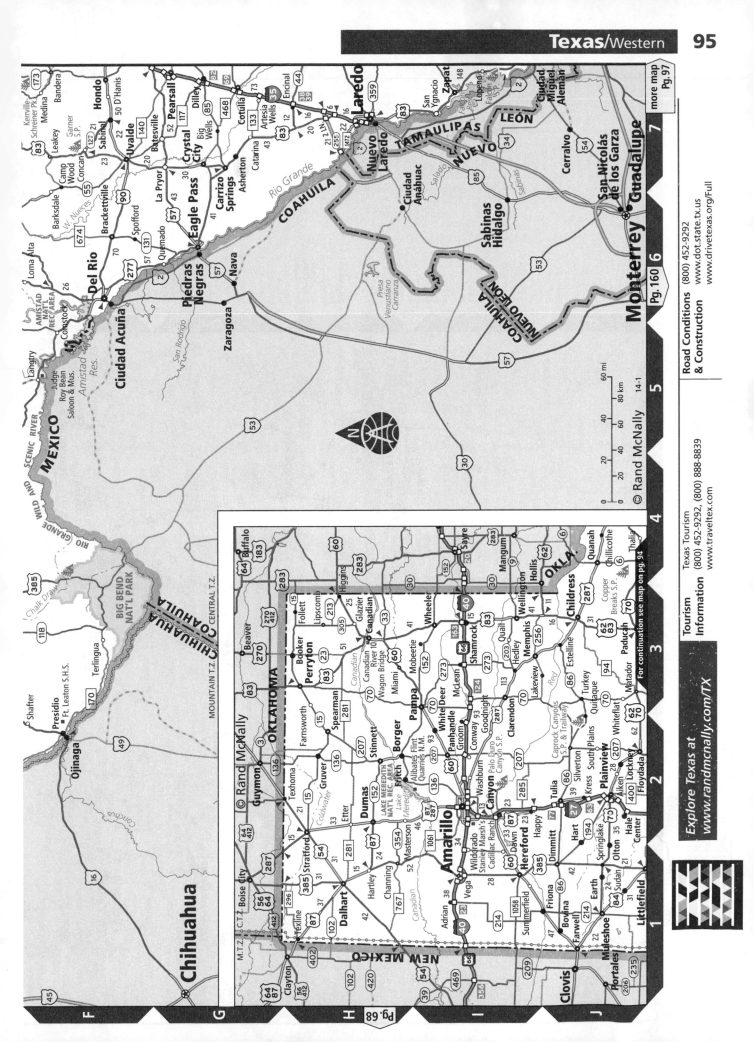

Nickname: The Lone Star State
Capital: Austin, E-9

**Texas state facts**

| | |
|---|---|
| Population: 25,145,561 (rank: 2nd) | Land area: 261,797 sq. mi. (rank: 2nd) |
| Largest city: Houston, 2,099,451, F-11 | Highest point: Guadalupe Peak, 8,749 ft., C-2 |

## Texas

### Cities and Towns

more map Pg. 94 • Pg. 85 • Pg. 16 • Pg. 48

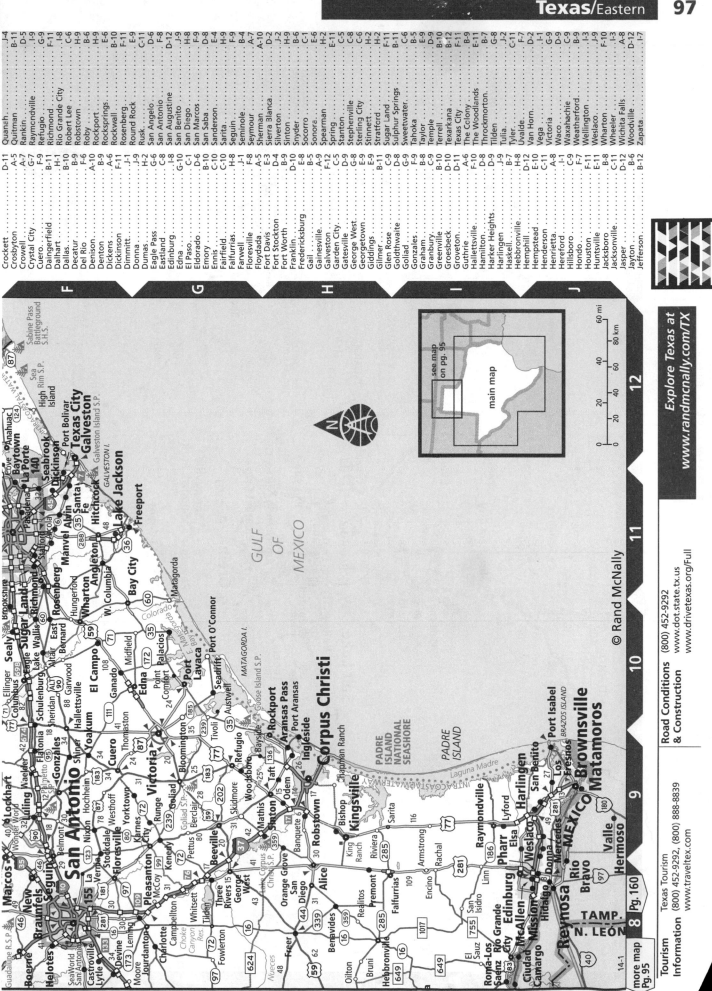

## Index

| Place | Grid | | Place | Grid |
|---|---|---|---|---|
| Quanah | A-7 | | Crockett | D-11 |
| Quitman | B-11 | | Crosbyton | A-5 |
| Rankin | D-5 | | Crowell | A-7 |
| Raymondville | I-9 | | Crystal City | G-7 |
| Refugio | G-9 | | Cuero | F-9 |
| Richmond | F-11 | | Daingerfield | B-11 |
| Rio Grande City | I-8 | | Dalhart | H-1 |
| Robert Lee | C-6 | | Dallas | B-10 |
| Robstown | H-9 | | Decatur | B-10 |
| Roby | B-6 | | Del Rio | F-6 |
| Rockport | H-9 | | Denison | A-10 |
| Rocksprings | E-6 | | Denton | B-9 |
| Rockwall | B-10 | | Dickens | A-6 |
| Rosenberg | E-10 | | Dickinson | F-11 |
| Round Rock | E-9 | | Dimmitt | J-1 |
| Rusk | C-11 | | Donna | J-9 |
| San Angelo | D-6 | | Dumas | H-2 |
| San Antonio | F-8 | | Eagle Pass | G-6 |
| San Augustine | C-12 | | Eastland | C-8 |
| San Benito | J-9 | | Edinburg | I-8 |
| San Diego | H-8 | | Edna | G-10 |
| San Marcos | E-9 | | El Paso | C-1 |
| San Saba | D-8 | | Eldorado | D-6 |
| Sanderson | E-4 | | Emory | B-10 |
| Sarita | H-9 | | Ennis | C-10 |
| Seguin | F-9 | | Fairfield | C-10 |
| Seminole | B-4 | | Falfurrias | H-8 |
| Seymour | A-7 | | Farwell | J-1 |
| Sherman | A-10 | | Floresville | F-8 |
| Sierra Blanca | D-2 | | Floydada | A-5 |
| Sinton | H-9 | | Fort Davis | D-2 |
| Snyder | B-6 | | Fort Stockton | D-4 |
| Socorro | C-1 | | Fort Worth | B-9 |
| Sonora | E-6 | | Franklin | D-10 |
| Spearman | H-2 | | Fredericksburg | E-8 |
| Spring | E-11 | | Gail | B-6 |
| Stanton | C-5 | | Gainesville | A-9 |
| Stephenville | C-8 | | Galveston | F-12 |
| Sterling City | C-5 | | Garden City | C-5 |
| Stinnett | H-2 | | Gatesville | D-9 |
| Stratford | H-1 | | George West | G-8 |
| Sugar Land | E-10 | | Georgetown | E-9 |
| Sulphur Springs | B-11 | | Giddings | E-9 |
| Sweetwater | C-7 | | Gilmer | B-11 |
| Tahoka | A-5 | | Goldthwaite | D-8 |
| Taylor | E-9 | | Goliad | G-9 |
| Temple | D-9 | | Gonzales | F-9 |
| Terrell | B-10 | | Graham | B-8 |
| Texarkana | A-12 | | Granbury | C-9 |
| Texas City | F-11 | | Greenville | B-10 |
| The Colony | B-10 | | Groesbeck | D-10 |
| The Woodlands | E-11 | | Groveton | D-11 |
| Throckmorton | B-7 | | Guthrie | A-6 |
| Tilden | G-8 | | Hallettsville | F-10 |
| Tulia | I-2 | | Hamilton | D-8 |
| Tyler | B-11 | | Harker Heights | D-9 |
| Uvalde | F-7 | | Harlingen | J-9 |
| Van Horn | D-2 | | Haskell | B-7 |
| Vega | I-1 | | Hebbronville | H-8 |
| Victoria | G-9 | | Hemphill | D-12 |
| Waco | D-9 | | Hempstead | E-10 |
| Waxahachie | C-10 | | Henderson | C-11 |
| Weatherford | B-9 | | Henrietta | A-8 |
| Wellington | I-3 | | Hereford | I-1 |
| Weslaco | J-9 | | Hillsboro | C-9 |
| Wharton | F-10 | | Hondo | F-7 |
| Wheeler | I-3 | | Houston | E-11 |
| Wichita Falls | A-8 | | Huntsville | D-11 |
| Woodville | D-12 | | Jacksboro | B-8 |
| Zapata | I-7 | | Jacksonville | C-11 |
| | | | Jasper | D-12 |
| | | | Jayton | B-6 |
| | | | Jefferson | B-12 |

see map on pg. 95

main map

0   20   40   60 mi
0   20   40   60   80 km

© Rand McNally

*Explore Texas at*
*www.randmcnally.com/TX*

more map Pg. 95

| | |
|---|---|
| **Tourism Information** | Texas Tourism (800) 452-9292, (800) 888-8839 www.traveltex.com |
| **Road Conditions & Construction** | (800) 452-9292 www.dot.state.tx.us www.drivetexas.org/Full |

Utah
state facts

Nickname: The Beehive State
Capital: Salt Lake City, C-4

Population: 2,763,885 (rank: 34th)
Largest city: Salt Lake City, 186,440, C-4

Land area: 82,144 sq. mi. (rank: 12th)
Highest point: Kings Peak, 13,528 ft., C-5

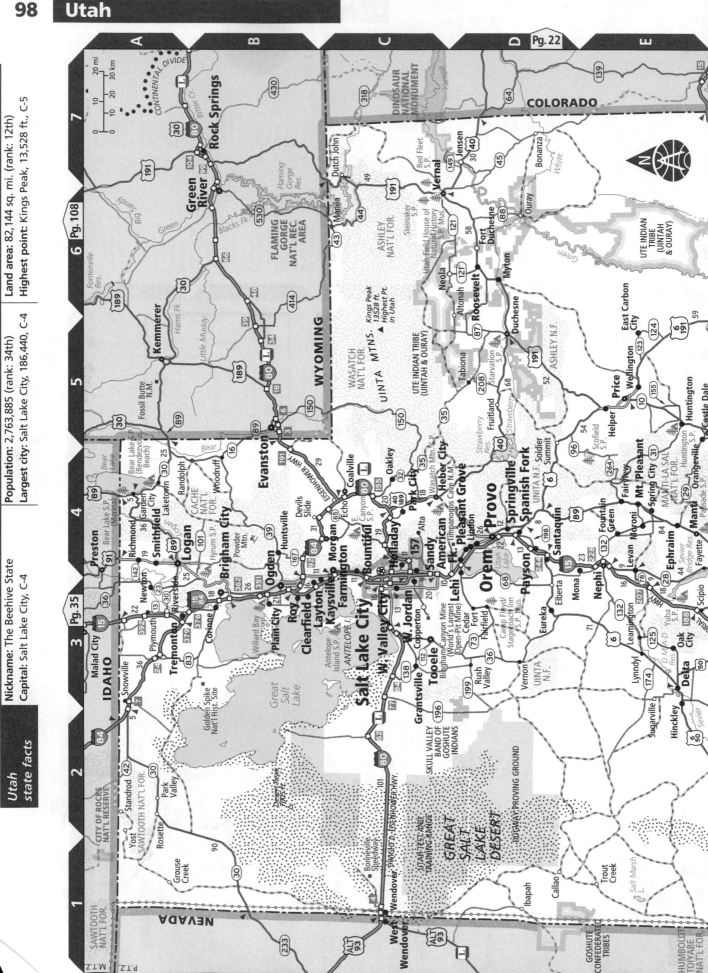

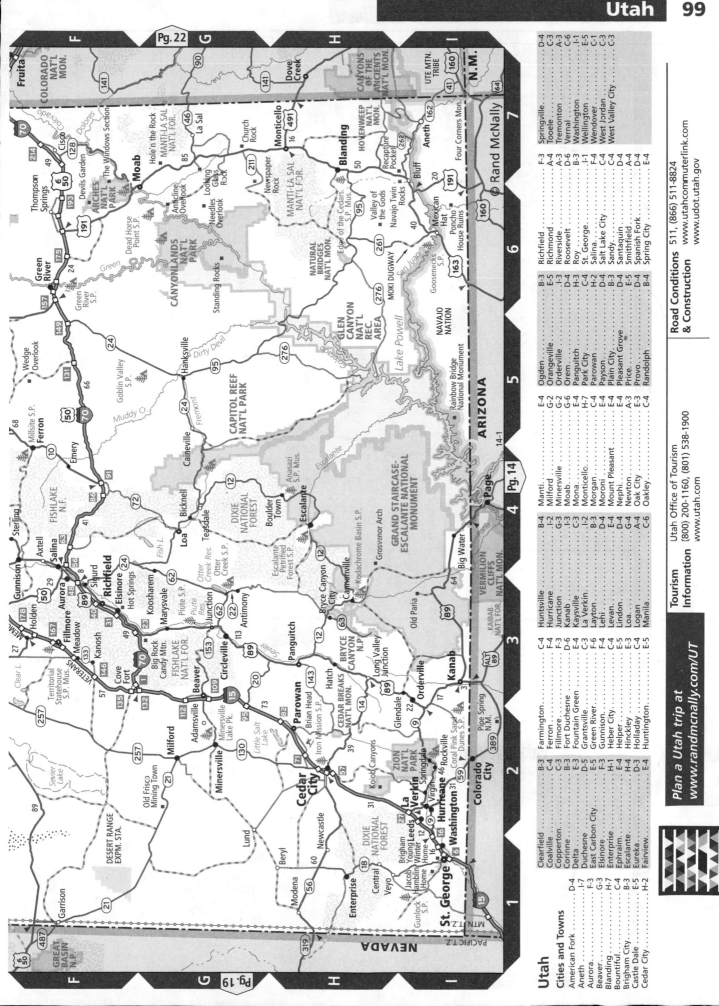

| | | |
|---|---|---|
| **Tourism Information** | Utah Office of Tourism (800) 200-1160, (801) 538-1900 www.utah.com | **Road Conditions & Construction** 511, (866) 511-8824 www.utahcommuterlink.com www.udot.utah.gov |

*Plan a Utah trip at*
**www.randmcnally.com/UT**

© Rand McNally

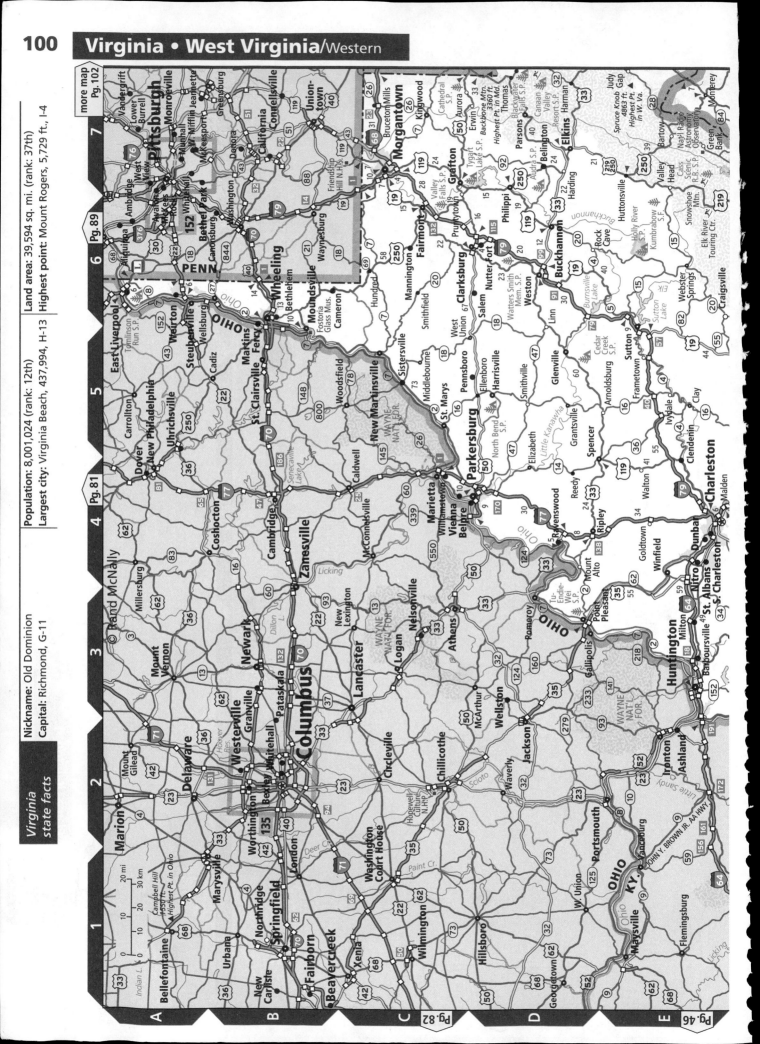

*Virginia*
*state facts*

Nickname: Old Dominion
Capital: Richmond, G-11

Population: 8,001,024 (rank: 37th)
Largest city: Virginia Beach, 437,994, H-13

Land area: 39,594 sq. mi. (rank: 12th)
Highest point: Mount Rogers, 5,729 ft., I-4

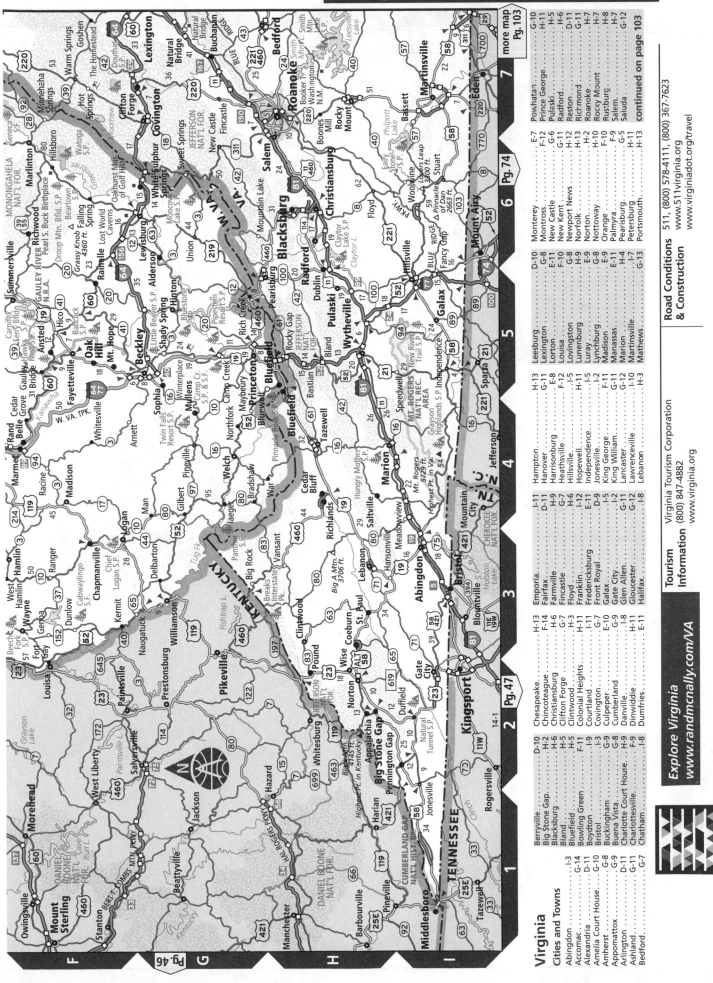

more map Pg. 103

### Road Conditions & Construction
511, (800) 578-4111, (800) 367-7623
www.511virginia.org
www.virginiadot.org/travel

### Tourism Information
Virginia Tourism Corporation
(800) 847-4882
www.virginia.org

*Explore Virginia*
www.randmcnally.com/VA

Pg. 74

Pg. 47

Pg. 46

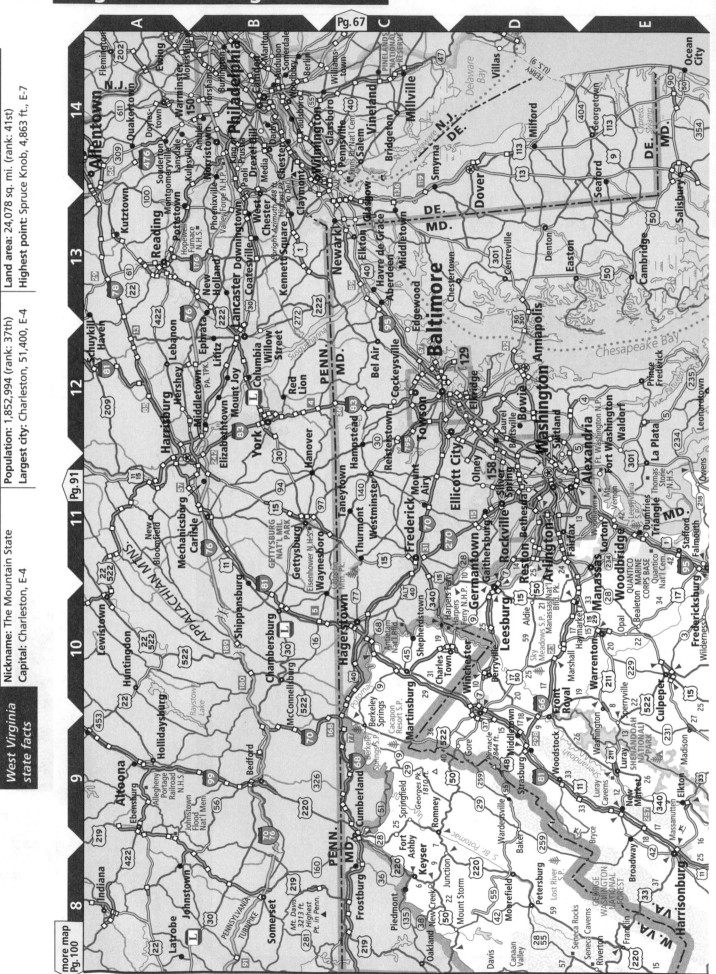

*West Virginia*
**state facts**

Nickname: The Mountain State
Capital: Charleston, E-4

Population: 1,852,994 (rank: 37th)
Largest city: Charleston, E-4

Land area: 24,078 sq. mi. (rank: 41st)
Highest point: Spruce Knob, 4,863 ft., E-7

more map
Pg. 100

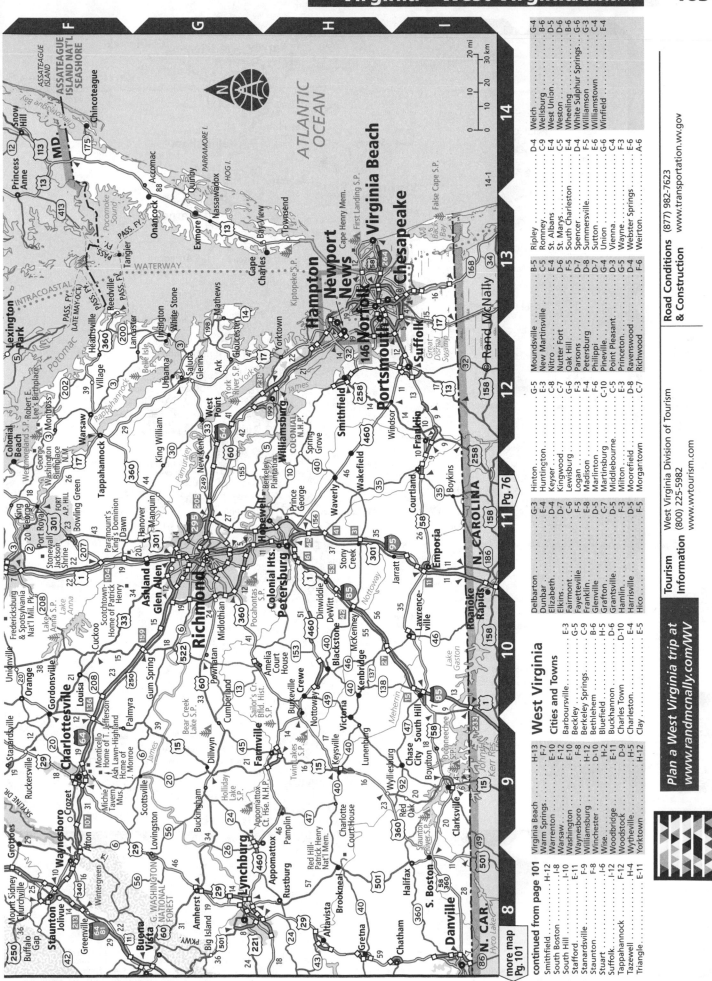

continued from page 101

more map Pg. 101

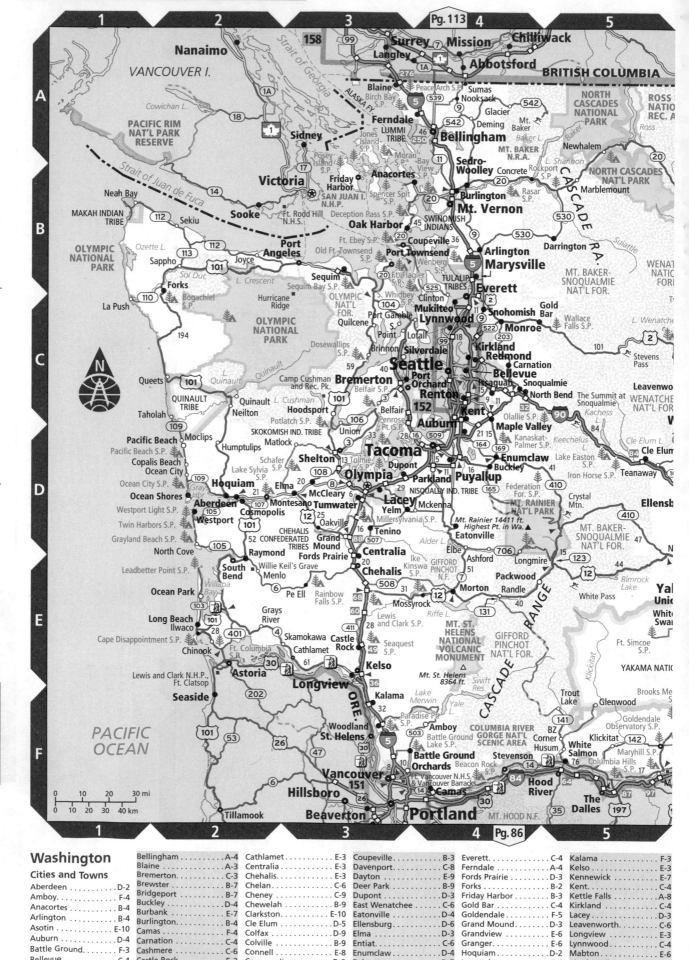

*Washington state facts*

Nickname: The Evergreen State
Capital: Olympia, D-3

Population: 6,724,540 (rank: 13th)
Largest city: Seattle, 608,660, C-4

Land area: 66,544 sq. mi. (rank: 20th)
Highest point: Mount Rainier, 14,411 ft., D-4

# Washington

## Cities and Towns

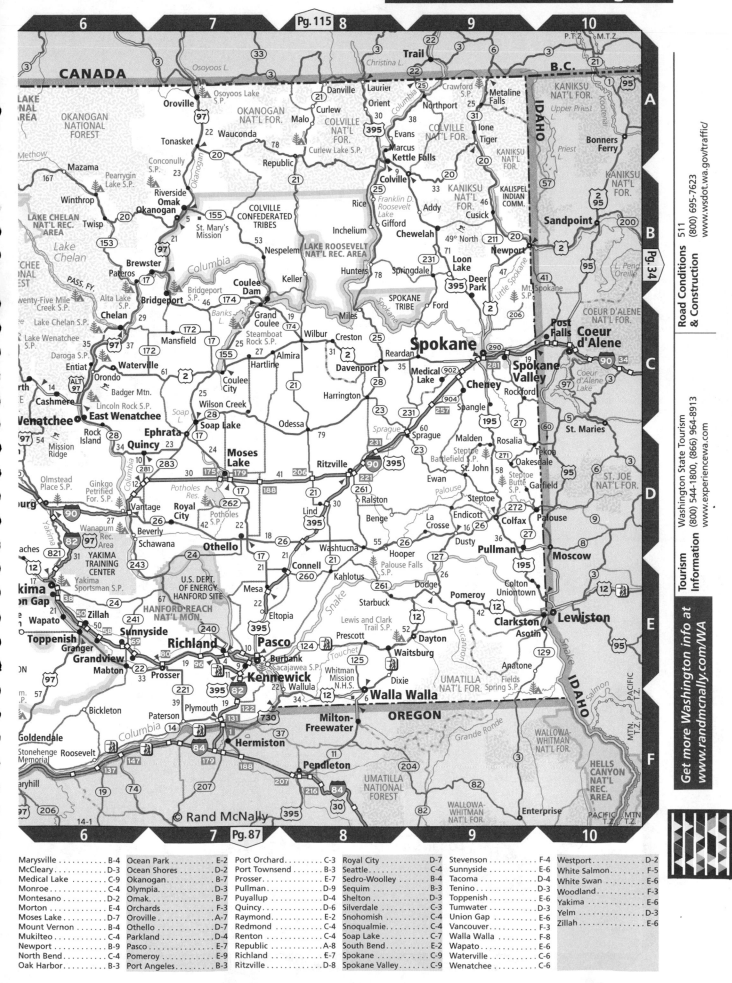

Road Conditions
& Construction
511
(800) 695-7623
www.wsdot.wa.gov/traffic/

Tourism
Information
Washington State Tourism
(800) 544-1800, (866) 964-8913
www.experiencewa.com

Get more Washington info at
www.randmcnally.com/WA

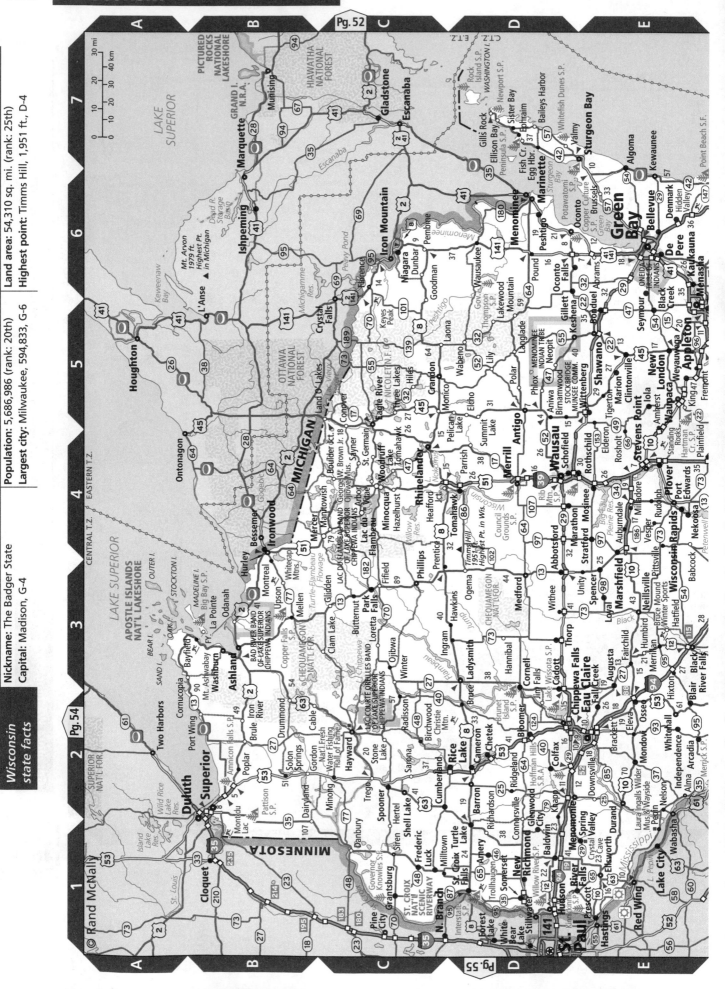

*Wisconsin state facts*

Nickname: The Badger State
Capital: Madison, G-4

Population: 5,686,986 (rank: 20th)
Land area: 54,310 sq. mi. (rank: 25th)
Largest city: Milwaukee, 594,833, G-6
Highest point: Timms Hill, 1,951 ft., D-4

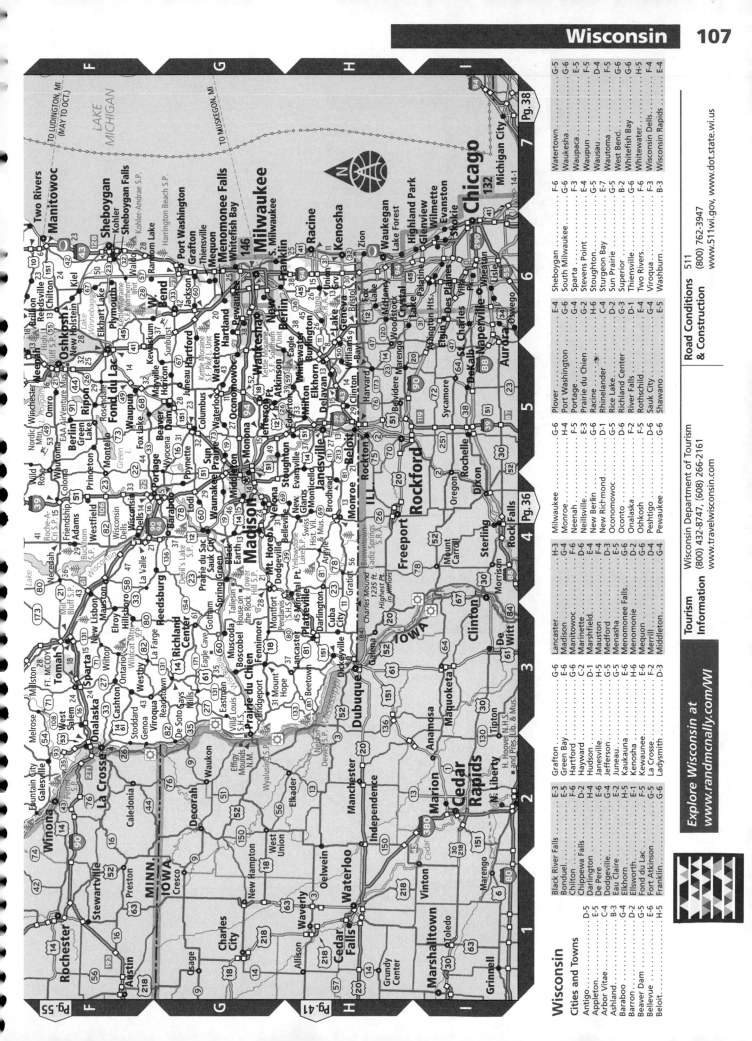

Pg. 38 · Pg. 36 · Pg. 41 · Pg. 55

**Tourism Information**
Wisconsin Department of Tourism
(800) 432-8747, (608) 266-2161
www.travelwisconsin.com

**Road Conditions & Construction**
511
(800) 762-3947
www.511wi.gov, www.dot.state.wi.us

Explore Wisconsin at
www.randmcnally.com/WI

## Wyoming

**Wyoming state facts**

Land area: 97,100 sq. mi. (rank: 9th)
Highest point: Gannett Peak, 13,804 ft., C-3

Population: 563,626 (rank: 50th)
Largest city: Cheyenne, 59,466, F-8

Nickname: The Equality State
Capital: Cheyenne, F-8

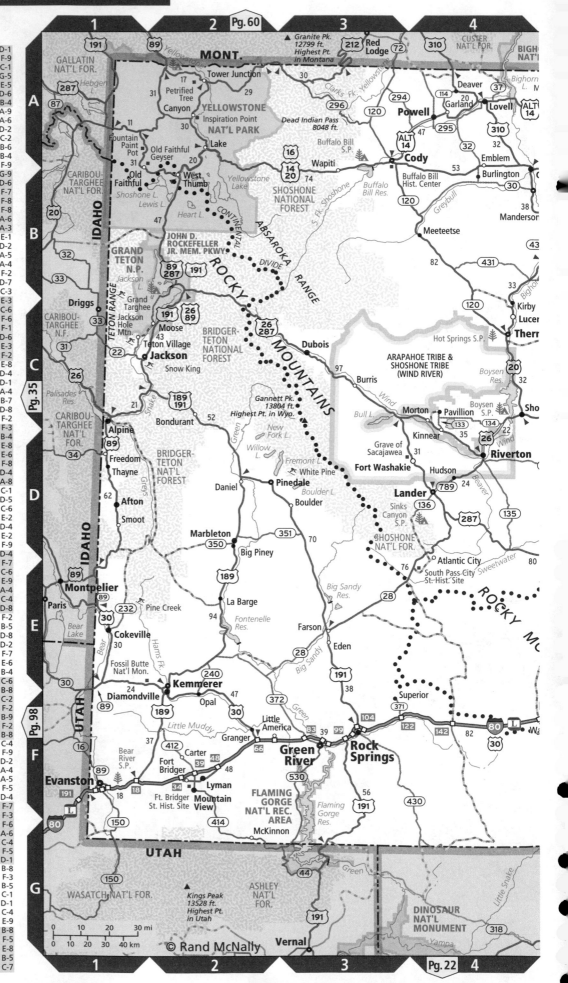

© Rand McNally

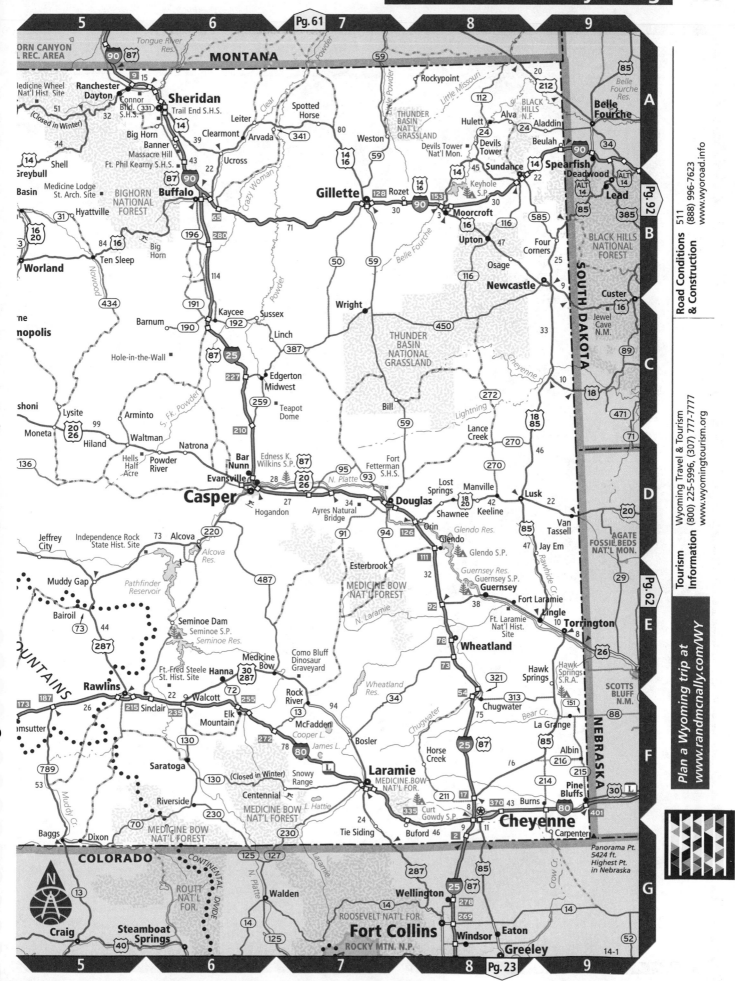

Pg. 61

MONTANA

Pg. 92

Pg. 62

Road Conditions 511
& Construction (888) 996-7623
www.wyoroad.info

Tourism Wyoming Travel & Tourism
Information (800) 225-5996, (307) 777-7777
www.wyomingtourism.org

Plan a Wyoming trip at
www.randmcnally.com/WY

SOUTH DAKOTA

NEBRASKA

COLORADO

Panorama Pt.
5424 ft.
Highest Pt.
in Nebraska

Pg. 23

14-1

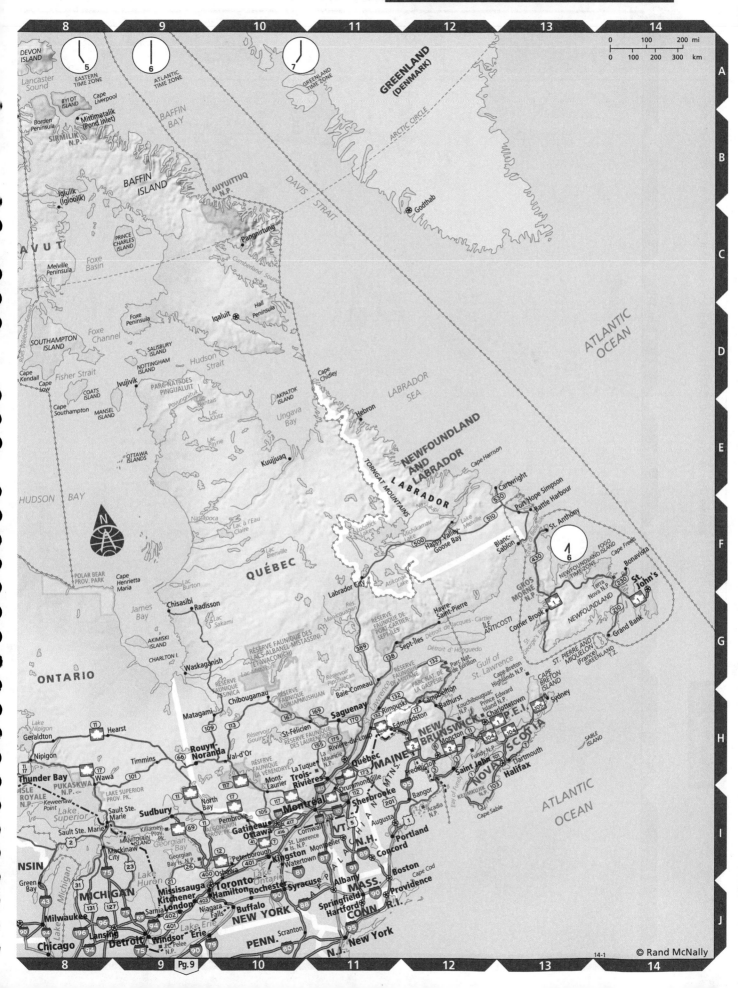

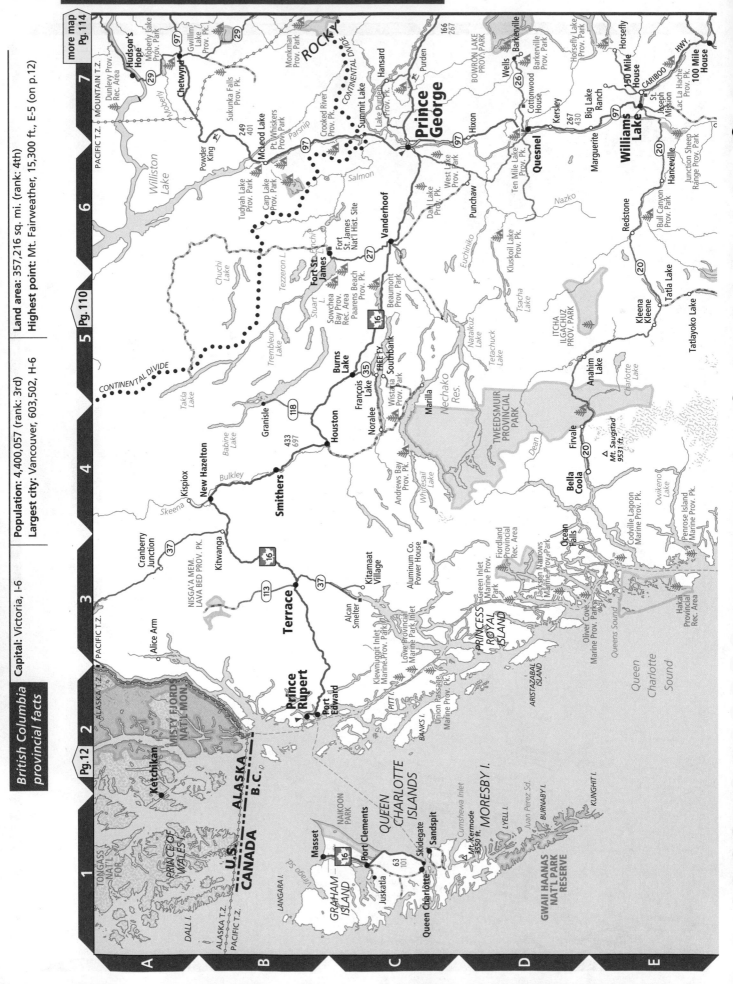

more map
Pg. 114

British Columbia *provincial facts*

Capital: Victoria, I-6 | Population: 4,400,057 (rank: 3rd) | Land area: 357,216 sq. mi. (rank: 4th)
Largest city: Vancouver, 603,502, H-6 | Highest point: Mt. Fairweather, 15,300 ft., E-5 (on p.12)

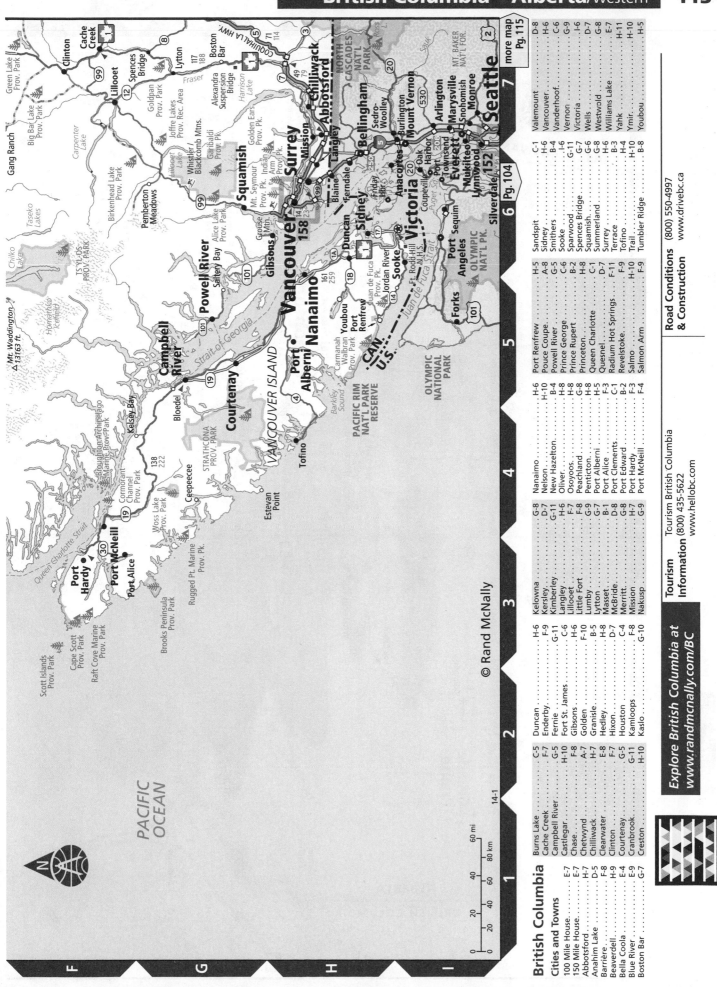

more map Pg. 115
Pg. 104

© Rand McNally

PACIFIC OCEAN

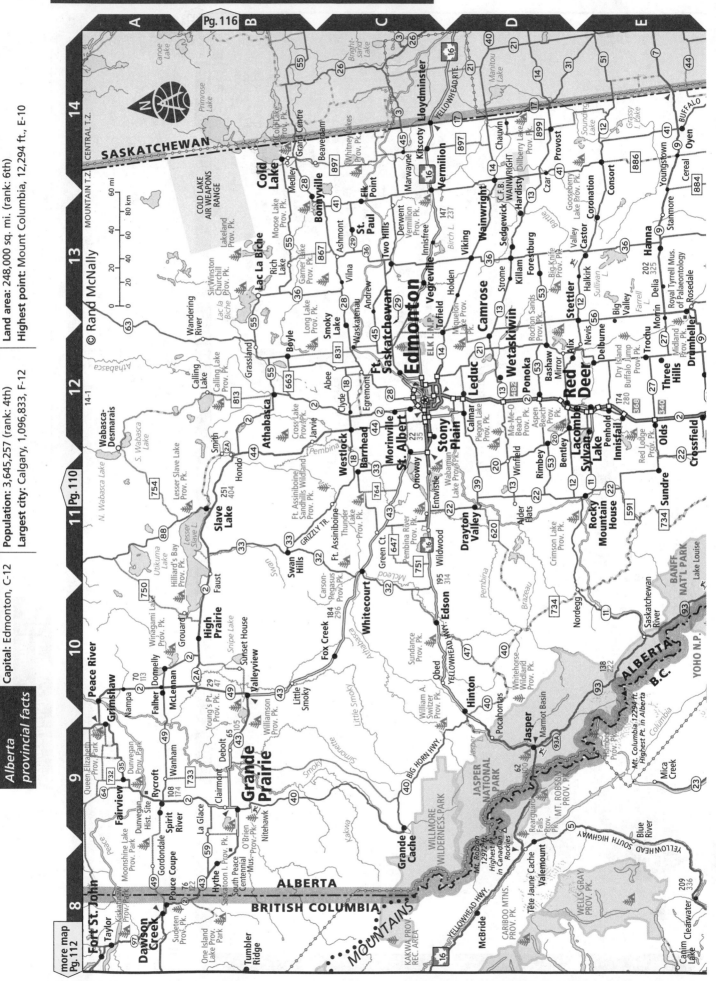

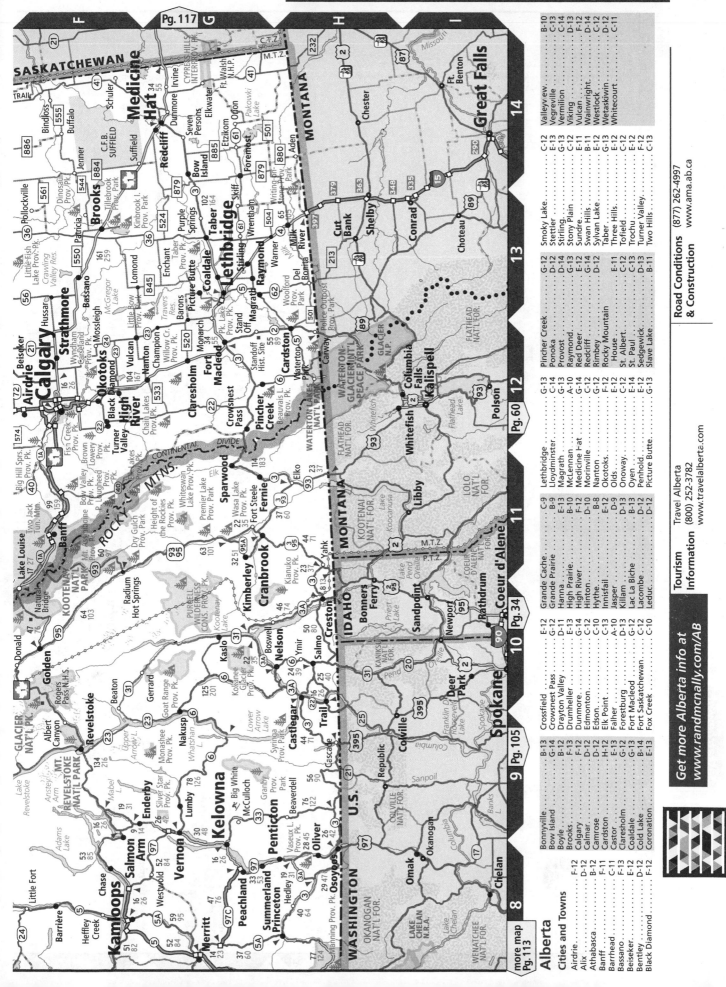

**Tourism** **Road Conditions**   (877) 262-4997
**Information** **& Construction**   www.ama.ab.ca

**Travel Alberta**
(800) 252-3782
www.travelalberta.com

*Get more Alberta info at*
**www.randmcnally.com/AB**

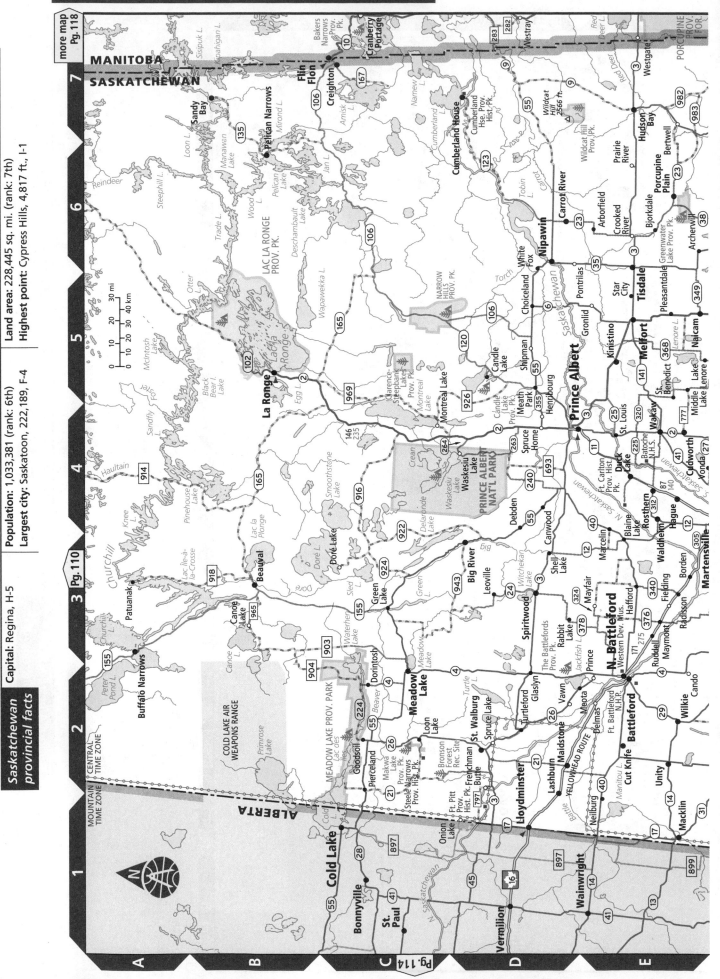

more map Pg. 118

Pg. 110

Pg. 114

**Saskatchewan provincial facts**

Capital: Regina, H-5

Population: 1,033,381 (rank: 6th)
Largest city: Saskatoon, 222,189, F-4

Land area: 228,445 sq. mi. (rank: 7th)
Highest point: Cypress Hills, 4,817 ft., I-1

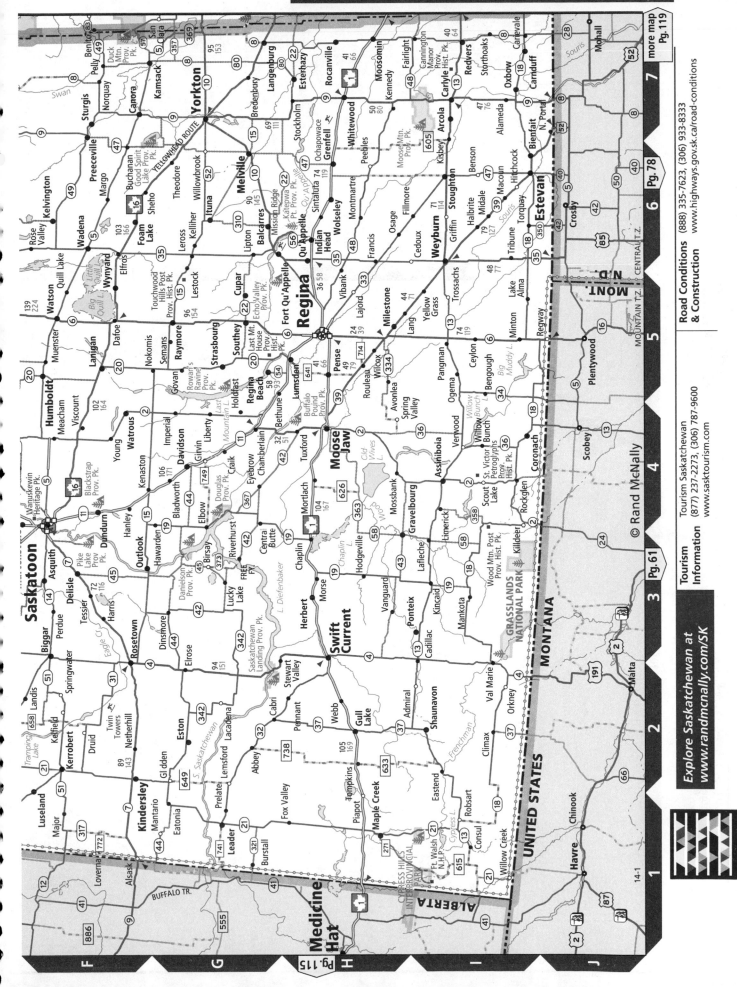

**Road Conditions & Construction**
(888) 335-7623, (306) 933-8333
www.highways.gov.sk.ca/road-conditions

**Tourism Information**
Tourism Saskatchewan
(877) 237-2273, (306) 787-9600
www.sasktourism.com

*Explore Saskatchewan at*
*www.randmcnally.com/SK*

Capital: Winnipeg, H-11 | Population: 1,208,268 (rank: 5th) | Land area: 213,729 sq. mi. (rank: 8th)
Largest city: Winnipeg, 663,617, H-11 | Highest point: Baldy Mountain, 2,730 ft., G-8

*Manitoba provincial facts*

## Saskatchewan
### Cities and Towns

| | |
|---|---|
| Arcola | I-7 |
| Asquith | F-3 |
| Assiniboia | J-4 |
| Avonlea | H-5 |
| Balcarres | G-6 |
| Battleford | E-2 |
| Beauval | B-3 |
| Bethune | G-5 |
| Bienfait | J-6 |
| Big River | D-3 |
| Biggar | F-3 |
| Blaine Lake | E-3 |
| Buffalo Narrows | A-3 |
| Cabri | G-2 |
| Canora | F-7 |
| Canwood | D-4 |
| Carlyle | I-7 |
| Carnduff | J-7 |
| Carrot River | D-6 |
| Central Butte | G-4 |
| Choiceland | D-5 |
| Coronach | J-4 |
| Craik | G-4 |
| Creighton | C-7 |
| Cudworth | E-4 |
| Cumberland House | D-7 |
| Cupar | G-5 |
| Cut Knife | E-2 |
| Davidson | G-4 |
| Debden | D-4 |
| Delisle | F-3 |
| Duck Lake | E-4 |
| Dundurn | F-4 |
| Eastend | I-2 |
| Eatonia | G-1 |
| Elrose | G-2 |
| Esterhazy | G-7 |
| Estevan | I-6 |
| Eston | G-2 |
| Foam Lake | F-6 |
| Fort Qu'Appelle | G-6 |
| Glaslyn | D-2 |
| Gravelbourg | H-3 |
| Green Lake | C-3 |
| Grenfell | H-6 |
| Gull Lake | H-2 |
| Hafford | E-3 |
| Hague | E-4 |
| Hanley | F-4 |
| Herbert | H-3 |
| Hudson Bay | E-7 |
| Humboldt | F-5 |
| Indian Head | H-6 |
| Ituna | G-6 |
| Kamsack | G-7 |
| Kelvington | F-6 |
| Kerrobert | F-2 |
| Kindersley | E-5 |
| Kinistino | B-5 |
| La Ronge | I-3 |
| Lafleche | H-3 |
| Langenburg | G-7 |
| Lanigan | F-5 |
| Lashburn | D-2 |
| Leader | G-1 |
| Leoville | D-3 |
| Lloydminster | D-1 |
| Lucky Lake | G-3 |
| Lumsden | H-5 |
| Luseland | F-2 |

## Manitoba
### Cities and Towns

| | |
|---|---|
| Amaranth | H-10 |
| Angusville | G-8 |
| Arborg | G-11 |
| Ashern | G-10 |
| Austin | H-9 |
| Baldur | I-9 |
| Beausejour | H-11 |
| Belmont | I-9 |
| Benito | F-7 |
| Berens River | I-6 |
| Binscarth | H-8 |
| Birch River | E-8 |
| Birtle | H-8 |
| Boissevain | I-9 |
| Bowsman | F-8 |
| Brandon | I-9 |
| Camperville | F-8 |
| Carberry | H-10 |
| Carman | I-9 |
| Cartwright | I-9 |
| Cormorant | C-8 |
| Cranberry Portage | C-7 |
| Crystal City | I-9 |
| Darlingford | I-10 |
| Dauphin | G-9 |
| Deloraine | I-8 |
| Douglas | H-9 |
| Duck Bay | F-8 |
| Elkhorn | I-8 |
| Elm Creek | I-10 |
| Elphinstone | H-8 |
| Emerson | I-11 |
| Erickson | H-9 |
| Eriksdale | G-10 |
| Ethelbert | G-8 |
| Fisher Branch | G-10 |
| Flin Flon | C-7 |
| Gilbert Plains | G-8 |
| Gimli | G-11 |
| Gladstone | H-9 |
| Glenboro | I-9 |
| Glenella | H-9 |
| Grand Rapids | E-9 |
| Grandview | G-8 |
| Gretna | I-11 |
| Gypsumville | F-10 |
| Hamiota | H-8 |
| Hartney | I-8 |
| Holland | I-9 |
| Inglis | H-8 |
| Inwood | H-11 |
| Kenville | F-8 |
| Killarney | I-9 |
| La Broquerie | I-11 |
| Lac du Bonnet | H-12 |
| Langruth | H-10 |
| Letellier | I-11 |
| Lockport | H-11 |
| Lowe Farm | I-11 |
| Lundar | G-10 |
| MacGregor | H-10 |
| Mafeking | F-5 |
| Manigotagan | G-11 |
| Manitou | I-10 |
| Matheson Island | G-11 |
| McCreary | G-9 |
| Melita | I-8 |
| Miniota | H-8 |
| Minitonas | F-8 |
| Minnedosa | H-9 |

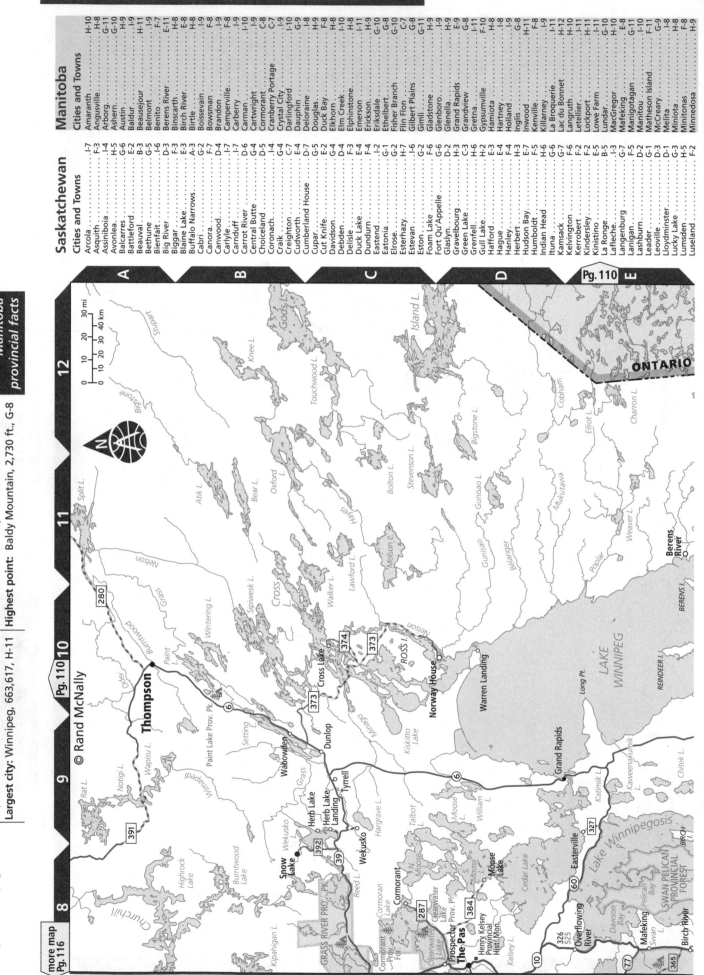

more map Pg. 116 — Pg. 110 — Pg. 110

© Rand McNally

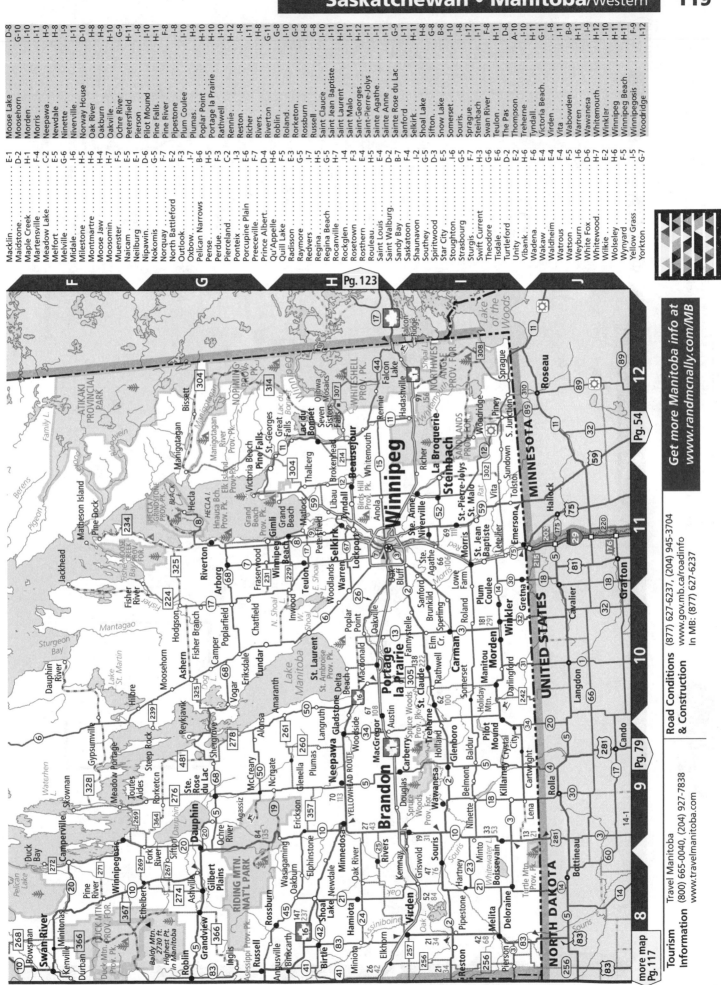

## Index

| Place | Grid |
|---|---|
| Macklin | E-1 |
| Maidstone | D-2 |
| Maple Creek | H-1 |
| Martensville | F-4 |
| Meadow Lake | C-2 |
| Melfort | E-5 |
| Melville | G-6 |
| Midale | I-6 |
| Milestone | H-5 |
| Montmartre | H-6 |
| Moose Jaw | H-4 |
| Moose Lake | D-8 |
| Moosehorn | G-10 |
| Moosomin | H-7 |
| Morden | H-11 |
| Morris | H-9 |
| Muenster | E-5 |
| Naicam | E-5 |
| Neepawa | H-8 |
| Neilburg | D-6 |
| Newdale | E-5 |
| Nipawin | D-6 |
| Ninette | G-6 |
| Niverville | I-6 |
| Nokomis | F-5 |
| Norquay | F-7 |
| North Battleford | D-3 |
| Norway House | I-11 |
| Oak River | D-10 |
| Oakburn | H-5 |
| Oakville | H-6 |
| Ochre River | H-4 |
| Outlook | F-3 |
| Oxbow | I-7 |
| Pelican Narrows | B-6 |
| Pense | H-4 |
| Perdue | F-3 |
| Petersfield | H-7 |
| Pierceland | C-2 |
| Pierson | H-8 |
| Pilot Mound | G-9 |
| Pine Falls | F-5 |
| Pine River | E-5 |
| Pipestone | E-1 |
| Plum Coulee | D-6 |
| Plumas | G-5 |
| Ponteix | I-3 |
| Poplar Point | F-7 |
| Porcupine Plain | E-6 |
| Portage la Prairie | F-8 |
| Preeceville | F-4 |
| Prince Albert | D-4 |
| Qu'Appelle | H-6 |
| Quill Lake | E-3 |
| Radisson | G-11 |
| Rathwell | E-2 |
| Raymore | F-5 |
| Redvers | I-7 |
| Regina | H-5 |
| Regina Beach | G-5 |
| Rennie | F-3 |
| Reston | I-7 |
| Richer | B-6 |
| Rivers | H-11 |
| Riverton | F-3 |
| Roblin | C-2 |
| Rocanville | H-7 |
| Rockglen | I-4 |
| Roland | I-3 |
| Rorketon | E-6 |
| Rosetown | F-3 |
| Rossburn | F-4 |
| Rosthern | E-4 |
| Rouleau | H-5 |
| Rivers | G-11 |
| Russell | I-7 |
| Saint Claude | H-5 |
| Saint Jean Baptiste | G-5 |
| Saint Laurent | H-7 |
| Saint Louis | E-4 |
| Saint Malo | I-6 |
| Saint Walburg | D-2 |
| Saint-Georges | F-3 |
| Saint-Pierre-Jolys | E-4 |
| Sainte Agathe | H-5 |
| Sainte Anne | H-4 |
| Sainte Rose du Lac | D-2 |
| Sandy Bay | B-7 |
| Sanford | F-4 |
| Saskatoon | F-4 |
| Selkirk | I-2 |
| Shaunavon | I-2 |
| Shoal Lake | G-5 |
| Sifton | G-5 |
| Snow Lake | B-8 |
| Somerset | D-3 |
| Souris | B-10 |
| Southey | E-5 |
| Sprague | F-7 |
| Spiritwood | D-3 |
| Star City | E-5 |
| Steinbach | H-3 |
| Stoughton | I-6 |
| Strasbourg | G-5 |
| Sturgis | F-6 |
| Swan River | E-6 |
| Swift Current | H-3 |
| Teulon | E-6 |
| The Pas | D-8 |
| Theodore | F-6 |
| Thompson | E-2 |
| Tisdale | E-2 |
| Treherne | E-2 |
| Turtleford | D-2 |
| Tyndall | H-6 |
| Unity | E-2 |
| Vibank | H-6 |
| Victoria Beach | G-11 |
| Virden | E-4 |
| Vita | E-4 |
| Wabowden | F-5 |
| Wadena | E-4 |
| Wakaw | E-4 |
| Waldheim | F-5 |
| Warren | I-6 |
| Watrous | F-5 |
| Watson | E-4 |
| Wawanesa | H-7 |
| Weyburn | I-6 |
| White Fox | D-6 |
| Whitemouth | H-7 |
| Whitewood | H-7 |
| Wilkie | E-2 |
| Winkler | H-6 |
| Winnipeg | G-11 |
| Winnipeg Beach | F-5 |
| Winnipegosis | I-5 |
| Wolseley | H-6 |
| Woodridge | H-11 |
| Wynyard | F-5 |
| Yellow Grass | I-5 |
| Yorkton | G-7 |

**Tourism Information**
Travel Manitoba
(800) 665-0040, (204) 927-7838
www.travelmanitoba.com

**Road Conditions & Construction**
(877) 627-6237, (204) 945-3704
www.gov.mb.ca/roadinfo
In MB: (877) 627-6237

Pg. 123
Pg. 54
Pg. 79
more map Pg. 117

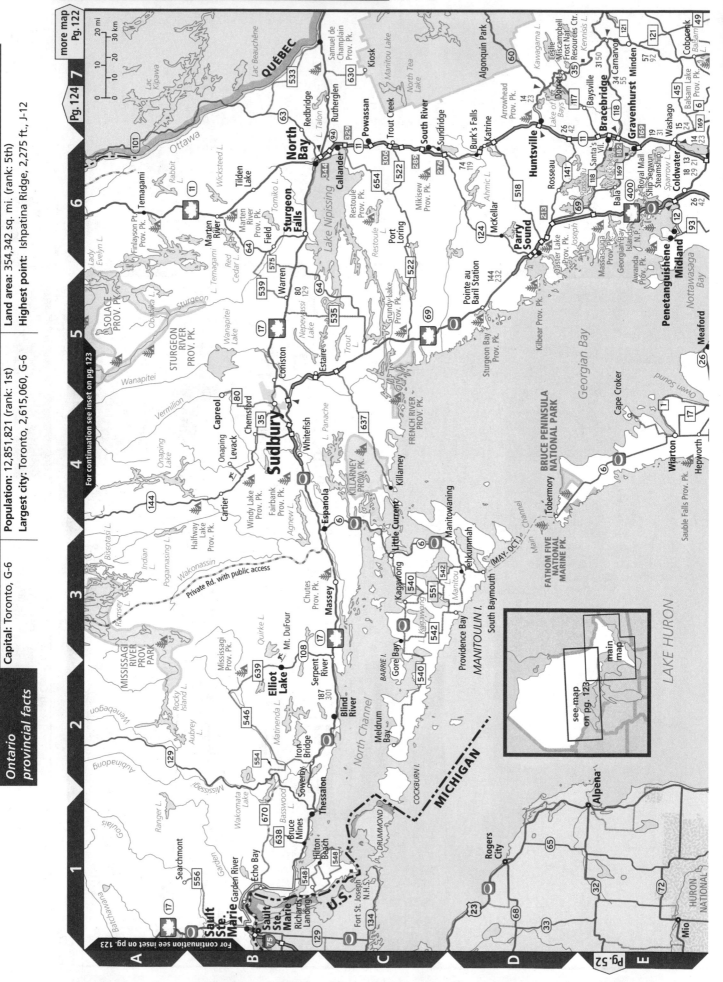

more map
Pg. 122

Pg. 124

## Ontario
### provincial facts

**Capital:** Toronto, G-6

**Population:** 12,851,821 (rank: 1st)
**Largest city:** Toronto, 2,615,060, G-6

**Land area:** 354,342 sq. mi. (rank: 5th)
**Highest point:** Ishpatina Ridge, 2,275 ft., J-12

20 mi
30 km

For continuation see inset on pg. 123

Private Rd. with public access

For continuation see inset on pg. 123

see map
on pg. 123

main
map

QUÉBEC

Ottawa

North Bay
Sudbury
Sault Ste. Marie
Parry Sound
Huntsville
Bracebridge
Gravenhurst
Midland
Penetanguishene

Georgian Bay

LAKE HURON

BRUCE PENINSULA NATIONAL PARK

FATHOM FIVE NATIONAL MARINE PK.

MANITOULIN I.

MICHIGAN

U.S.

HURON NATIONAL

LAKE ERIE

UNITED STATES

MICH.

NEW YORK

PENNSYLVANIA

N

FOREST

© Rand McNally

more map Pg. 123

Pg. 88

Pg. 81

Pg. 53

**Capital:** Toronto, G-6 | **Population:** 12,851,821 (rank: 1st) | **Land area:** 354,342 sq. mi. (rank: 5th)
| **Largest city:** Toronto, 2,615,060, G-6 | **Highest point:** Ishpatina Ridge, 2,275 ft., J-12

*Ontario provincial facts*

## Ontario

### Cities and Towns

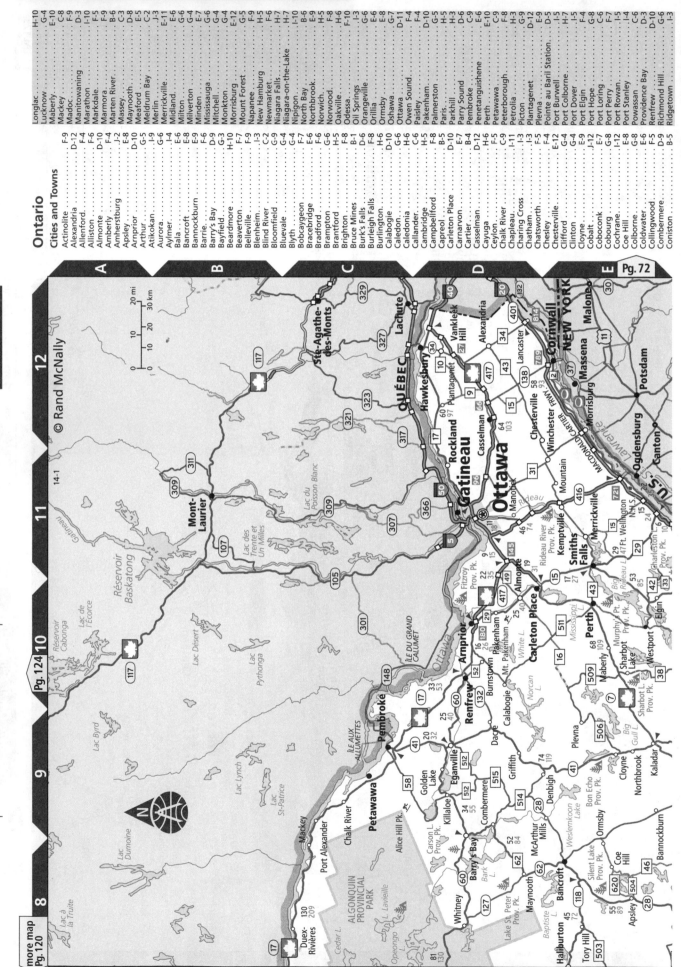

© Rand McNally

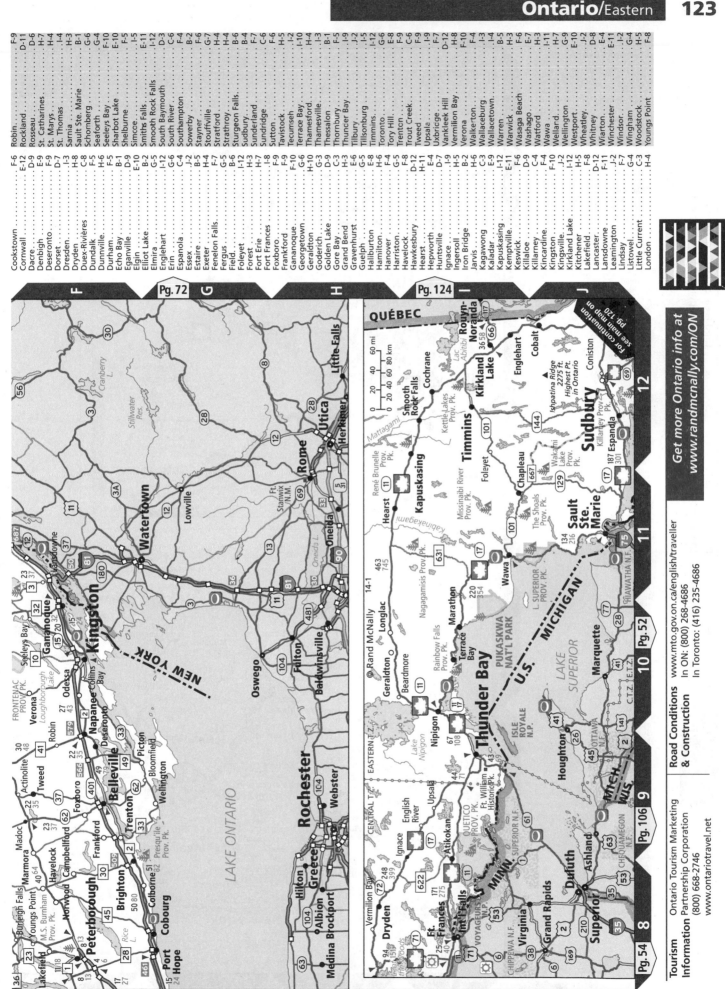

For continuation see main map on pg. 120

Get more Ontario info at
www.randmcnally.com/ON

**Tourism** Ontario Tourism Marketing
**Information** Partnership Corporation
(800) 668-2746
www.ontariotravel.net

**Road Conditions**
**& Construction**
www.mto.gov.on.ca/english/traveller
In ON: (800) 268-4686
In Toronto: (416) 235-4686

## Québec

Land area: 527,079 sq. mi. (rank: 2nd)
Highest point: Mont d'Iberville, 5,420 ft.

Population: 7,903,001 (rank: 2nd)
Largest city: Montréal, 1,649,519, F-3

Capital: Québec, D-6

Québec *provincial facts*

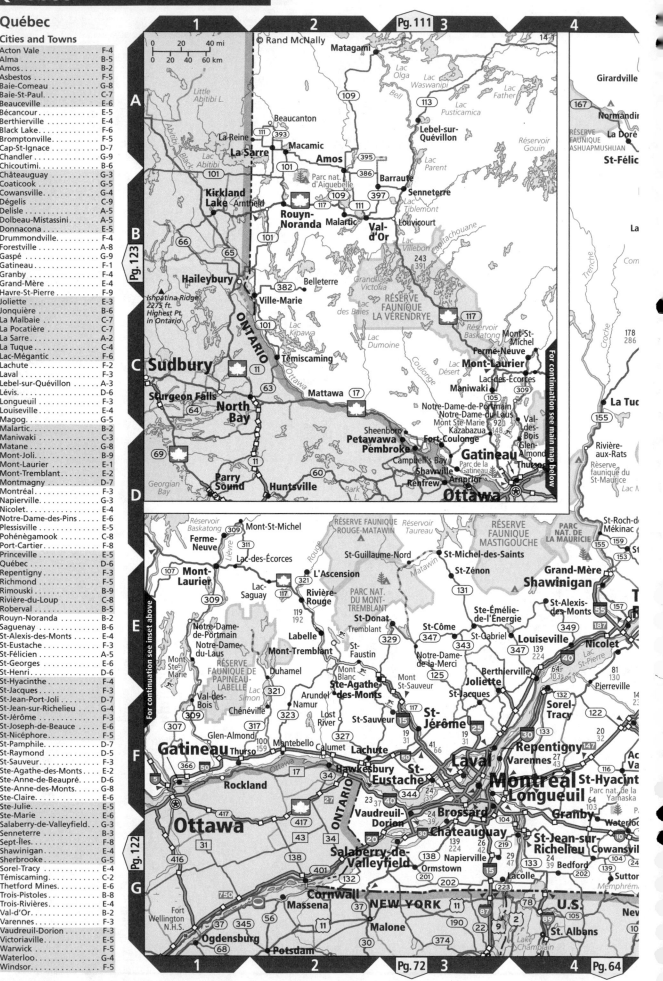

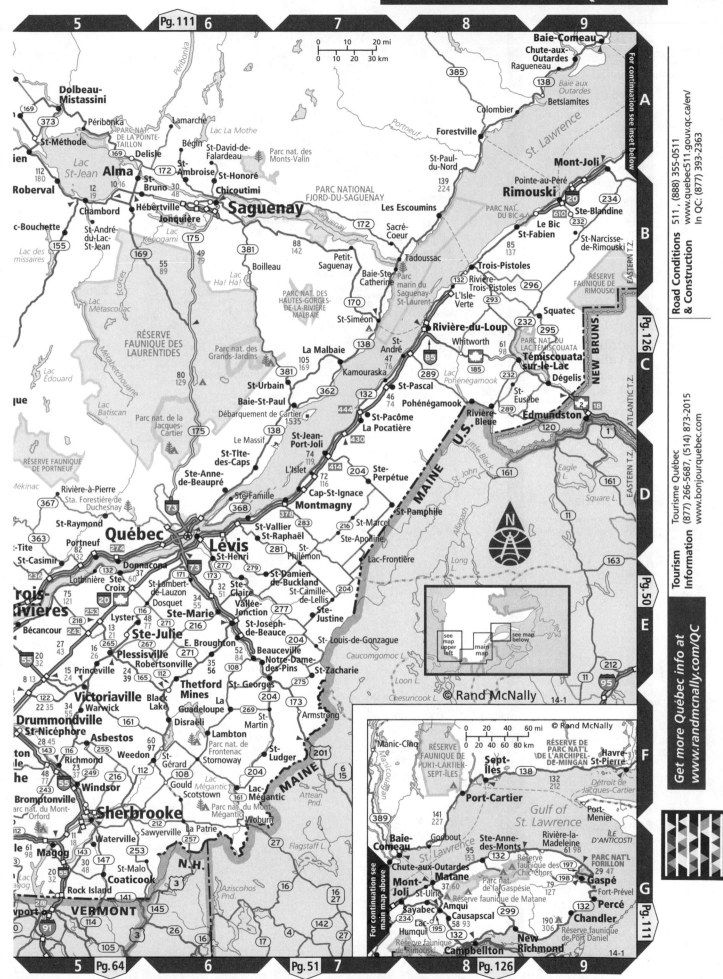

For continuation see inset below

Pg. 126
Pg. 50
Pg. 111

© Rand McNally

## New Brunswick

## Newfoundland and Labrador

## Nova Scotia

## Prince Edward Island

**NEW BRUNSWICK**
Population: 751,171 (rank: 8th)
Largest city: Saint John, 70,063, E-4
Land area: 27,587 sq. mi. (rank: 11th)

**NEWFOUNDLAND & LABRADOR**
Population: 514,536 (rank: 9th)
Largest city: St. John's, 106,172, B-9
Land area: 144,353 sq. mi. (rank: 10th)

**NOVA SCOTIA**
Population: 921,727 (rank: 7th)
Largest city: Halifax, 390,096, F-6
Land area: 20,594 sq. mi. (rank: 12th)

**PRINCE EDWARD ISLAND**
Population: 140,204 (rank: 10th)
Largest city: Charlottetown, 34,562, D-6
Land area: 2,185 sq. mi. (rank: 13th)

Pg. 111

Pg. 125

Pg. 50

### Map labels

St. Lawrence
Baie-Comeau
Ste-Anne-des-Monts
Forestville
Matane
Parc nat. de la Gaspésie
Réserve faunique des Chic-Chocs
Mont-Joli
Rimouski
Amqui
Lac Matapédia
Réserve faunique de Matane
Trois-Pistoles
QUÉBEC
Campbellton
Dalhousie
Belledune
Pointe-Ver
Rivière-du-Loup
Réserve faunique de Rimouski
Sugarloaf Prov. Pk.
Bathurst
Témiscouata-sur-le-Lac
Kedgwick St-Quentin
Mt. Carleton Prov. Pk.
Dégelis
Edmundston
Mt. Carleton 2680 ft. Highest Pt. in New Brunswick
Nepisiguit Bay
La Pocatière
Pohénégamook
Nictau
Miramichi
Douglastown
St-Pamphile
Grand Falls (Grand Sault)
Little S.W. Miramichi
Caribou
Plaster Rock
NEW BRUNSWICK
Renous
Rogersville
Presque Isle
Perth-Andover
Blackville
Acadie Siding
Juniper
Blissfield
Doaktown
Harcourt
Florenceville
Boiestown
Hartland Covered Br.
Hartland
Woodstock
Cross Creek
Nashwaak Bridge
Houlton
Mt. Katahdin 5268 ft. Highest Pt. in Maine
Upper Hainesville
Millville
Keswick Ridge
Chipman
Minto
Fredericton
Millinocket
Kings Landing Hist. Settlement
Oromocto
Thomaston Corner
Harvey
Tracy
Sussex
Hampton
Welsford
St. Croix
Oromocto Lake
Lawrence Station
St. Stephen
St. George
Saint John
Dover-Foxcroft
Lincoln
Calais
St. Croix I. Int'l Hist. Site
St. Andrews
Bay of Fundy
Old Town
Orono
Brewer
Skowhegan
Bangor
Hampden
Passamaquoddy Bay
CAMPOBELLO I.
Roosevelt Campobello Int'l Park
North Head
Bridgetown
Pittsfield
Fairfield
Waterville
Winslow
Bucksport
Buckport
Ellsworth
Machias
GRAND MANAN I.
Annapolis Royal
Port-Royal N.H.S.
Digby
Centreville
Belfast
Tiverton
Weymouth
Camden
Westport
Mavilette
Salmon River
KEJIMKUJIK N.P.
Rockland
Thomaston
ACADIA NAT'L PARK
Bar Harbor
ACADIA NAT'L PARK
Hebron
Yarmouth
Carleton
Ellenwood Lake Prov. Pk.
Tusket
Shelburne
Wedgeport
Pubnico
Shag Harbour
Barrington Bay
ATLANTIC OCEAN
QUÉBEC / MAINE
U.S.
ME.
Penobscot Bay
Eagle L.
Long L.
Square L.
EASTERN T.Z. ATLANTIC T.Z.

0 10 20 30 mi
0 10 20 30 40 km

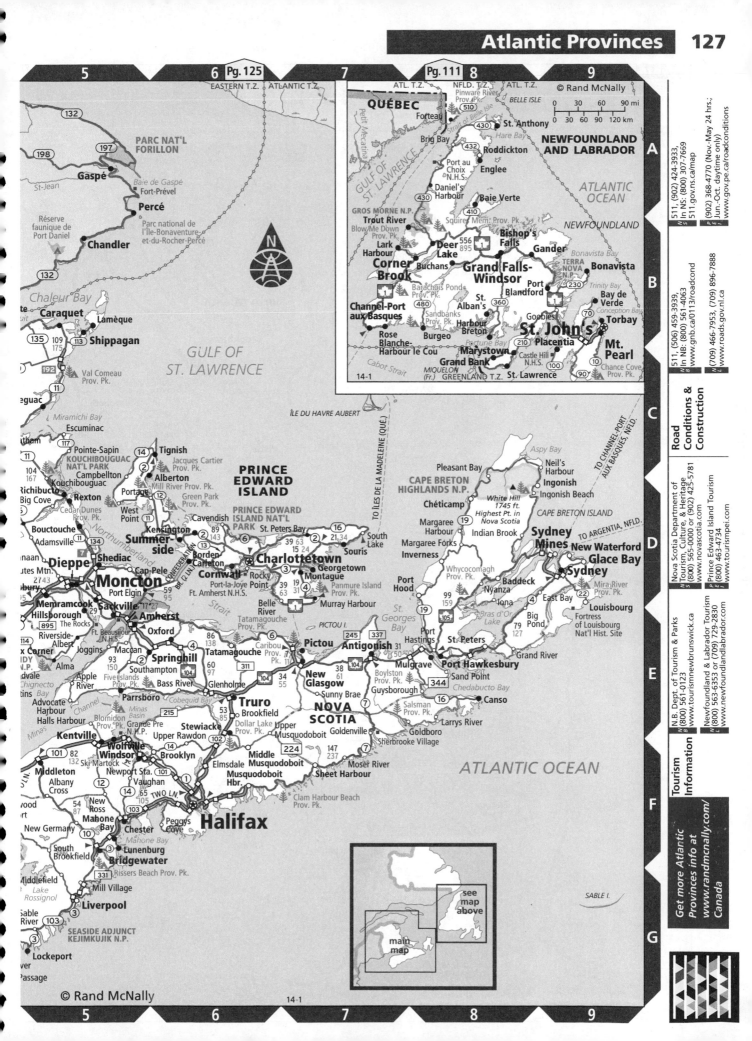

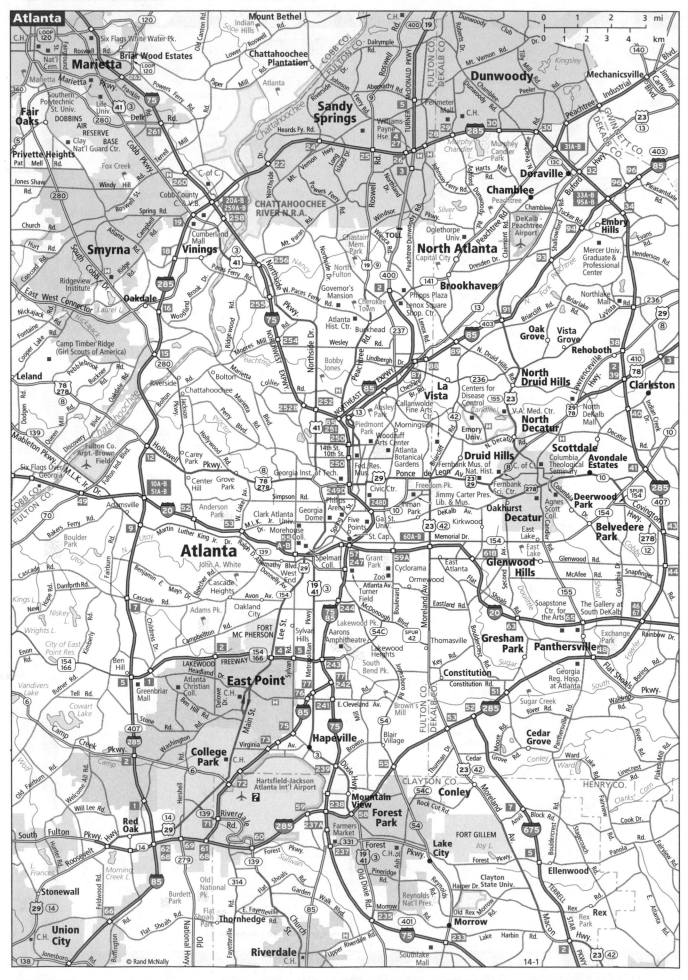

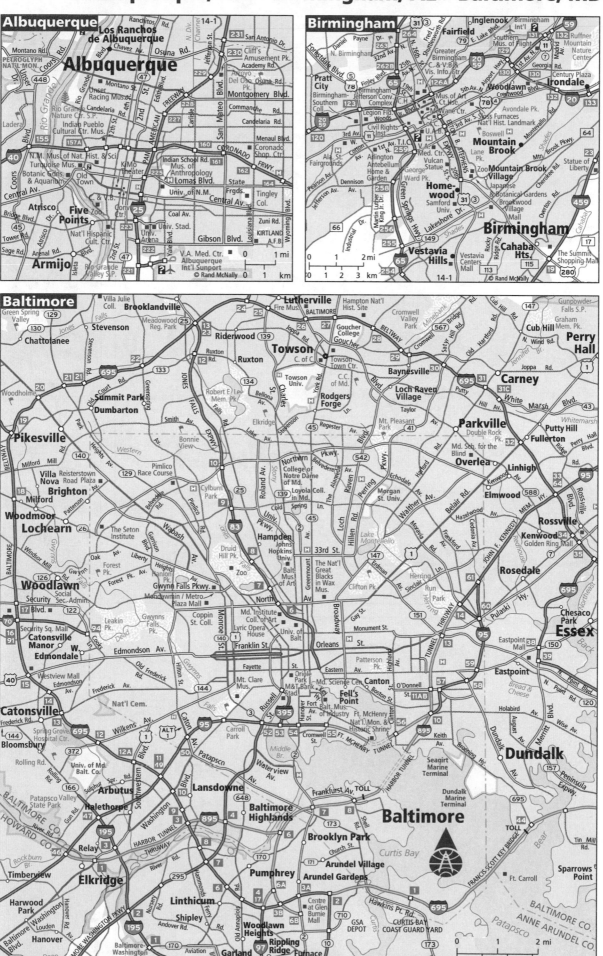

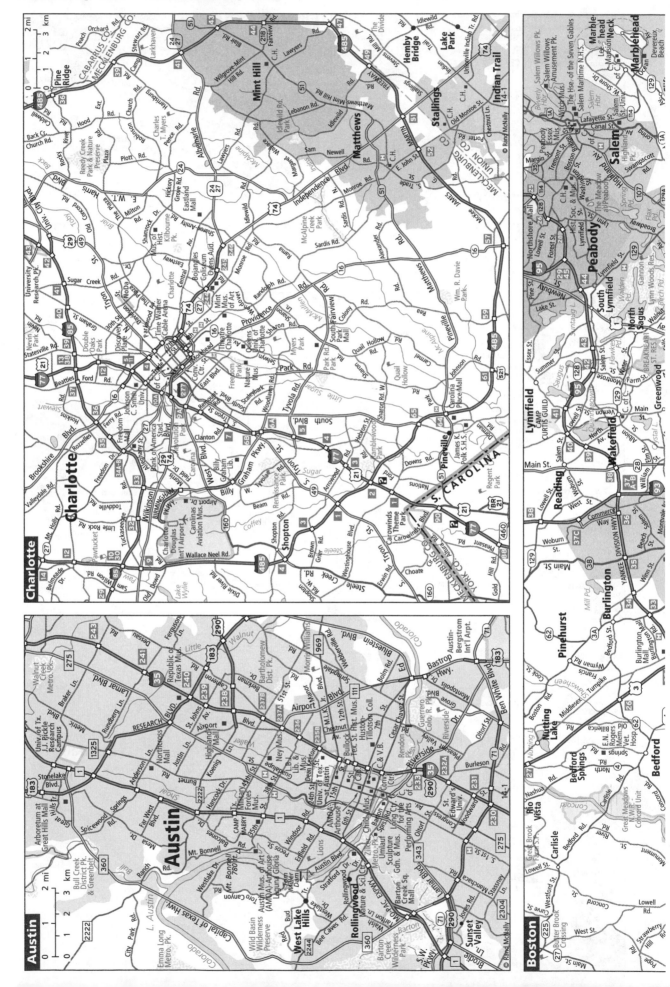

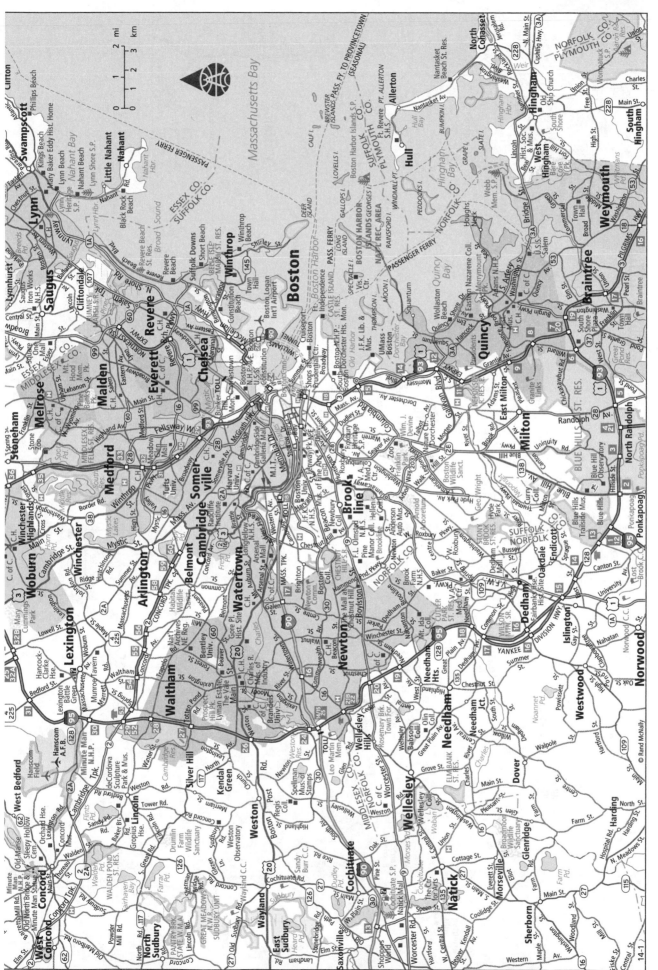

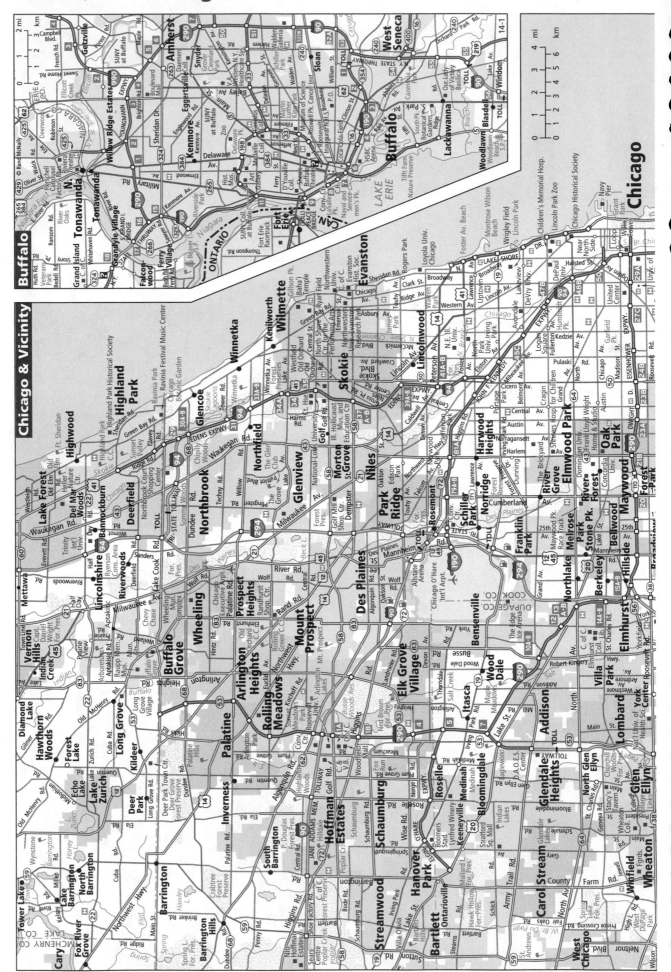

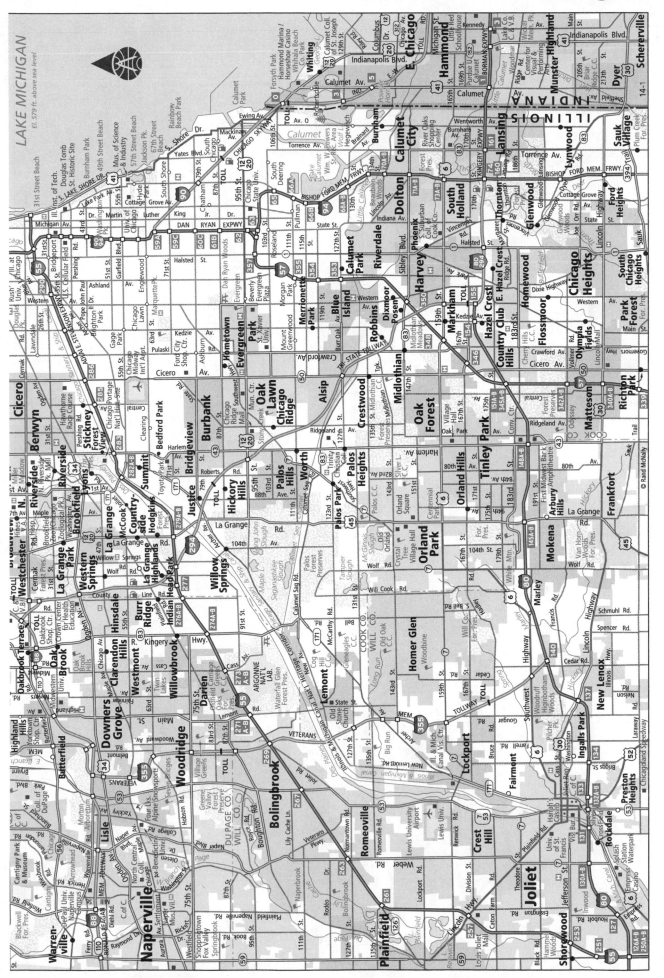

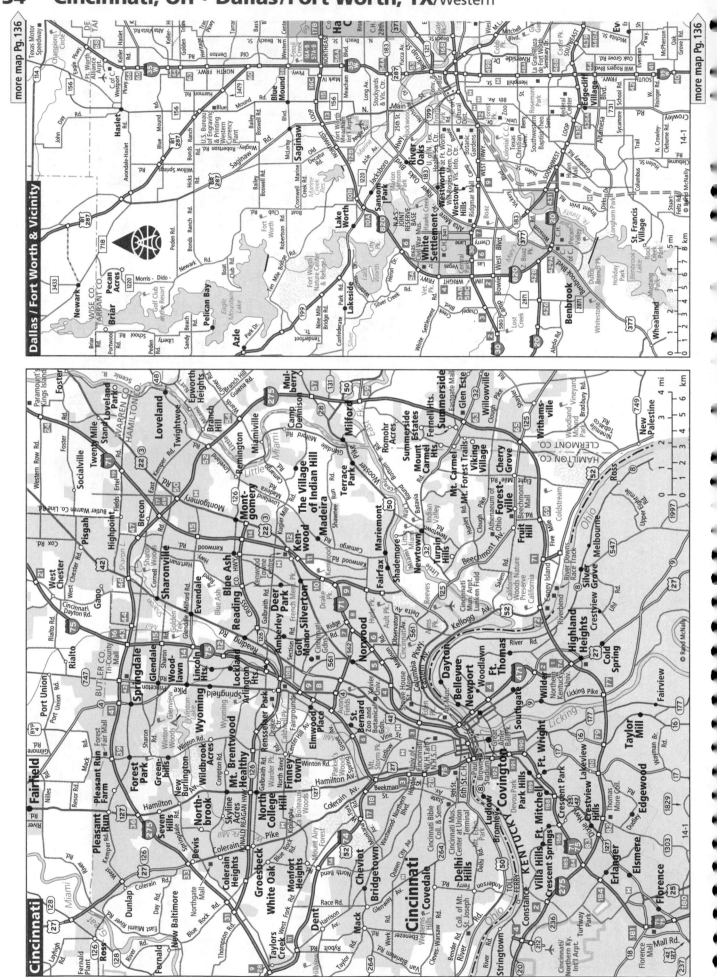

more map Pg. 136

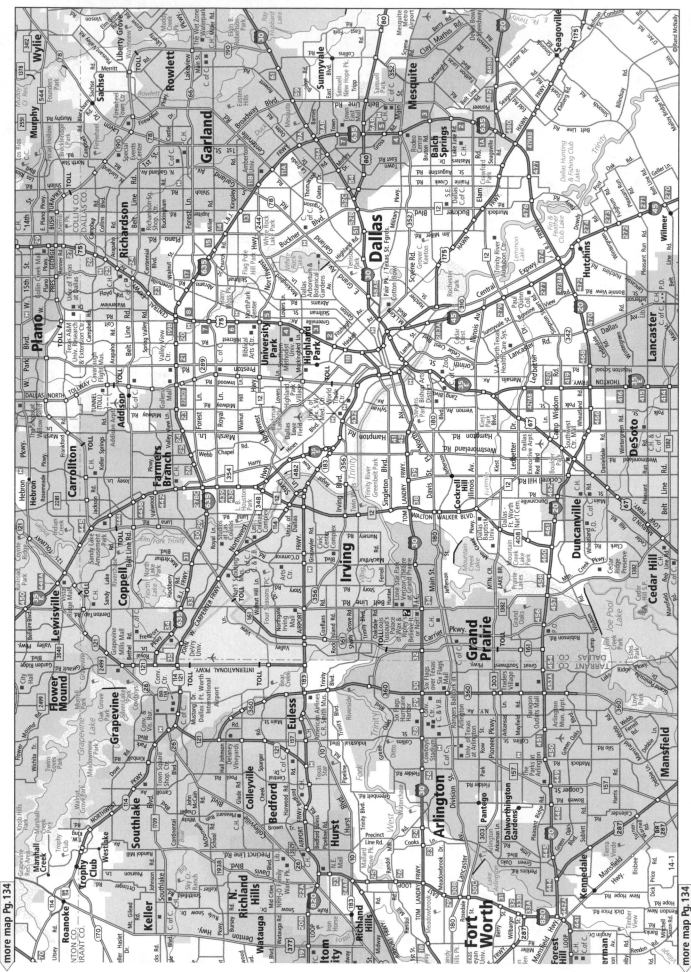

more map Pg. 134

more map Pg. 134

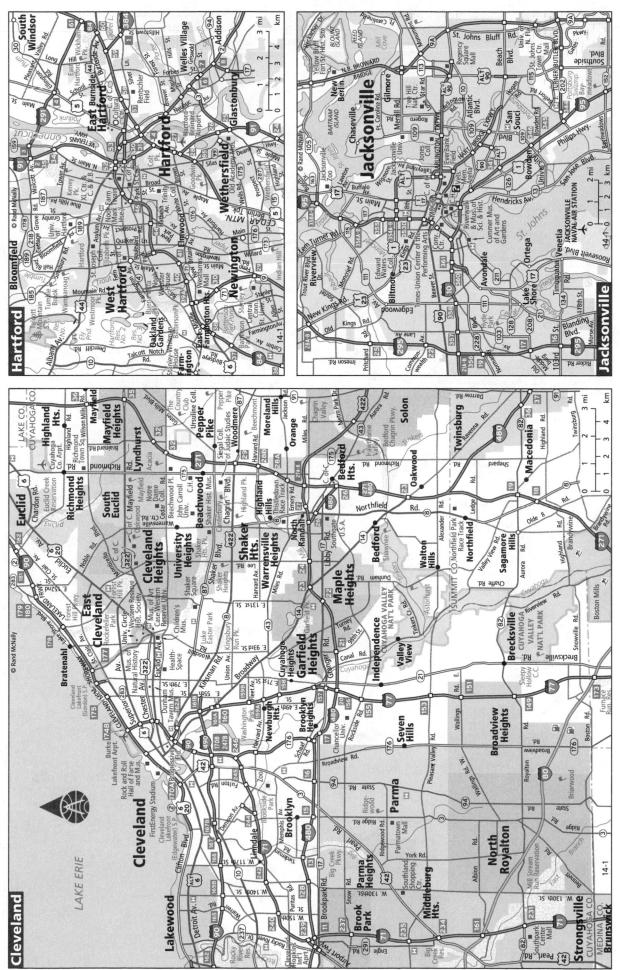

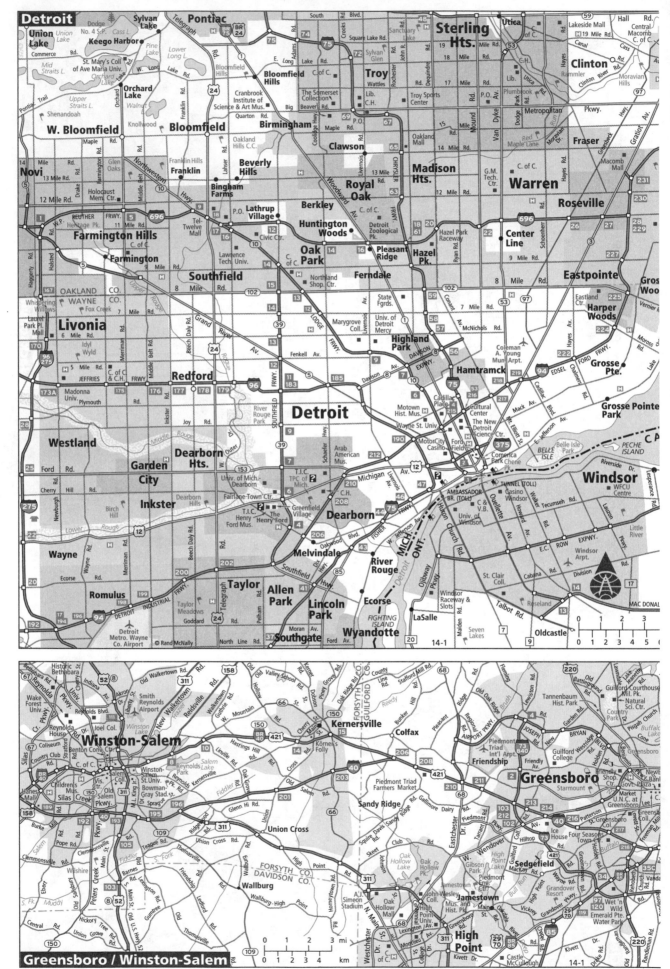

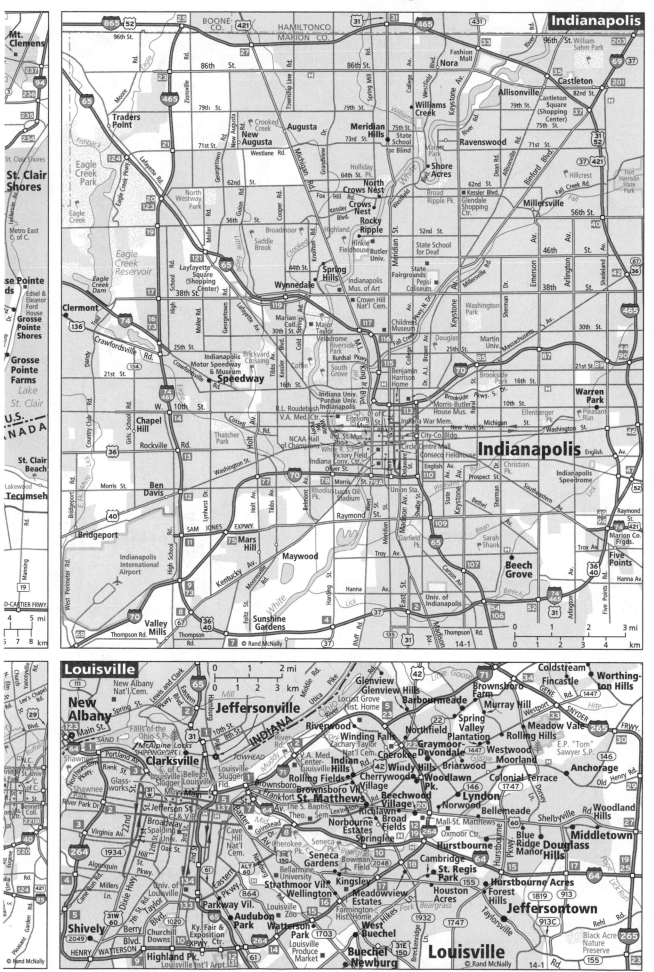

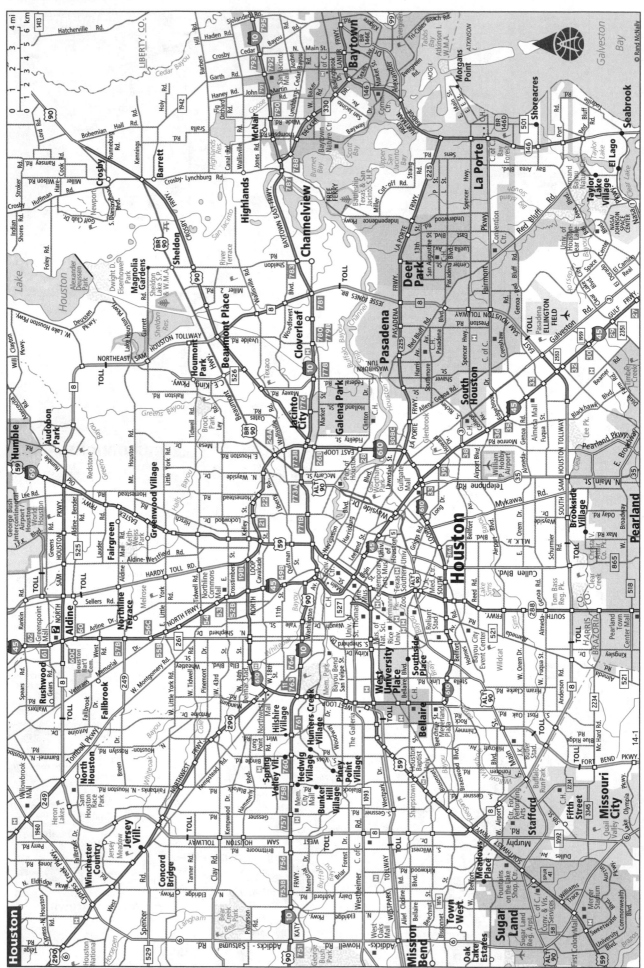

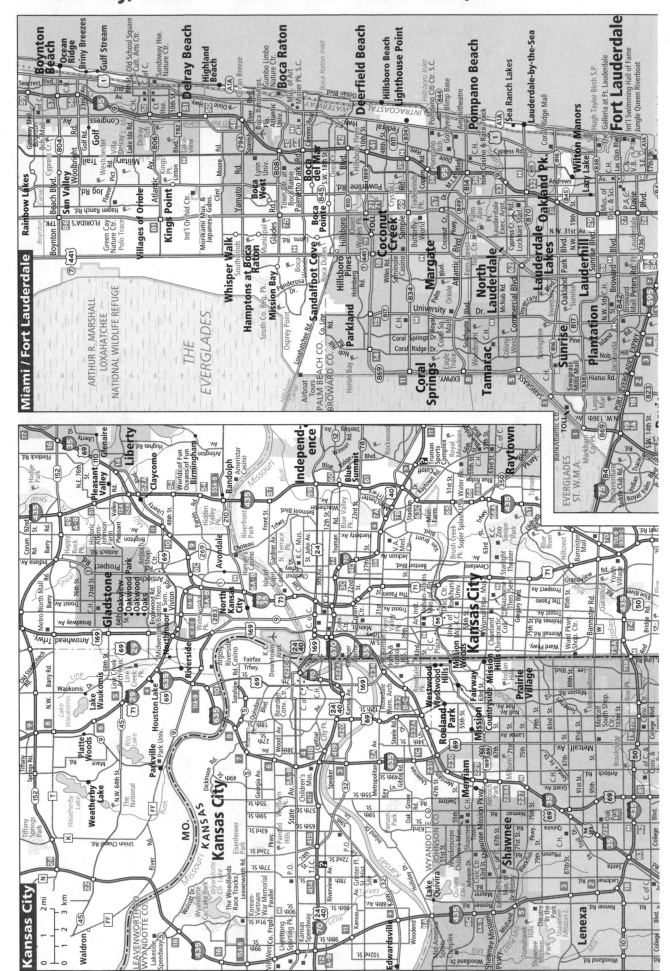

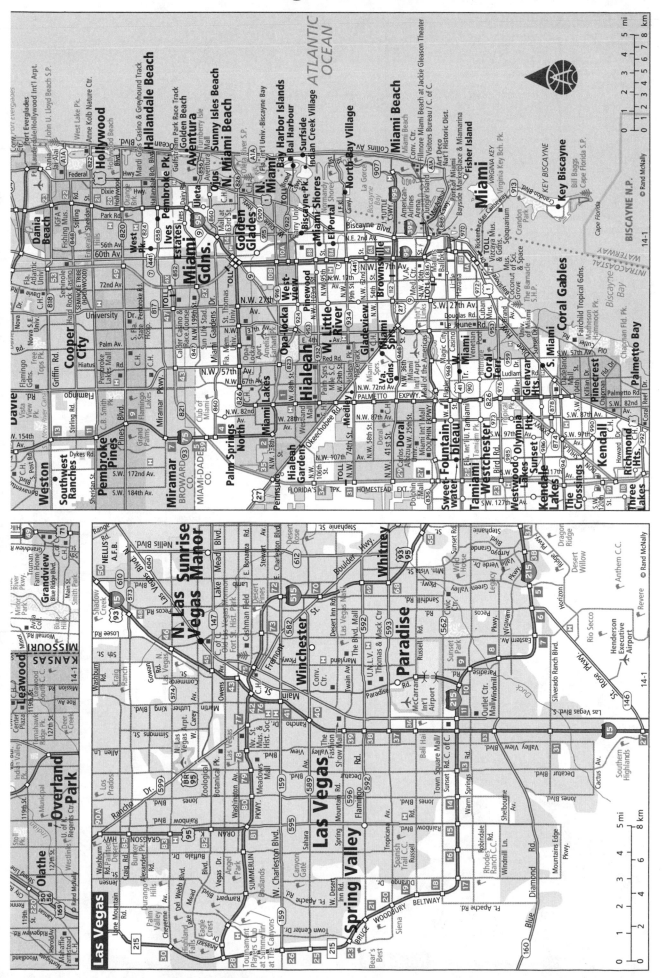

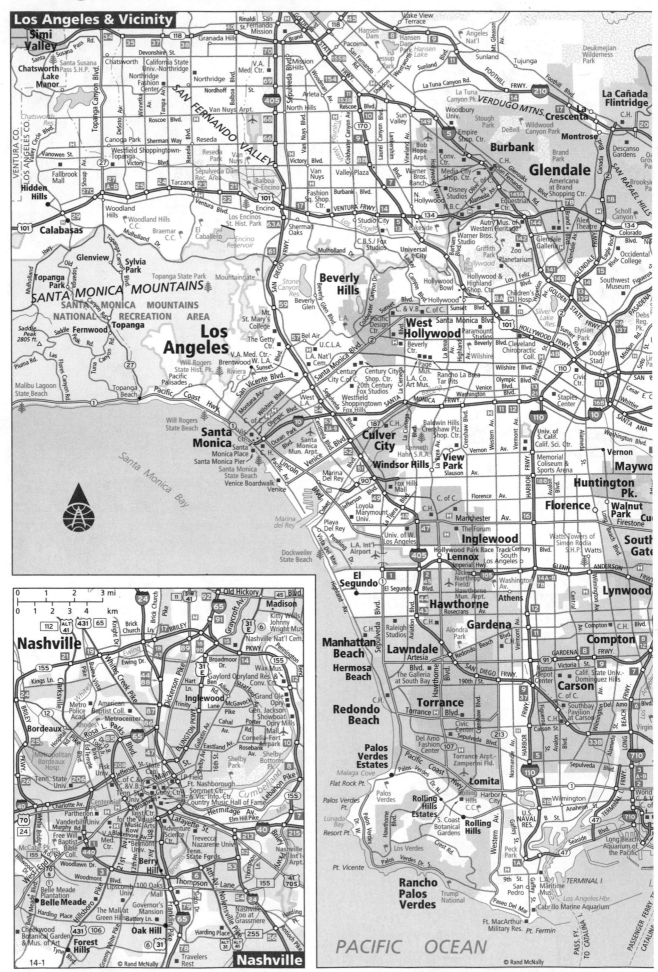

Los Angeles & Vicinity

Nashville

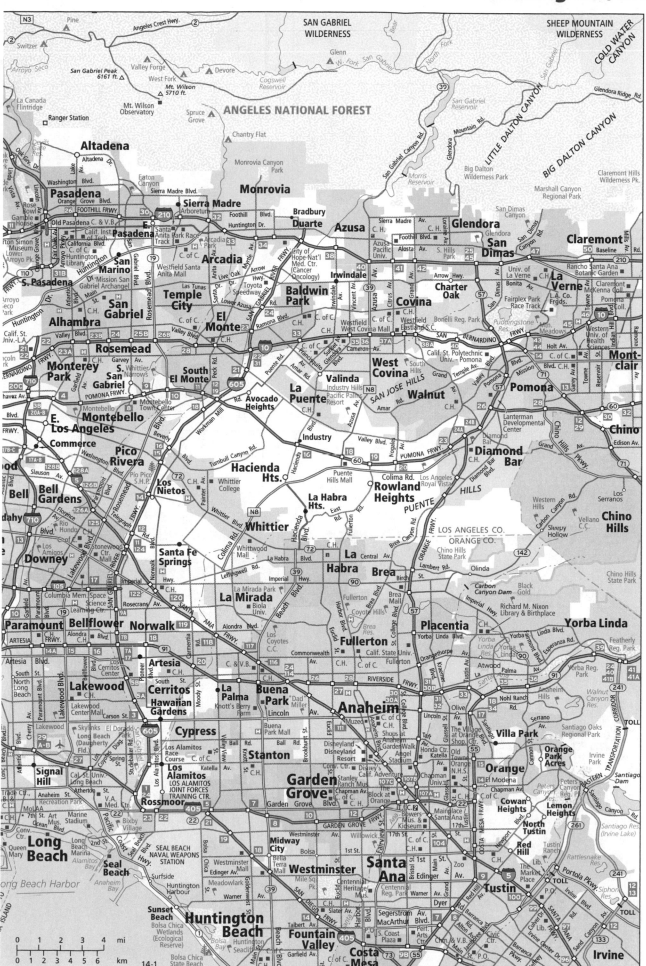

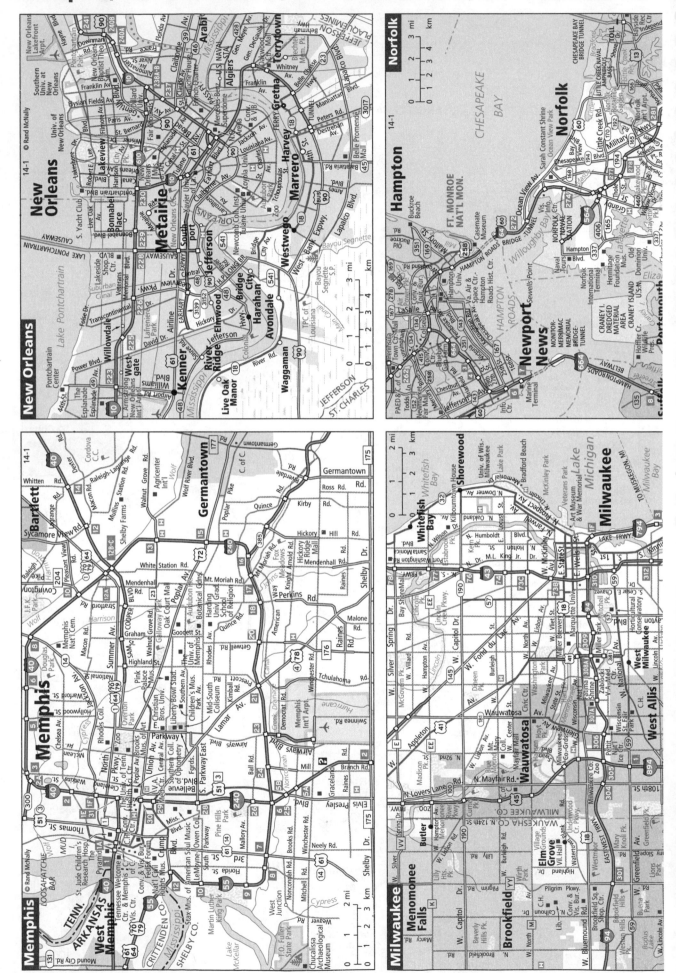

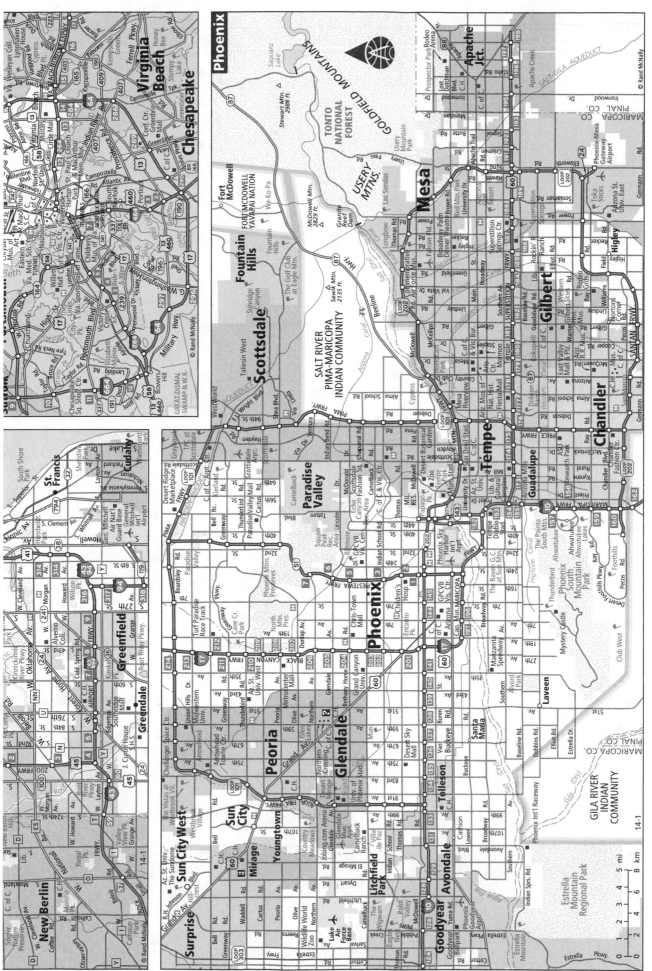

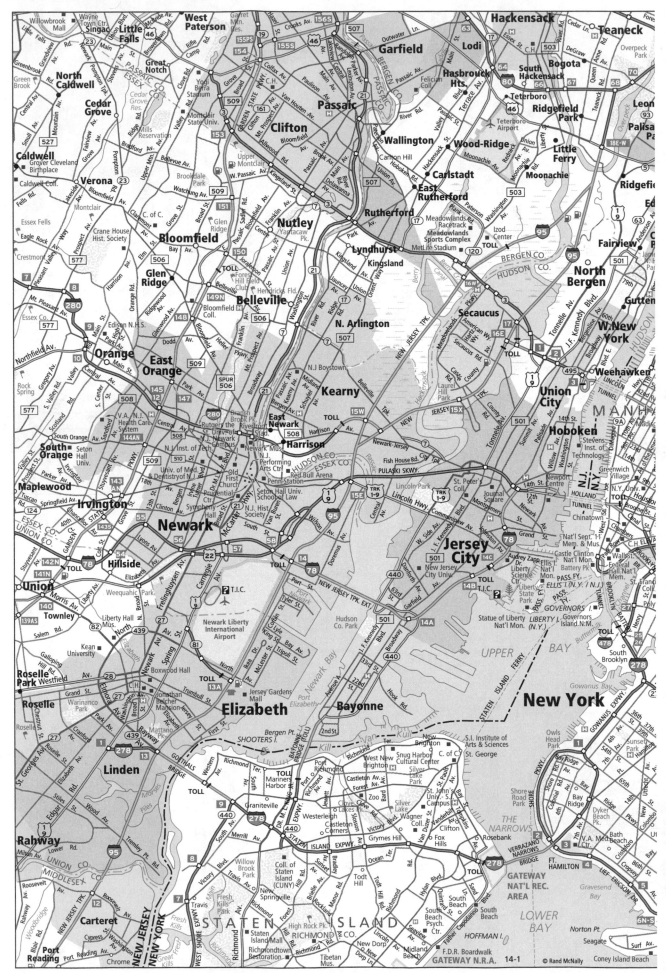

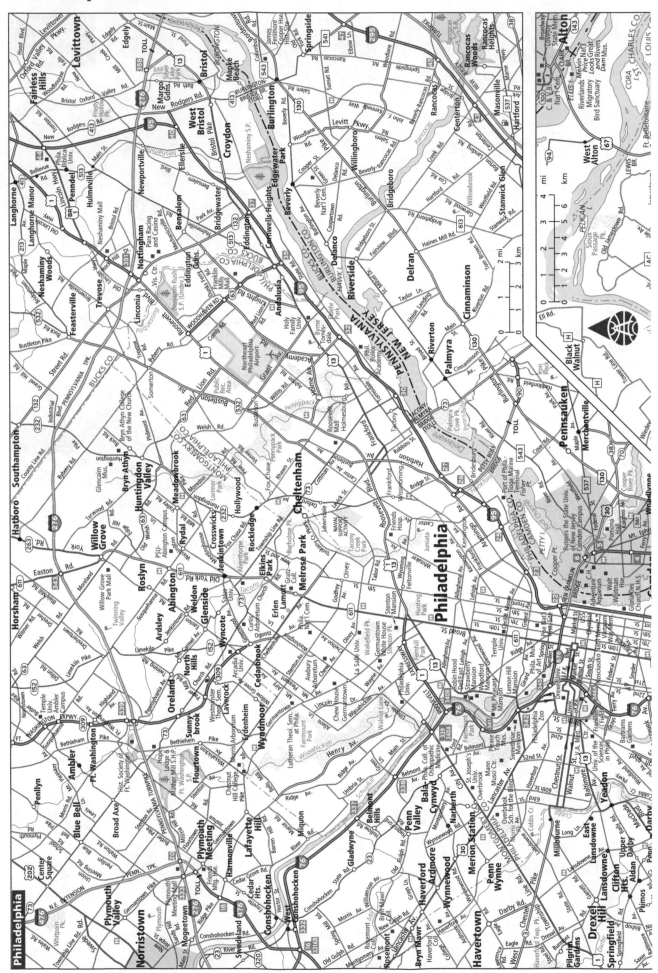

Philadelphia

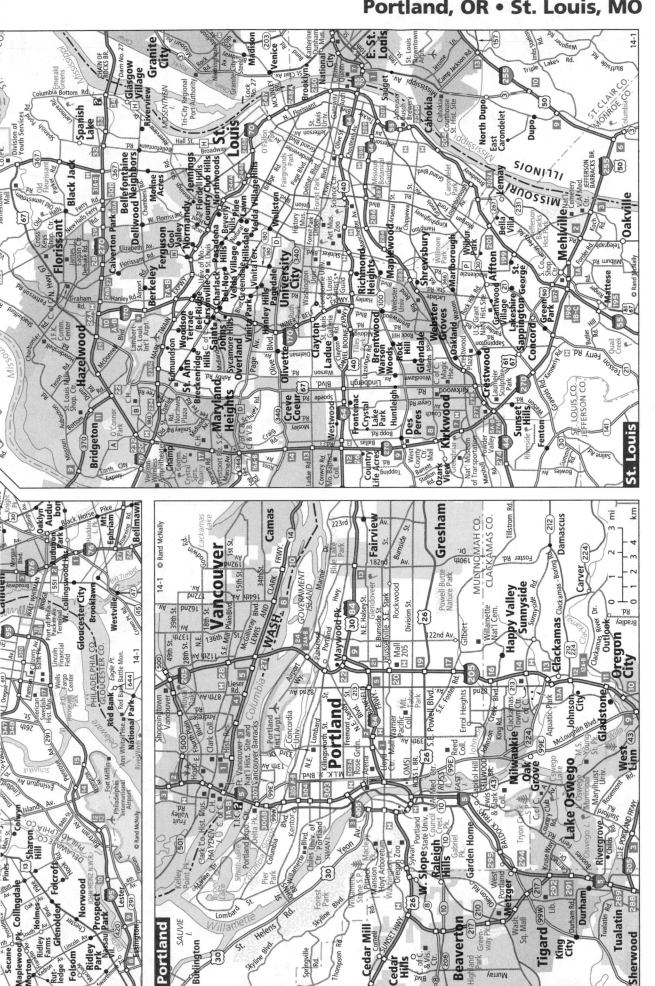

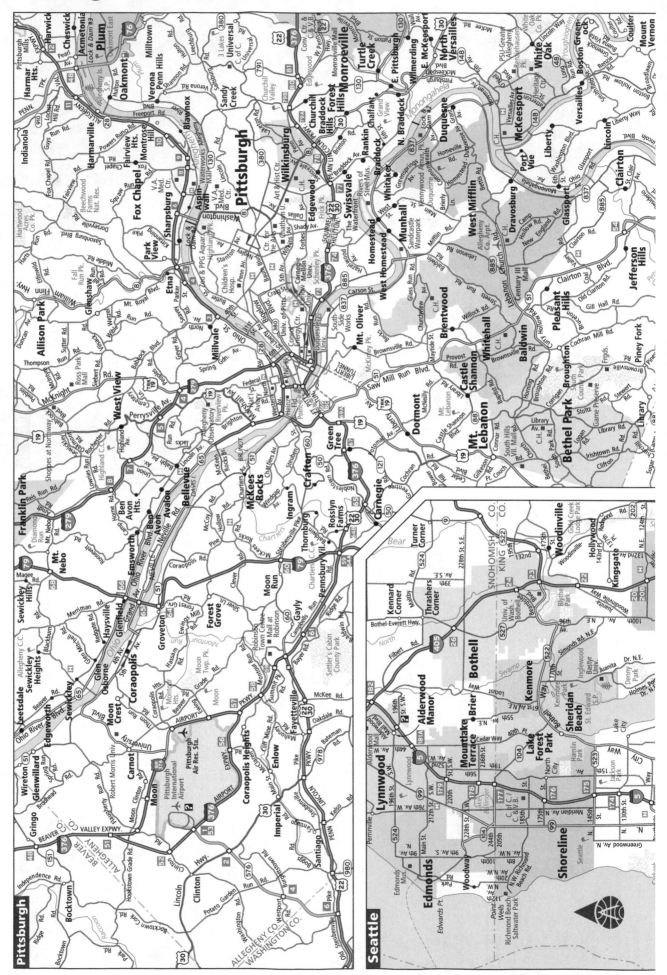

Pittsburgh

Seattle

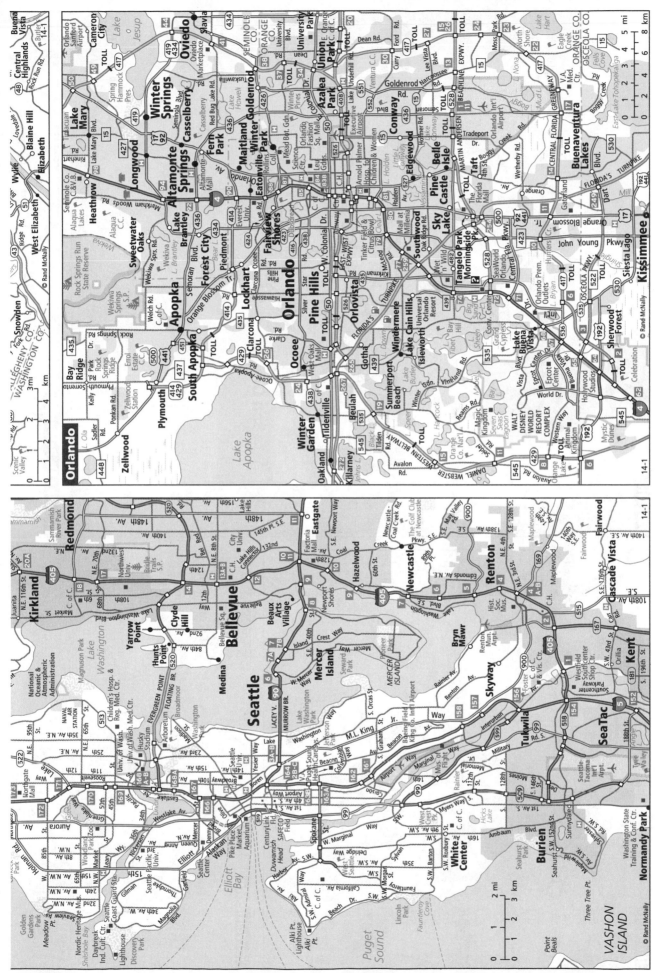

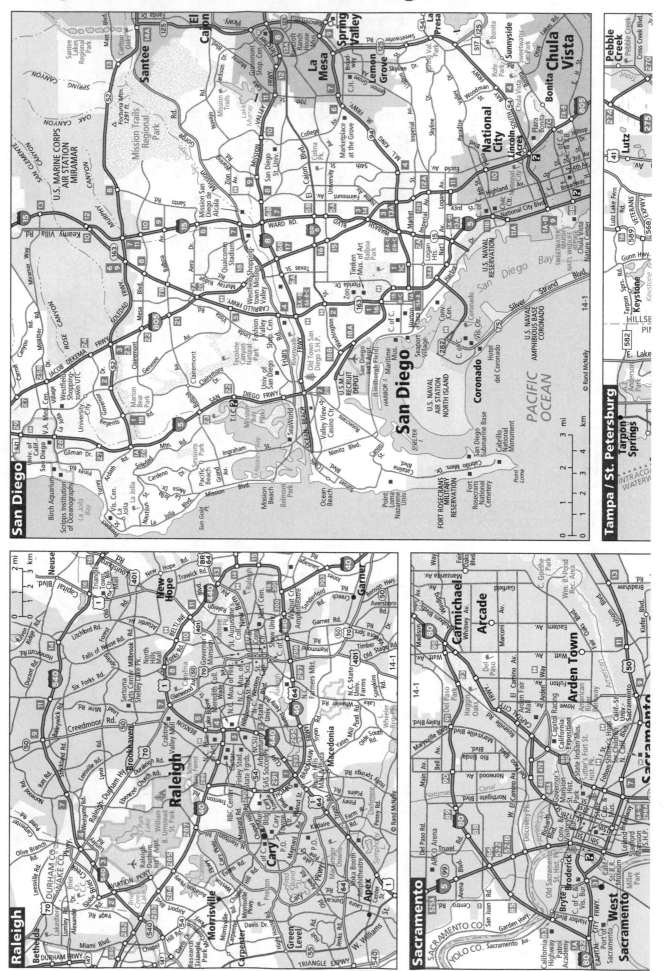

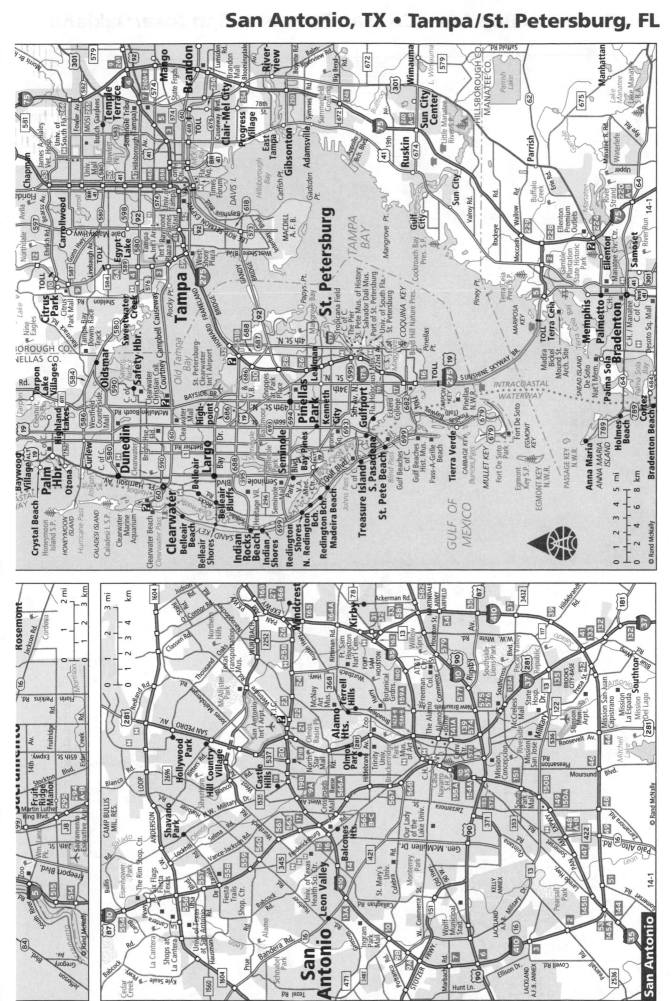

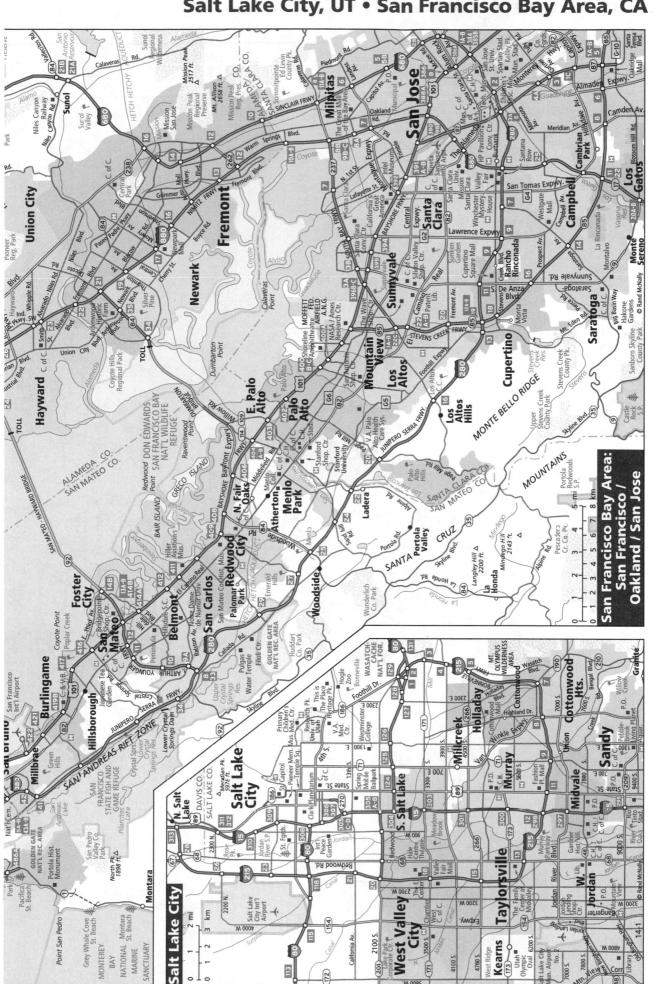

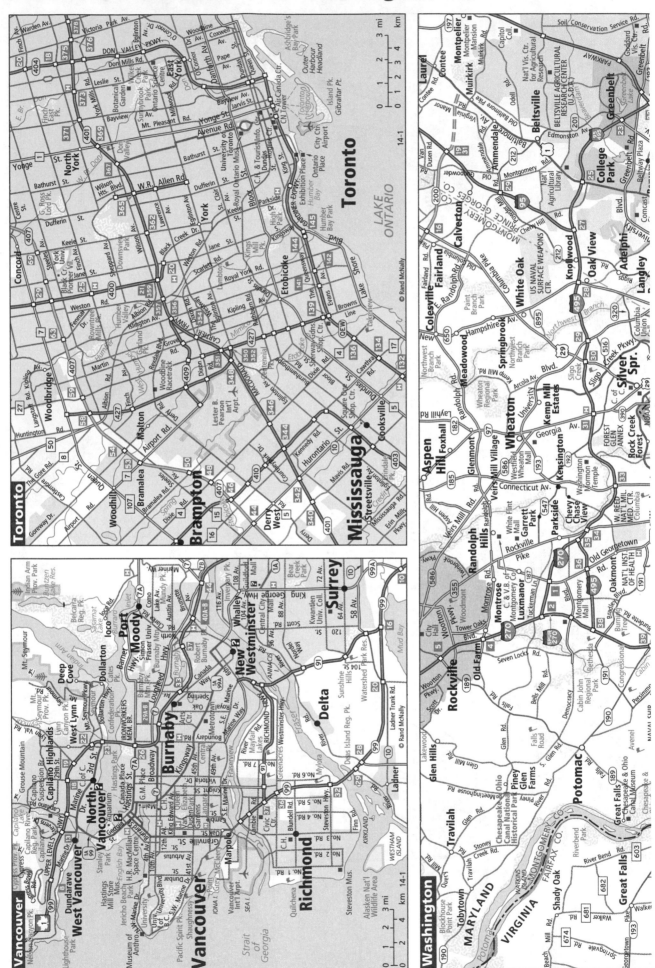

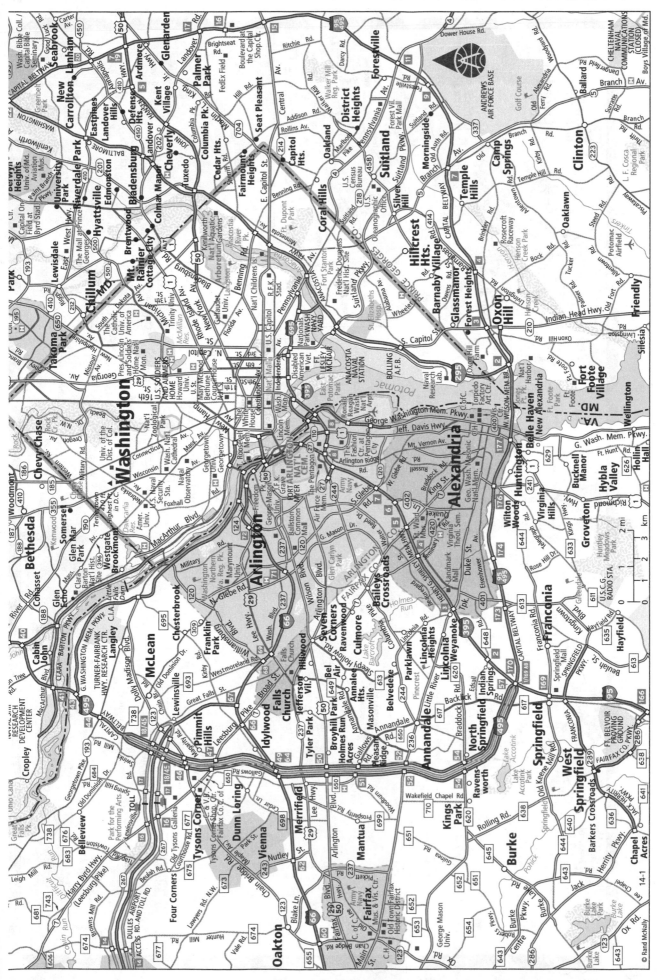

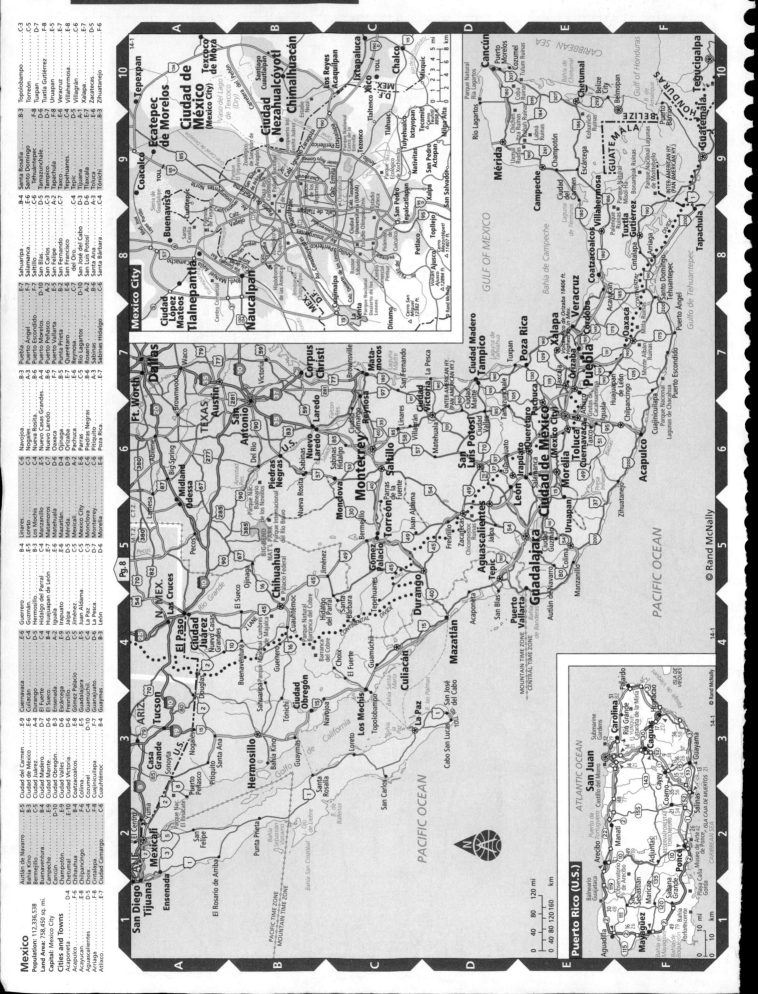

### Mexico City

### Puerto Rico (U.S.)